The Short Oxford History of the British Isles

General Editor: Paul Langford

From the Vikings to the Normans

Edited by Wendy Davies

The Short Oxford History
of the British Isles

General Editor: Paul Langford

From the Vikings
to the Normans

Edited by Wendy Davies

OXFORD
UNIVERSITY PRESS

OXFORD
UNIVERSITY PRESS

Great Clarendon Street, Oxford OX2 6DP

Oxford University Press is a department of the University of Oxford.
It furthers the University's objective of excellence in research, scholarship,
and education by publishing worldwide in

Oxford New York

Auckland Bangkok Buenos Aires Cape Town Chennai
Dar es Salaam Delhi Hong Kong Istanbul Karachi Kolkata
Kuala Lumpur Madrid Melbourne Mexico City Mumbai Nairobi
São Paulo Shanghai Taipei Tokyo Toronto

Oxford is a registered trade mark of Oxford University Press
in the UK and in certain other countries

Published in the United States
by Oxford University Press Inc., New York

British Library Cataloguing in Publication Data

Data available

Library of Congress Cataloging in Publication Data

Data applied for

ISBN 0–19–870050–4 (hbk)
ISBN 0–19–870051–2 (pbk)

10 9 8 7 6 5 4 3 2 1

Typeset in Minion
by RefineCatch Limited, Bungay, Suffolk
Printed in Great Britain by
T.J. International Ltd, Padstow, Cornwall

General Editor's Preface

It is a truism that historical writing is itself culturally determined, reflecting intellectual fashions, political preoccupations, and moral values at the time it is written. In the case of British history this has resulted in a great diversity of perspectives on both the content of what is narrated and the geopolitical framework in which it is placed. In recent times the process of redefinition has positively accelerated under the pressure of contemporary change. Some of it has come from within Britain during a period of recurrent racial tension in England and reviving nationalism in Scotland, Wales, and Northern Ireland. But much of it also comes from beyond. There has been a powerful surge of interest in the politics of national identity in response to the break-up of some of the world's great empires, both colonial and continental. The search for new sovereignties, not least in Europe itself, has contributed to a questioning of long-standing political boundaries. Such shifting of the tectonic plates of history is to be expected but for Britain especially, with what is perceived (not very accurately) to be a long period of relative stability lasting from the late seventeenth century to the mid-twentieth century, it has had a particular resonance.

Much controversy and still more confusion arise from the lack of clarity about the subject matter that figures in insular historiography. Historians of England are often accused of ignoring the history of Britain as a whole, while using the terms as if they are synonymous. Historians of Britain are similarly charged with taking Ireland's inclusion for granted without engaging directly with it. And for those who believe they are writing more specifically the history of Ireland, of Wales, or of Scotland, there is the unending tension between so-called metropolis and periphery, and the dilemmas offered by wider contexts, not only British and Irish but European and indeed extra-European. Some of these difficulties arise from the fluctuating fortunes and changing boundaries of the British state as organized from London. But even if the rulers of what is now called England had never taken an interest in dominion beyond its borders, the economic and cultural relationships between the various parts of the British Isles would still have generated many historiographical problems.

This series is based on the premiss that whatever the complexities and ambiguities created by this state of affairs, it makes sense to offer an overview, conducted by leading scholars whose research is on the leading edge of their discipline. That overview extends to the whole of the British Isles. The expression is not uncontroversial, especially to many in Ireland, for whom the very word 'British' implies an unacceptable politics of dominion. Yet there is no other formulation that can encapsulate the shared experience of 'these islands', to use another term much employed in Ireland and increasingly heard in Britain, but rather unhelpful to other inhabitants of the planet.

In short we use the words 'British Isles' solely and simply as a geographical expression. No set agenda is implied. It would indeed be difficult to identify one that could stand scrutiny. What constitutes a concept such as 'British history' or 'four nations history' remains the subject of acute disagreement, and varies much depending on the period under discussion. The editors and contributors of this series have been asked only to convey the findings of the most authoritative scholarship, and to flavour them with their own interpretative originality and distinctiveness. In the process we hope to provide not only a stimulating digest of more than two thousand years of history, but also a sense of the intense vitality that continues to mark historical research into the past of all parts of Britain and Ireland.

Lincoln College PAUL LANGFORD
Oxford

Contents

List of Illustrations

Acknowledgements

Viking arm-rings from Dinorben Quarry, Anglesey
By permission of National Museums and Galleries of Wales

Pharaoh sentences his chief baker to be hanged; from the Old English
Illustrated Hexateuch, BL MS Cotton Claudius Biv, fo.59ʳ
By permission of the British Library

Carved whalebone plaque found in the Viking burial at Scar, Orkney
Crown copyright. Reproduced by permission of Historic Scotland

Plan of the Viking fort at Repton, from J. Haywood ed., *The Penguin
Historical Atlas of the Vikings*
Reproduced by permission

A hogback tombstone, panel type
© Oxford University School of Archaeology

Viking Age buildings during excavation, Fishamble Street, Dublin 1981.
From *The Viking Age Buildings of Dublin Part II: Illustrations* (1992)
Courtesy Patrick Wallace, National Museum of Ireland, Dublin

Map of York, from Richard Hall, *The Book of Viking York* (English Heritage/
Batsford, 1996)
Reproduced by permission

Map of Dublin, from *Viking and Medieval Dublin* by Curriculum
Development Unit (The O'Brien Press Ltd, Dublin, 1988)
Reproduced by permission

Map of Wallingford, from M. Biddle and D. Hill, *Antiquaries Journal*, 1971
(vol. LI, pt1)
Reproduced by permission

Towns in 1100, from Barbara Harvey ed., *The Twelfth and Thirteenth
Centuries* (Short Oxford History of the British Isles), Oxford University Press,
2001

The eleventh-century shrine of the Stowe Missal, lower face
Courtesy the National Museum of Ireland, Dublin

'The relationships and arrangements within a theoretical multiple estate', from Michael Aston, *Interpreting the Landscape* (Routledge, London, 1985) Reproduced by permission

Map of Shapwick, Somerset, from Michael Costen, *The Origins of Somerset* (Manchester University Press, 2002) Courtesy Michael Costen

Map showing the distribution of surviving Irish ringforts, from Matthew Stout, *The Irish Ringfort* (Four Courts Press, 2000) Reproduced by permission

An Illustration from the Old English Hexateuch, BL MS Cotton Claudius Biv, fo.13^r By permission of the British Library

An eleventh-century illustration of a feast, BL MS Cotton Tiberius Cvi, fo.5^v By permission of the British Library

The east face of Muiredach's Cross, Monasterboice, Co. Louth Courtesy Duchas, The Heritage Service of the Departments of Art, Heritage, Gaeltacht and the Islands

The opening of Psalm 1 in the Psalter and Martyrology of Rhigyfarch (Trinity College Dublin MS 50, fo. 35^r) By permission of Trinity College Library, Dublin

Cross-carved grave-marker from St Davids Crown copyright. Royal Commission on the Ancient and Historical Monuments of Wales

Lebor na hUidre (Dublin, Royal Irish Academy, MS 23E25 (1129), fo. 39^r) By permission of the Royal Irish Academy ©RIA

St Dunstan's Classbook: MS Auct. F. 4. 32, fols 1^v, 10^r, 22^r Reproduced by permission of the Bodleian Library, University of Oxford

Colchester Castle. Courtesy Anthony Kersting

The Pictish cross-slab at Glamis Copyright Royal Commission on the Ancient and Historical Monuments of Scotland

List of Contributors

BARBARA E. CRAWFORD is Honorary Reader in Medieval History at the University of St Andrews. Her main research activities focus on the historical links between Scotland and Scandinavia in the Viking and medieval periods. Her publications include the multi-disciplinary *Scandinavian Scotland* (1987) and the major excavation report, *The History and Excavation of a Royal Norwegian Farm at the Biggings, Papa Stour, Shetland* (1999). She is the editor of *Scandinavian Settlement in Northern Britain* (1995), a book of essays on the place-names of Norse settlement, and her current contributions to publications of national importance include *The New Penguin History of Scotland, New Dictionary of National Biography, The Oxford Companion to Scottish History*, and *A New History of the Isle of Man*.

WENDY DAVIES is Pro-Provost, European Affairs, and Professor of History at University College London. She has written on early Welsh, Breton, Irish, English and European history and archaeology, and is currently working on rural communities in northern Spain in the tenth century. Her publications include *Wales in the Early Middle Ages* (1982), *Small Worlds: The Village Community in Early Medieval Brittany* (1988), *A Breton Landscape*, with Grenville Astill (1997).

ROBIN FLEMING is Professor of Medieval History at Boston College. She is the author of *Kings and Lords in Conquest England* (1991) and *Domesday Book and the Law: Society and Legal Custom in Early Medieval England* (1998). She has been awarded fellowships by the Harvard Society of Fellows, the Bunting Institute, the Institute for Advanced Study at Princeton, and the John Simon Guggenheim Memorial Trust.

JOHN GILLINGHAM studied history at Oxford and Munich Universities. He is Emeritus Professor of History at the London School of Economics and Political Science where he taught for more than thirty years. He is Director of the Battle Conference on Anglo-Norman studies which meets annually on the field of the battle of Hastings. His most recent books are: *The Angevin Empire* (2001); *The English in the Twelfth Century: Imperialism, National Identity and Political*

Values (2000); with Ralph A. Griffiths, *Medieval Britain: A Very Short Introduction* (2000); and *Richard I* (1999). He contributed to *Medieval Warfare: A History*, ed. Maurice Keen (1999); and wrote the medieval chapters in *The Young Oxford History of Britain and Ireland* (1996).

DAVID GRIFFITHS is a Fellow of Kellogg College, Oxford, and lectures in Archaeology at the Department for Continuing Education, Oxford University. He also teaches Medieval Archaeology at the Institute of Archaeology, University College London. A graduate of Durham University in history and archaeology, and formerly a visiting researcher at Tromsø University, Norway, his research interests include Britain, Ireland, and Scandinavia in the early medieval period. He is currently working on the archaeology of non-urban coastal trading sites, and also edits the journal *Anglo-Saxon Studies in Archaeology and History*.

DÁIBHÍ Ó CRÓINÍN is Associate Professor in the Department of History, National University of Ireland, Galway, specializing in early medieval Irish and European history. He is the author of numerous books and articles, including *Early Medieval Ireland, 400–1200* (1995), and is editor of the Royal Irish Academy's *New History of Ireland*, vol. 1, covering prehistoric and early medieval Ireland.

HUW PRYCE is Reader in History at the University of Wales, Bangor. His publications include *Native Law and the Church in Medieval Wales* (1993) and the edited volume *Literacy in Medieval Celtic Societies* (1998). He has recently completed a forthcoming edition of documents (with the assistance of Charles Insley), *The Acts of Welsh Rulers, 1120–1283*.

PAULINE STAFFORD is Professor of Medieval History at the University of Liverpool. She has published extensively on the history of early medieval England and on the history of queens in the early middle ages, most recently *Queen Emma and Queen Edith: Queenship and Women's Power in Eleventh-Century England* (1997). Her other publications include *Unification and Conquest: a Political and Social History of England in the Tenth and Eleventh Centuries* (1989); *The East Midlands in the Early Middle Ages* (1986); and *Queens, Concubines and Dowagers: the King's Wife in the Early Middle Ages* (1983).

Frontispiece Viking arm-rings from Dinorben Quarry, Anglesey.
By permission of National Museums and Galleries of Wales.

Introduction

Wendy Davies

Vikings and Normans

The period covered by this book, from AD 800 to 1100, or thereabout, is defined by two phases of attack from beyond the islands of Britain and Ireland, the first by Vikings from Scandinavia and the second by Normans from northern France.

Viking raiding began in the 790s and in a sense continued for nearly 300 years, although it is conventional to differentiate a 'first Viking Age' during the ninth century from a 'second Viking Age' in the late tenth and early eleventh. In truth there was barely a decade until the 1090s when some part of Britain or Ireland was not subject to these raids: although England was free from the onslaught for much of the tenth century, Ireland experienced a fresh wave of attacks from the beginning until the middle of that century, followed by Scotland and then Wales; Norse and Hiberno-Norse fleets remained active in the Irish Sea in the eleventh century and both Welsh and Irish rulers used Scandinavian mercenary warriors for much of that time.

The Norman attack was quite different, and for some parts of Britain was extremely rapid. The conquerors came in 1066 and within a few years had effected the conquest of England. Conquest of Wales began by 1070, but, although there was plenty of consequent settlement in the south of the country by 1100, it took most of the following 200 years to complete the takeover. Ireland was different in yet another way: conquest did not begin for another hundred years but such was the interest of Norman, or rather by now 'English', lords in Ireland in the 1170s that kings of England began, and thereafter continued, to include it in their dominions. And as for Scotland:

although here, as in Wales, there were Norman expeditions in the generation following the conquest of England, they were largely concentrated on the border zone, and there never was a Norman conquest of Scotland.

Questions about the impact of these raiders, invaders, and conquerors have dominated the writing of history of these islands for centuries. Were there thousands of Vikings or merely a few boatloads? Were the raids wildly exaggerated by 'biased' 'monastic' chroniclers, who were both too selfish and too self-absorbed to appreciate the constructive entrepreneurial spirit of the incomers, who brought colonization of new lands, greatly enhanced market activity and new networks of long-distance trade, boat-building, and urban life? Did they stimulate the development of the Scottish, and then the English, monarchies? Did they wipe out Christian religious life and learning, or rather bring an enhanced vocabulary and enrich the insular languages? Did the Norman conquerors simply take over the administrative mechanisms of the Old English state, changing personnel but scarcely changing the system at all? Or did the Conquest overthrow everything that was truly English and introduce new and 'superior' systems from the continent? Did they enslave and enserf a free English people? Once settled, and at some level 'Anglicized', how far did they come to dominate the Celtic peoples of these islands? Or rather, did they strive to bring 'civilization' to the rude and barbarous peoples of the west and north? Were they genuine allies of a reforming papacy, bringing truth and light to corrupt and backward churches, or did they use the language of reform purely to assist the political process, embedding themselves and their powers in the landscape—of England and Wales especially?

Fashion has veered from one extreme to another, with late twentieth-century writers emphasizing the benefits that came with the Vikings and—rather oddly—tending to emphasize both Anglo-Norman continuities from the Old English state and also Anglo-Norman oppression in Celtic lands. But there are clearly different camps, most strikingly with reference to the Norman impact: there remain pro-English and pro-Norman parties. And while archaeologists tend to be pro-Viking, those who work mostly with written texts have a greater tendency to emphasize the destruction the Vikings brought.

This is of course a very crude characterization, but the bold lines should give some context to the pieces that follow. All the contributors to this volume are touched by these debates and all discuss, in different ways and with different approaches, the fundamental questions of the extent and nature of the external impact.

Other concerns of previous generations

Although the question of external impact is central, past historians have had other preoccupations too. In these the differences between historians of England and those of Ireland, Scotland, and Wales figure much more sharply. The diversity is reflected by the fact that some of the issues are taken up by contributors to this book, but many are not.

For generations of English historians, issues of freedom have been central. Were English peasants of the sixth and seventh centuries free and did they become more and more enserfed, particularly in the tenth and eleventh centuries? Issues of lordship are related: did the powers of lords extend? How did they extend? Did they become territorialized? What obligations did lords demand from their dependants, and did these increase over time? What of lords? What made a lord? Who constituted the aristocracy, and what size was it? Could people enter these ranks and leave them? How big was the slave population? Interestingly, and surprisingly, these fundamental questions of social structure are barely touched in the Irish, Scottish, and Welsh historiography of this period, and when they are they are mainly treated in the context of customary law—the law tracts declare this or that; therefore this must be the way that society functioned, so many historians have supposed. This difference is partly to be explained by the fact that English writers of the early eleventh century were themselves conscious of the core issues, and their concerns have attracted the attention of generations of historians; it is also partly to be explained by the fact that there is an exceptionally large surviving corpus of early Irish law, and the way that this is framed has had a dominant influence on the shape of early Irish history writing. However, there are other kinds of reason: historians of England, particularly in the second half of the twentieth century, have been more influenced by French historians than have their

Celtic counterparts, who have often—perhaps understandably—followed more nationalist trails.

The militarization—or otherwise—of the aristocracy is a comparable case, although there has been much discussion of warrior bands and warrior societies in Celtic countries. The imposition of military obligations on whole communities in late Saxon England, or parts of communities, has been a long-standing matter of dispute; it gets a brief mention in discussion of Ireland and Wales. The context here is often the development of royal power. While political consolidation and emerging monarchies have been a major interest in all parts, the mechanics and machinery of the growth of royal power have been much more of an English interest. So too the existence of community institutions and their utilization—or destruction—by kings; the notion of a free people, organizing their own business in rural villages, belongs very much to the myth-making of the English, but not the Celtic, past. The contrast arises partly because of the presence of professional lawyers in early Wales and Ireland, especially the latter, and because of their role in the localities; they left less room for community decisions. But it also arises because of the development of the English parliament and the particularities of eighteenth- and nineteenth-century English colonial history. Since it was the English parliament that presided over Irish and Welsh affairs, primitive democracy in Britain and Ireland could only—it appears—have English roots.

In the latter part of the twentieth century writers on Ireland and Wales, though not Scotland, have made a case for increasing commercial exchange and more markets, in an attempt to bring them into the English and continental mainstream of economic development. This has not been entirely successful and the authors of this volume make a very useful contribution towards a more balanced picture.

Lastly, mention needs to be made of two areas that have been prominent in the literature, but are not so controversial. The important role of the family, and particularly of the extended family, has not so much been discussed and debated as assumed appropriate for Scotland, Ireland, and Wales, especially in the twentieth century, under the influence of social anthropology; for England there is some classic literature on the declining role of the kin, in the face of the rise of lordship, for which a thorough examination is long overdue.

Again, contributors to this volume make some subtle points about this subject—that neighbours were important too, for example. The final prominent theme of the histories of the last century is that of the Irish impact on Europe, an impact which began already in the seventh century but was especially notable in the ninth and continued through the tenth and eleventh. Again, this is not controversial and has been noted by many writers, of different backgrounds. The point is important and is sometimes underplayed; it is well made in this volume too.

England versus the rest

In writing this book we have tried to get away from the English-dominated view of the 'British Isles' that has so characterized English history writing; and we have intentionally looked at the development of the islands from the viewpoints of those who know Ireland, Scotland, and Wales as well; indeed, three of the contributors live and work in these countries.

The raiders that came in the 790s and after may have launched their raids at the four areas of Ireland, Scotland, Wales, and England, but they did not set their attack on a single—or on four—kingdoms. Whether we consider the year 800 or the year 1100, there were many political units, many kingdoms, in Britain and Ireland, though the pattern of 1100 was very different from that of 800. As Pauline Stafford makes clear below, the political geography of Britain and Ireland was exceptionally volatile in this period. Even in 1100, we need to think in terms of tens of kings, and other rulers too—lords with regalian rights—although by then the single kingdom of England had largely taken shape (though there was still some change of English territory to come in the Scottish border area in the twelfth century). Indeed, the establishment of the polities of England and Scotland, of a shape very similar to those we know in the early twenty-first century, is one of the main developments of the period covered in this book, and one that sharply differentiates those countries from Ireland and Wales.

As Pauline Stafford also says, it may be that the limited source material that we have emphasizes differences between the regions or creates an appearance of difference where in reality there was none. The point is very well made, but in some respects—even where our evidence is fragmentary—there clearly *were* differences between England and the lands to the north and west. First, and obviously, there were linguistic differences: a Germanic language dominant in England by this period, Celtic languages dominant in the rest, although with an increasing incidence of Norse in the Northern Isles. There were also differences in the way legal judgments were made, especially as between Ireland and the rest; this had a major bearing on the relationship between kings, lawyers, and people. As Huw Pryce points out, by the early eleventh century religious institutions in England were simply not the same as those in the north and west; nor—as Dáibhí Ó Cróinín shows—was something as basic as the practice of writing. Patterns of consumption were strikingly divergent in England, Robin Fleming reveals, as were levels of urbanization—a point made in different ways by Barbara Crawford, David Griffiths, and John Gillingham.

The sources

Pauline's point about sources, however, is extremely important and is one to remember. Taking Britain and Ireland as a whole, the problem is not so much one of absence or paucity of sources but of unevenness (see Dáibhí Ó Cróinín's discussion below, for manuscripts that survive, and for the kinds of text that must have been lost). Considerable quantities of written material survive from England and Ireland, of very varied character—laws, annals, histories, saints' Lives, poems, stories, sermons, scholarly discussions of academic issues, letters, charters (England much more than Ireland), wills (England only), and so on; however, there is virtually none of the official documentation (such as government records) that characterizes more modern centuries (the closest equivalent of such texts in this period is the record of his resources made for the English king in 1086, the Domesday Book; it is of unique and exceptional value, but even this extraordinary text has gaps and ambiguities). By contrast there is very little material from Wales, and what there is is dominated by material from the south-east. There is some good archaeology from Scotland but hardly any written material at all—we largely have to deal with highly inadequate fragments, although there is a small but significant corpus of inscriptions on stone from this period, in Roman, ogam, and runic alphabets. While inscriptions on stone survive from England and Ireland too, in some numbers in the latter case, those from south and central Wales and from the Isle of Man—like the Scottish corpus—are particularly significant, given the paucity of other records from those parts.

We should not, of course, forget the archaeology, or physical evidence of other kinds. Considerable archaeological work has been undertaken in England and we have in-depth studies of a wide range of sites and of thousands of artefacts. Some classic sites of our period were excavated in Ireland in the mid-twentieth century, and the excavation of Dublin later in the century is of outstanding importance. There has been very good recent analysis of art and artefacts too, and some pioneering environmental work. However, overall, the volume of available data is much less than survives from England. Material from Wales is again thin; despite careful attention on the ground, it is very difficult to locate surviving material remains of this period; the important sites of Llandough, Llan-gors, and Llanbedrgoch, excavated in the late 1980s and 1990s, are a notable exception. Material of this period from Scotland is also thinner than that from England and Ireland, but there are very important Viking sites on the Northern and Western Isles, as well as the exceptional monastery, bishopric, and town of Whithorn in Galloway.

Add to these differences of source material the physical differences of land and landscape, which are fundamental to the character of Ireland, Scotland, England, and Wales and to regional differences within those countries (see below, pp. 13–14). Whether the land has mountain, bog, cultivable lowland, or a long coastline makes a difference to the density of settlement, to the kind of living people could make, and to ease of communication. In fact, the availability of cultivable land tended to increase overall in our period, thanks to an improving climate, as did the availability of bodies to work it, thanks to steadily increasing populations in Ireland and in midland and southern England (see below, pp. 97–8). But this was not sufficient to reduce the contrasts between the essential nature of, for example, highland Scotland and south-east England, or western Ireland and mid-Wales.

There is therefore no doubt that both the variety of the physical character of the different countries and the unevenness in the availability of information make sustained comparison difficult. With that in mind, read on.

Figure 1.0 Pharaoh sentences his chief baker to be hanged; from the Old English Illustrated Hexateuch, BL MS Cotton Claudius Biv, fo. 59ʳ.

1

Kings, Kingships, and Kingdoms

Pauline Stafford

During the ninth, tenth, and eleventh centuries the political landscape of Britain and Ireland was dominated by kings and divided into the kingdoms they ruled. The simplicity of that statement masks a political geography which fluctuated dramatically and kings and kingships whose powers varied enormously. Around 800, within what is now England, for example, there were kings of Kent, of the East Anglians, of the Mercians, of the West Saxons, of the Northumbrians, and of the West Welsh (Cornwall). Several of these kingdoms were themselves formed of older and smaller units—in Northumbria for example, the Deirans (roughly modern Yorkshire), and the Bernicians to their north. In the course of these centuries most of these kingdoms disappeared, to be replaced by a single kingdom of the English.

Within what we would recognize as Wales, there were, amongst others, kings of the people of Gwynedd, of Powys, of Dyfed, of Brycheiniog. Between the ninth and eleventh centuries many of these often came under the rule of a single overking, usually based in Gwynedd. That overkingship had not, however, replaced other kingships permanently by 1100. In what is now Scotland the ninth century saw a Pictish overkingship of much of the east and south, and in the west 'Scottish' (i.e. Gaelic) kings in Dalriada, and a British kingship in Strathclyde. During the later ninth and tenth centuries the Pictish overkingship seems to have been taken over by Scottish kings. Kingships in Strathclyde/Cumbria, Galloway, and perhaps Moray survived into the eleventh century, or were newly established. (An almost total

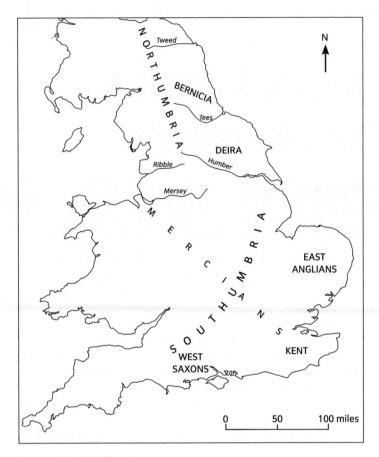

Figure 1.1 English kingdoms *c.*800–1100.

lack of written sources makes the early history of north Britain particularly obscure.) In Ireland the 185 tribes and kings of later antiquarian tradition had gone by 800, if they had ever existed. By the tenth century there were still many kingships. But here too wide overkingships developed, or were already in place, of, for example, the peoples of Leinster, Munster, Connacht. In the eleventh century overkingship was still contested among the most powerful provincial dynasties.

'Ireland', 'Wales', 'Scotland', and 'England' are used here in their modern geographical and political sense. They are potentially misleading terms when applied to these centuries. The 'English' kingdom

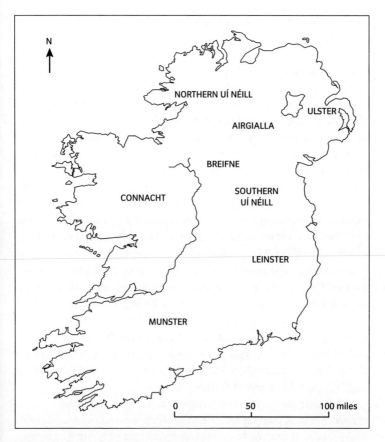

Figure 1.2 Irish provincial overkingdoms.

of the Northumbrians, for example, stretched well to the north of the modern Scottish border, the 'Scottish' kingdom of Strathclyde sometimes to its south. In the west of Britain in the early tenth century the power of English overkings was extending into what is now south-east Wales. Some Welsh kings at this date were being drawn into relations of tribute with kings of the English. The bearings of our modern political geography require reorientation when approaching this period.

Some of this rethinking should acknowledge the importance of geography itself. There is a fundamental difference within Britain between the lowland south and east and the highland north and west.

The English kingdom was essentially a political development of those lowland regions; when it extended north and west of the Pennines and of the Humber and Mersey its control was always different. Neither the geography of Ireland nor its political pattern divides so neatly, though the fertile plain of Brega in the east has a special significance. Like the Humber estuary and its extensive marshy extensions, the Mounth, the central highland region of Scotland, was a geographical boundary often reflected in political ones. The mountainous interior of Wales was a factor which turned some of its kingdoms west to the Irish Sea, and others south and east towards England. The tributary nature of early tenth-century southern Welsh kings has a geographical logic. Other aspects of early political geography are more surprising. The Irish Sea united as much as it divided. Long before AD 800 eastern Ireland, the Western Isles, north-west and south-west Wales, Man, north-west England, and western Scotland had links through settlement, cultural contact, and political interchange. Viking activity in the Irish Sea reflected rather than created these links. In the early tenth century a Viking dynasty linking York and Dublin was one political expression of them. Another was the recurring exile and flight within this area of candidates for kingship and of other political figures: Gruffudd ap Cynan from Gwynedd at the end of the eleventh century or the sons of Harold, king of the English, after the defeat at Hastings in 1066.

Important as physical geography was, however, other factors shaped political geography. Overkings built up wide rule of varying degrees of stability; the brute facts of terrain are only one key to their understanding. The southern Welsh kings may have been turned east by geography. But in the ninth and early tenth centuries they were seeking alliance and protection against the expansion of the northern Welsh rulers of Gwynedd, Rhodri Mawr and his sons, and they sought it from West Saxon kings, like Alfred and Athelstan, who were themselves rapidly extending their rule. There were many Rhodris, Alfreds, and Athelstans in these centuries; the ninth-century Irish overkingship of the eastern-based Uí Néill kings like Máel Sechnaill (846–62), or its Pictish counterparts and their tenth- and eleventh-century MacAlpin successors in Scotland. These overkingships could cross geographical boundaries and create different patterns. In the early tenth century the southern Welsh kings appear as part of a West Saxon overkingship. In the mid-eleventh century, they would be

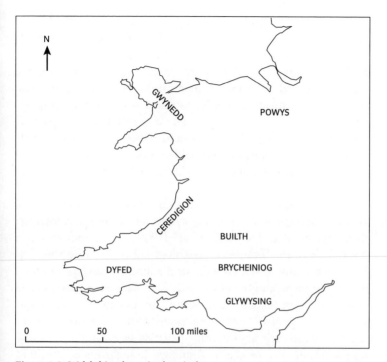

Figure 1.3 Welsh kingdoms in the ninth century.

under that of Gruffudd ap Llywelyn of Gwynedd. The Tees if not the Humber was a geographically logical boundary of the kingdom of the Scots. The activities of Southumbrian kings ensured that the English kingdom stretched north of this, albeit tenuously. Kings as much as geography made the political shape of Britain and Ireland.

So too, perhaps, did cultural factors, the ethnic identities of peoples in particular. Much of the political terminology of these centuries refers to peoples and often links kings with them. Kings are different from lords in being rulers of *peoples*. The immediate impression is again of complexity. So Æthelwulf was king of the West Saxons, his son an underking of the people of Kent. In Ireland there were the Ulaid (Ulstermen), the Laigin (Leinstermen), and groups of peoples like the Airgialla (eastern hostages). These already seem to be 'peoples' rather than tribes, larger in scale, with wider shared identities and ones by which they were regularly identified by others. If 'tribes' can be seen as the small-scale basic building blocks of political development in Ireland, these 'peoples' are already shaped by that political development. But there are other terms which seductively accord with our own notions of political geography. 'Britannia/Britons', 'Cymry', 'Wales/Walenses' for the Welsh; for the Irish: the 'men of Ireland', 'Ireland' (Erenn/Ériu), found in poetry, and whom Máel Sechnaill is recorded as ruling at the time of his death, and Domnall ua Néill in 980; and for the English 'Angelcynn' (angle-kin), or 'Anglo-Saxons', whom Æthelwulf's son and early tenth-century descendants were said to rule. There were not only wide kingships, but notions of wider peoples whom those kings ruled.

Historians have recently shown great interest in these notions, and are cautious about how we should understand and interpret them. When Máel Sechnaill is called 'king of Ireland' this is a description of the breadth of his power, not of an office which he held. Such terms do not have the firm political meanings which we would give them, and sometimes they have different meanings from those we might impose. 'Angelcynn' for example, is no simple synonym for 'England' but a term coined to describe a very specific late ninth- and early tenth-century situation in which the West Saxons, Mercians, and people of Kent were brought under one king. There are other names which are now lost but which had significance then. 'Alba', the Gaelic word for the island of Britain, is used in the tenth century in Scotland. It too may have been newly minted to cover the kingdom ruled by Kenneth MacAlpin's successors, the product of this Scottish warlord's takeover of, or union with, the last Pictish overkings in the mid-ninth century. The breadth of currency of these notions cannot be known, nor how real a political identity they denote. Some of them, like 'Ireland' or 'Britons', are common in the literature. Others, like 'Anglo-Saxon', are newly formed, but out of widely used elements, 'Angle' and 'Saxon', which obviously carried a freight of meaning. Their creation and sudden appearance suggests that political identities were manipulable; the use of older components and ideas in them shows the boundaries of such manipulation and the raw material of them. That raw material was loyalty and identification. Political geography may have been shaped in the mind as well as on the ground and the battlefield.

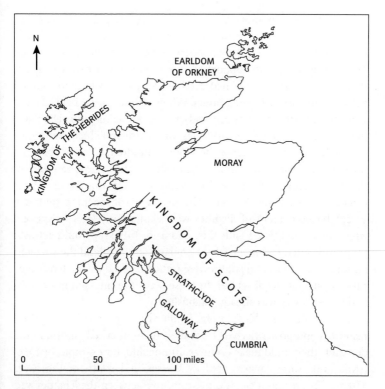

Figure 1.4 Scotland AD *c.*1000.

Kingship, overkingship, and monarchy

By AD 800 kingship was an established and central political fact in Britain and Ireland. It is tempting to begin by dividing these kingships into 'Celtic' and 'Germanic/Anglo-Saxon'. The temptation should be resisted. Much is common to them all. In most, if not all, cases kingship was already on a scale which precluded the face-to-face, everyday, regular contact of so-called 'tribal' kings—though there may have been many more of these in Ireland than in Britain. Larger-scale kingships placed a distance between king and people which underlines a fact central to our understanding of early kings, namely that for many if not most of the aspects of life, the inhabitants of early Britain and Ireland could function perfectly well without them. Kin were far more important, as were neighbourhoods. The duties and links of kinship were everywhere more formal and important than now. Contemporary norms and values put strong pressure on people to support their kin with resources, with aid if they were attacked or harmed. Arable and pastoral farmers worked with kin but also with neighbours. When disputes arose between and within kindreds, and between and among arable or pastoral groupings, there was a need for meetings and processes which could deal with and settle these—hence the English hundred, lathe, or soke, the northern English and southern Scottish *scir*, the Cumbrian *kadrez*, the predecessors of the Welsh commote and *cantref*, the Irish *comaithches* (neighbourhood). The problems of reaching mutually acceptable settlement of disputes were acute. Early laws were overwhelmingly concerned with this, and a lord or king could act as a judge or arbiter. In some parts of England and Scotland the *scirs* and hundreds where local disputes were settled centred by the tenth century or later on royal estates. In these areas the interaction of royal and local activity was already established.

By this date all kings were landlords; a proportion of their resources and power derived from their own inherited lands and the demands they could make on these. In England, for example, by 1066, royal lands were concentrated in Wessex and south of the River Thames. There was a significant scattering between the Thames and the Humber, less between Humber and Tees, and little that we know of to the north of that. This pattern resulted from the disappearance of other kingships, of which the West Saxon was the inheritor, and specifically from the family unions which lay behind the bringing together of Wessex, Mercia, and Kent, where royal land was mostly situated. This land not only provided royal resources. Through its local administrators if not occasional royal visits it provided a virtual royal presence, which was lacking in northern England. The record of 1086 known as Domesday Book allows us to see the extent and pattern of royal holdings for one brief moment in England; we have nothing comparable from elsewhere in these islands and it is difficult thus to make comparisons. Where evidence is available for Wales, that is from the south-east, extensive scattered royal estates are again identifiable. We cannot say whether overkings of Gwynedd acquired estates outside their own ancestral kingdoms as West Saxon kings did; the likelihood is not. A similar scattering has been noted in parts of

Scotland, though here the evidence is late and the situation may have developed after AD 1100.

In addition to their own lands all kings could claim hospitality and sustenance from their people, which translated into real demands for food, renders, and upkeep. The amount of this, who could and could not take it, were issues addressed by English charters and laws and by Irish agreements between kingdoms. The fact of them was clearly accepted. These payments separate kings from other lords. Kings were more than lords of tenants or heads of kindreds, though their origins may lie in both. The king's general relationship with and responsibility for his people underlie these wider demands. They were the basis for the elaboration of others: in England, for example, for the maintenance of bridges, roads, and fortifications, i.e. for the needs of royal armies; in Ireland for the forced labour which built and maintained roads. The *Mabinogi*, possibly of the late eleventh century, has the early king Maelgwn exploiting fiscal districts. It presumably projects contemporary practice into a quasi-mythical past. On this basis in the early eleventh century English kings faced with Viking attacks called for payments from all land to pay mercenaries—the so-called Danegeld. Land on which geld was not paid was declared forfeit. Irish kings by the same date were hiring mercenaries. It is not clear whether they took general and widely based payments of this sort in order to do so, though it has been argued that some Irish kings took general levies by the eleventh century. In 1106 the *Annals of Ulster* referred to a land unit, a *trícha cét* (perhaps comparable with the Welsh *cantref*), as a basis for this levying.

As such demands and levies make clear, kings were warriors, expected to defend their peoples, but also often aggressive and predatory leaders of warbands. Whatever may have been the case with the earliest Irish kings, the warlike nature and function of many of them are clear by the ninth century, as in England, Wales, and Scotland. A foray against neighbouring peoples is a recurring feature of the early stages of reigns of both Scottish and Irish kings. It appears almost as a semi-ritual, an extension of the rites by which a man became a king and proved himself. But it was also part of the resources of kingship, since raiding was about plunder and tribute. It was kings who were expected to respond to Viking attack. Failure here was a factor in the disappearance of several individual kings of Mercia in the ninth century. Success, which may often have grown in the telling, was a feature of some of the successful dynasties like that of Kenneth MacAlpin, Alfred, perhaps of Brian Bóruma (Brian Boru). The latter's wars were in truth between Irish kings, with Vikings only an additional complication. It was part of the twelfth-century nationalist and royalist retelling of the story which made them Irish versus Vikings. Alfred had already shaped the story himself in this way in ninth-century Wessex. Brian's battles against Irish kings were the common coin of struggles between kings, and increasingly for the prize of overkingship, throughout these islands. Only later nationalist historiography has written tenth-century West Saxon aggression north of the Humber as attempts to unify England.

These basic attributes of kingship were common. So too, by this date, was the phenomenon of overkingship. This was a wider rule which involved the domination of other kings, though the term should also be applied to rapidly expanding kingships where other kings were temporarily replaced. Rhodri Mawr (844–78) began as king of Gwynedd in 844, to which Powys was added in 855 and Seisyllwg in 872. His grandson Hywel Dda began as a king of Dyfed in 904, to which he added Seisyllwg c.920 after the death of his brother and Gwynedd in 942 after the death of his cousin. Ecgberht had blood claims on the kingdom of the West Saxons and probably Kent; he became briefly king of the Mercians after defeating their king in battle. His great-grandson Edward began as king of the West Saxons, became king of Mercia after the death of his sister who ruled there, and took over the kingdom of the East Angles after a series of military campaigns. Máel Sechnaill of the Uí Néill (846–62) was a similarly aggressive and successful warrior, building up an overkingship which led the *Annals* at his death to accord him the title of 'king of Ireland'—a claim which bears comparison with the *Anglo-Saxon Chronicle's* statement that Alfred at his death was 'king over all Angelcynn, except that part which was under Danish domination'.

As these instances show, overkingship was built on blood and battle—the personal claims based on kinship, the reduction of other kingdoms to tributary status through military activity, and the maintenance of the loyalty of followers through the resources which resulted. These overlordships might then be held together by the same means. Underkingships were often in the hands of family members, as when Ecgberht's son held Kent under his father or in the very complex arrangement which bound Wessex and Mercia through the marriage of Æthelflæd, Alfred's daughter and Edward's sister, to a Mercian king. In eleventh-century Scotland, Duncan, Malcolm II's son, held Strathclyde. Remoter relatives held parts of the Uí Néill hegemony, just as some tenth-century English ealdormen (local rulers, and at least in principle royal appointees), like Æthelweard of West Wessex or Ælfhere of Mercia, were royal kin. Marriage was an essential part of these very personal politics. In the first half of the eleventh century Macbeth married Gruoch, a descendant of Malcolm I; the marriage was one element in the strategies and circumstances which brought Macbeth to the Scottish kingship. The claims of Hywel Dda and his descendants on Dyfed came from Hywel's wife Elen, and those of Llywelyn, father of Gruffudd, on Gwynedd were strengthened by his marriage to Angharad, daughter of Maredudd, and may even have derived from her. Tenth-century kings of Wessex/ England were determined serial monogamists, seeking politically strategic matches with daughters of ealdormen. Edgar, who started from a power base in Mercia and then acquired Wessex, discarded two wives as his needs and aspirations changed. Raiding, ravaging, and the threat of it kept tributary kingdoms in line. The men of York were first brought to submission by Athelstan in the 920s, then ravaged by West Saxon kings in the mid-tenth century when their leading men chose other kings. The plunder of battle and raiding provided one of the cements which held kingdoms and overkingdoms together.

Overkingships—or hegemonies as they are often now called—were thus built on the personal ties of kinship and marriage. They were built on success in battle—and, like that success, could as easily be undone as built up. They were held together by the internal bonds of followers who supported the successful, and were as likely to desert when other stars were rising. At its most caricatured, this sort of political configuration was unstable, and could mushroom and disappear as rapidly. Its building blocks were the smaller kingdoms and lordships which were brought into tribute and/or friendship by these means. These set boundaries of a sort, but the blocks could, at least in this caricature, be assembled and reassembled in fluctuating patterns. This type of kingship was common to Britain and Ireland in the early middle ages, as it was common to much of western Europe at this date. It is characterized by an exercise of royal power which is likely to be intermittent if nonetheless potentially harsh—tribute, hostages, forced works, ravaging—and by personal bonds and fluctuating geographical extent. Its milder face is the distribution of treasure—mild to the receiver if not to those from whom it is taken—and the bonding rituals of feasting or hunting.

It is now often compared to and contrasted with territorial rule. Here the activity of the ruler is felt regularly—in taxation, military service, through agents and agencies which are responsible for these and for the king's responsibility for and interference in the working of local courts. If hegemony is characterized by extensive and intermittent rule, this is rule which is regular and in depth. The fluctuating nature of overlordship is replaced by firmer territorial boundaries. Historians are less and less inclined to discuss this as the growth of governmental institutions, but rather as the intensification of royal activity, the increase in its incidence, the development of a situation in which kings become an increasingly important part of the habits of mind and thought-world within which the powerful made their choices and decisions. These changes may be linked to others, though they have no necessary causal connections. A more restricted pattern of succession may develop, in which the political unit is not divided and reassembled at every succession. There may be a greater sacralization of kingship, one which exalts it and stresses its uniqueness, so that, once kingship is acquired, claims to it on the part of others become more and more difficult. The sum total of these differences could be said to distinguish two different types of wide rule by one king—overkingship and monarchy. In some respects these are ideal types—and kingship continued to show features of both long after this period. Personal links and bonds, marriage as a mechanism of politics, war for plunder, and the distribution of that plunder to cement loyalties are recurring features of personal rule in all periods. Conversely, even within a wide overkingship, there were often core areas, heartlands where the layering and intensification of the exercise of power implied in the monarchical model may always have been a feature—thus, for example, in Wessex as part of a wider England, or in eastern Scotland, especially what is now Fife, within the Scottish overkingship. The first conclusion from a comparison of the kingships of Ireland and Britain at this date must be that the fundamentals of kingship and the mechanisms of overkingship are remarkably similar. Already, however, some different if not divergent development can be seen. Historians have been inclined to identify such divergence even more clearly in the areas of succession and law.

Succession to the throne

Kings were normally of royal birth, with claims through blood. The royal genealogies which are such a feature of Welsh and Irish sources are ample testimony to this. Fewer of them have survived from England, but they tell the same tale. A king was legitimized through his ancestry; his authority and some of the material basis for his power came through blood inheritance. Royal blood, however, flows through many veins. How much of it is necessary for succession, whether preference is given to older or younger heirs, to brothers or sons, through how many generations claims live on—all these and more are questions to which there can be different answers. Historians have been inclined to see the divergences here within Britain and Ireland as leading to fundamentally different political development. Pictish matriliny, Irish, and especially Welsh wide kinship claims have been identified as weakening, leading to bitter dispute. English succession, by contrast, is seen as settling in the tenth if not the ninth century into a more orderly pattern, even a deliberately planned one. There are still many questions here. Were the Picts matrilineal? Did the Scots and some of the Irish practise a system of alternating succession with the kingship passing between different branches of the descendants of Kenneth and of the Uí Néill respectively? Or is this a pattern imposed on what is really a struggle by royal descendants to make good a claim before they become too remote to attract sufficient support? Did the fact that Welsh kinship in general recognized the claims of a wider family, descending from a more remote ancestor, lead to more bitter disputes here? Or is that dispute rather the result of the emergence of overkingship and an intensified effort to obtain it? Was the fact that brother succeeded brother from the mid-ninth century in Wessex a deliberate strategy, offsetting intra-family fighting? Or was it an accidental development, stoking considerable tension?

Whatever the answers to these questions, what is common to all succession at this date is that it rarely if ever followed strict rules and was everywhere a subject of intense dispute and rivalry. Power was a major determinant of succession, or rather power and authority. All these kingships were, loosely speaking, 'elective'. That did not entail any notion of democracy. It did mean that there was a pool of eligible (literally choose-able) candidates, not just one obvious one, and that that pool was determined by varying combinations of blood/birth and competence, i.e. resources, warrior ability, and other kingly attributes. It also meant that a new king had to be acceptable to the elites who would sustain his rule, whether secular or clerical, and in particular to those whose task was formally to inaugurate or instate him, i.e. to participate in the ceremonies which made him a king and separated him from other lords. A king needed support, and questions of eligibility and thus legitimacy affected his success in mustering it. Legitimacy and the factors which determined that were as important as swords and resources in attracting and retaining that support; the two cannot really be separated. In ninth-century eastern Ireland, candidates were almost always Uí Néill family members; in tenth-century Gwynedd, candidates were direct descendants of Rhodri or married into his line; Kenneth's descendants dominated tenth- and eleventh-century Scotland as did Æthelwulf's in Wessex and ultimately the kingdom of the English. These families clearly established a claim which it was hard, though not impossible, to overturn. The very success of overkingships made them tempting prizes. They could strengthen a dynasty and its hold on the throne, but also intensify or provoke struggle within it or from rivals to supplant it.

Succession dispute is a common feature of all these kingships. Sometimes this was between families. In late tenth- and eleventh-century Ireland Brian Bóruma, king of Munster, and his descendants became a rival dynasty which eventually supplanted the Uí Néill in the east. Sometimes it was within families. Thus among the West Saxon, later English, family every succession between 955 and 1042, and most of those between 899 and 1100, was disputed, usually within the royal family. In tenth- and eleventh-century Gwynedd the picture is similar, though the family in question is a wider one; and, as in Wessex/England, succession questions and dispute led to the murder of royal kin. In Scotland, too, Malcolm II (1005–34) murdered his way to the throne. Arguments about suitability for kingship may have been involved in some of these disputes. Was a king a good warrior? Could he provide defence against Vikings? The latter may well have been a factor in ending some individual reigns in ninth-century Mercia, or in commending a man like Alfred in relation to his young nephews. The importance of proving oneself warlike is underlined by the forays which Uí Néill kings of Tara or Scottish kings undertook soon after their accessions. But forays are about resources as well as proof of suitability, and brute force could transfer kingdoms and kingship, as it did in eleventh-century England, where conquest twice delivered the throne to intrusive dynasties—the Danish one of Cnut and the Norman one of William.

Much attention has been devoted to succession practices. The critical questions are not simply, however, whether certain practices lead to more or less dispute—dispute seems to be the norm—but whether dispute is a factor allowing or encouraging the continual dismantling and reassembling of overkingships. The question is not so much *how* people succeeded, but *to what* they succeeded and whether the 'how' has a critical impact on the 'what'. The impact of disputes on the kingdoms which these kings ruled varied. In Wales, the death of a king usually dismantled the overlordship which he had assembled. So, for example, when Maredudd died, Gwynedd was claimed by Llywelyn, a remote descendant of a grandson of Rhodri, who at some point married Maredudd's daughter. But the rest of Maredudd's overlordship was claimed by other descendants of Rhodri. Gruffudd ap Llywelyn later reassembled Maredudd's power—but only through battle. The stable political unit was Gwynedd, which was fought over but not divided. The significance of succession practice here is that it opened the possibility of dismantling on the death of every overking. No narrow dynasty became permanently identified with a wider unit within which intensification of loyalties and activity could then occur. In Ireland, Uí Néill candidates claimed a wide overkingship with some degree of success up to the ninth century. From the ninth to the eleventh century, however, their power was hotly contested, especially by the kings of Munster. Once again at the level of the overkingship, as opposed to the smaller kingdoms, there was no continuity of existence and association with a particular family. Here, as perhaps in Wales, the survival of powerful rival kingdoms was important. Tadc, son of Brian Bóruma, continued to make his own claims to the kingship acquired by his half-brother Donnchadh. He sought refuge and help from Diarmait of Leinster. Would division among the sons of Brian have had the same significance without the presence of Diarmait and Leinster?

Bitter struggle and exile of candidates was a feature of the Scottish/ Alba and West Saxon/English situation. In the eleventh century

Scottish exiles sought refuge to the south in Northumbria. English royal blood fled across the Channel to Flanders or Normandy, and, after 1066, to Dublin. Whether succession dispute divided the Scottish kingdom is difficult to say. Moray and Strathclyde may have emerged or re-emerged during eleventh-century struggle, but it is not clear whether they were powerful enough to be a Leinster in north British politics. Alba like Gwynedd or Munster remained undivided; but its kings' wider overkingship may have passed on with it more often than happened in Wales. Wessex passed in the line of Æthelwulf. Between 850 and the 950s, Kent and Mercia were added to this, largely held together through family. This was a common feature of overkingships; Brian made his son an underking of Dublin, and Scottish sons may have ruled in the eleventh century in Strathclyde. The West Saxon-Mercian arrangement was particularly successful. In spite of disputes which came very close to dividing it in the 920s and 950s, it held. In England, as eventually in Scotland, other king-ships which made up the earlier overkingships disappeared. Though eleventh-century conquest came close to dividing the kingdom again, especially in 1035, the wider unity survived.

The decisions against division were taken by the elites. No candidate for succession could ever be credible without sufficient support from them. Their attitudes and aims determined the outcome of succession dispute, not merely who won, but what he acquired. In England, and perhaps in Scotland, supporters sought control of the enlarged overkingship of the English, not the reassertion of other, older kingships. By the tenth century the dynasty united both Mercian and West Saxon/Kentish royal blood, which may have helped. A key factor may simply be habit. The West Saxon/Mercian/Kentish polity lasted for long enough to become the accepted prize for which candidates fought. Mercian nobles may have sought their own king in the 950s or 1030s, but this was apparently to make him king of the English, not to go it alone. That decision, not the succession practice which produced dispute, was critical.

Kings and law

Kings, as we have seen, were not essential to the working of law, arbitration, and justice. Disputes were settled locally in courts which met and operated locally. Kin and community provided their own policing. Elaborate systems of surety underpinned the system. Kin, friend, or lord stood guarantor for the individual in a variety of circumstances—for the payment of fines after settlements were agreed, for a person's good conduct or word and for the specific operation of these, in marriage negotiations or buying and selling, for example. The extent to which kings had become involved in, or been drawn into, the law and its workings is a second area where historians have seen divergence, between on the one hand Wales and Ireland, where the king's concern with the law was minimal, and on the other England, where it developed strongly. (Once again Scottish documentation is virtually non-existent.) The problem here is the very different nature of the surviving texts. They may mask fundamental similarities across all these systems and in the kings' involvement in them.

From Wales and Ireland on the one hand we have extensive legal tracts covering in great detail such topics as the working of systems of surety, the levels and nature of fines for personal injury, theft, status, and court procedures. These texts survive in much later documents, but in the Irish case in particular painstaking work has uncovered and is continuing to uncover their earlier layers. These are apparently statements of custom—'how we do things'—not legislation as we would understand it—'how we are going to do things from now on'. These legal tracts are schoolbooks, designed to train lawyers, and to serve as handbooks for lawyers. The Welsh and Irish laws were never neutral records of what everybody did. They fulfil the didactic need for comprehensive statements, arguably filling in spaces and certainly tidying up what was almost certainly a messier practice. In the case of Irish law, by the later middle ages, when the surviving texts were written, they were archaic and remote from practice. Some may already have been so by the tenth and eleventh centuries. The Irish canonical tracts, like *Senchas Már*, had probably already been written by the eighth century. In both Ireland and Wales, all these tracts are lawyers' tracts, produced by and for a secular learned legal class, almost caste, who were the legal experts in these societies. The survival of the odd reference to such people in early Scotland suggests that here too, or at least in some parts, a similar situation pertained.

The nature of the texts and the people for whom they were produced is crucial. Their attempt at comprehensiveness is part of their general purpose—to deal as fully as possible with the questions on which a lawyer might be called for guidance. Their lists of fines and the intricacies of suretyship are guidance precisely for the conduct of arbitration, where settlement could only be achieved if it were seen to be just and honourable. The lawyer provided the guidance as to what 'everyone did' which made such acceptance easier. In the case of Irish law, it has been argued that the language of the law may even have been functionally archaic and separate from the everyday. Like religious ritual it worked to give authority through difference, through the mystique and awe of the court. The Irish texts thus give a picture of the law as timeless, unchanging, static—if not remote from everyday life and rather archaic.

What is missing from both the Welsh and Irish material is the law in practice. There are virtually no records of what happened in courts, of the procedures in action in individual cases. The richness of the texts masks a real poverty. We know very little about how these laws worked, though the saga and other narrative literature offer historians possibilities of advance here.

The situation in England is radically different, or rather the textual evidence is. Here there was no learned class, no specialized lawyers before AD 1100. There were, of course, courts where settlements were made. Here the expertise was that of the leading men of the local community. They were important in the process of arbitration, and also in the making of any final judgment. Such men were the judgment makers, as opposed to legal experts, in the Welsh and Irish system too. In England they also provided the expertise; they were expected to have some knowledge of the law, and the best of them were probably well versed in it. Courts usually also had a president, or judge. By the tenth and eleventh centuries many such judges in England had some link with the king. At the level of the shire, ealdormen (local rulers, and perhaps royal appointees) and bishops sat as judges. These men could give final judgment, bring the case to final settlement. This required authority—which might derive, as with the legal experts, from knowledge of the law, but also from social or other rank. We owe most of our surviving legal texts to the interest in the law of late tenth- and eleventh-century bishops, in particular Archbishop Wulfstan of York and Gundulf of Rochester. But the non-professional nature of all these men involved in English courts means that no group produced texts which provided the comprehensive treatments which would be useful in the training of others. A handful of tracts do survive which show that the system was fundamentally similar to that in Wales and Ireland—like the tracts on status and surety from *c.*1000. But there is nothing to compare with the lawyers' books.

What *have* survived from early England are records of disputes in courts and laws—sometimes misleadingly called 'codes' by modern historians—associated with the names of kings, like the laws of Alfred, Æthelred II, and Cnut. The latter are varied, and only the law of Cnut from this period, and just possibly that of Alfred, should be thought of as codes in the sense of bringing earlier practice together, confirming, and in places changing it. Most of the surviving English laws belong to the late ninth, tenth, and early eleventh centuries. This is partly an accident of collection—the interests of Archbishop Wulfstan in the early eleventh century ensured the collection of many of them. But the later collections confirm the impression that after the early 1020s there were no more which were seen as important enough to be committed to writing. The tenth-century texts are varied. Many are concerned with theft and methods of dealing with thieves. Related in essential ways to this, many are concerned with procedures—the regular holding of courts, and the procedures for bringing people to justice. In both cases they build on existing procedure, seek to regularize it, or to confirm it or to change it slightly—but always to throw the weight of royal authority behind it. A few are sets of instructions to royal officials about, for example, the distribution of alms from royal estates or the taking of oaths of loyalty or the collection of royal dues. It is difficult to believe that such instructions did not continue into the eleventh century—it is simply that the impulse to record them, and the desire to present kings as lawgivers which lies behind that, was less strong. A few laws are concerned with what we would consider moral issues—dues to be paid to churches or Sunday buying and selling. Much of this points to the importance of tenth-century ecclesiastical reform and its royal ideology in the English situation.

These laws do make some changes, or affirmations. But on the whole they reiterate rulings and regularize procedures. The latter is not insignificant. Knowing when and where a court would meet is a central issue in the processes of self-help by which these societies regulated themselves. Agreement about whose oath counted for what was important when oath helping was central to judgments—and here, as elsewhere, the English laws are obviously in the same world as the Welsh and Irish, attempting to remove points of contention in order to make lasting settlement more likely.

But what is so striking at first sight about these laws, and seems to distinguish them from the Welsh and Irish, is the activity of the king, and of his officials. They are issued in the king's name. In them he appears, significantly, controlling his own servants. He adds his authority to the respect which all should pay to the church and its precepts. He underlines the community's own mechanisms for dealing with theft and violence. And in doing so it is not so much that he makes new law as that he takes responsibility for—or at least proclaims his responsibility for—the maintenance of the peace and order which civil society in general was organized to provide. By the ninth and tenth centuries the English consecration ritual for a king associated all these functions with him. In the earliest versions he enjoined them on his people. By the end of the tenth century he promised this peace and order before he was crowned and anointed. And the threefold promise—to suppress theft, to maintain peace and order, to protect the church—is precisely what the English laws of the tenth century are about. By the early eleventh century this same language shaped criticism of kings and played a crucial part in the exile and return of Æthelred and the acceptance of Cnut. These laws are just one sign that English kingship was, by the early eleventh century and in some eyes at least, being separated from the individual English king.

All this makes the difference between England on the one hand and Wales and Ireland on the other look very sharp. On one side, royal orders about cattle rustling, royal servants, and oaths of loyalty to the king; on the other what are often seen as arcane statements about offences by and against dogs and about bee swarms, or labyrinthine rules on surety.[1] It is a contrast compounded by the survival

---

[1] Irish Canonical Collection, probably reflecting native law, printed and trans. F. Kelly, *A Guide to Early Irish Law* (Dublin, 1988), 354–5; Bechbretha §§ 45–9, ibid. 356–7.

in England of records of disputes in court. Here the law in action looks dynamic and rational beside, for example, strange lists of compensations related to trees, which judge that a cow hide should be paid for stripping oak bark sufficient to tan a woman's sandals, an ox hide if it were enough for a man's.[2] But we should be wary. Ownership of trees and bees, and damage to and by animals, were critical questions in rural economies. Precise notions of levels of compensation were essential to the acceptance of a settlement as honourable and thus to its permanence. Such questions must have been significant in England too, but the lack here of comprehensive texts such as the lawyers' books means that documentation of them has not survived. English royal laws themselves need careful treatment. They are part of tenth-century royal ideology and are no simple and straightforward guide to royal activity. The same basic system and processes underlie the English texts. We can sometimes see that, and not merely in the tracts on status or surety. Alfred's laws deal with dogs disappearing after committing offences and their owners' liability, and rule on whether a tree which fell and killed a man belongs to the victim's kin or the original owner. We are on the floor of the same courts where Irish or Welsh lawyers were providing guidance which could lead to honourable and acceptable settlement.[3] Whereas Alfred's laws are a selection—perhaps of the king's own judgments—the Welsh and Irish tracts seek to be exhaustive. But if Alfred's laws represent his own judgments, perhaps there is a fundamental difference here, and one of the degree of royal involvement.

In England kings were clearly involved in the law and its procedures. The laws are ideological, but they gave the king real responsibilities, for guaranteeing courts and their meetings, for example, and underline his traditional role as judge. Is this a real contrast with Irish and Welsh kings, where a legal learned class rivalled and squeezed out royal authority and stunted its development? The simple existence of a class of lawyers, even one committed to its own survival and status, is no automatic inhibition to royal power. We need to examine the legal activities of Irish and Welsh kings. Irish kings were judges—and not merely for their own

[2] F. Kelly, 'The Old Irish Tree List', *Celtica*, 11 (1976), 107–24 at 109.
[3] Alfred §§ 23 and 13, printed D. Whitelock (ed.), *English Historical Documents*, I, 2nd edn. (London, 1979), 411–12.

followers and tenants. In the documents which regulate relations between kingdoms, like that between the Airgialla and the Uí Néill overlords, this is clear. As in England, consecration was a point where royal duties and roles were enunciated. Irish kings, like their English counterparts, declared the peace in a *rechtge* issued at their inauguration or at times of plague and war. Though the principle is the same, this appears to be a more temporally and geographically restricted thing than the English kings' generally promulgated peace. The Irish tracts on kingship make the king a judge in general and enjoin him to act with wisdom and counsel. *Airecht*, the tract on court procedure, makes the king the ultimate judge and promulgator of judgment.[4] Is Alfred very different when he announces his judgments? The Irish annals are explicit in their association of the king and law giving and by implication perhaps peacekeeping. The lack of charters and court records makes it difficult to know whether there was any Irish parallel for the intensifying, habit-forming royal activity of tenth- and eleventh-century England. The limited nature of the *cáin* points in one direction; the annals in another. In 1040 the *Annals of Inisfallen* record that the king of Munster proclaimed laws against theft, manual labour on Sunday, feats of arms, and cattle movement, whilst under 1068 these *Annals* state that 'no better (laws), were enacted in Munster for a long time' than those of Toirdelbach Ua Briain. The annals may flatter, we may have ideology and propaganda—as indeed we have in some English law. But these are kings doing what English kings had done.

The chief differences then may be textual. The learned legal profession preserved laws as lawyers wanted and needed to remember them; if kings were originally associated with any of them, that seems to have been irrelevant. In Wales, however, an apparent memory of royal authority is enshrined in the later texts, where the origin of the law tracts is linked with Hywel Dda in the mid-tenth century. Laws could be associated with kings who, as far as we know, never issued any. After 1066 the 'Laws of King Edward' seem to mean no more than 'hallowed tradition'. Hywel's name may carry the same significance, or be later royalist propaganda projected into a mythical past. But Hywel was in contact with English kings in their tenth-century lawmaking stage. He and his advisers may well have sought to imitate

---

[4] F. Kelly, 'An Old Irish Text on Court Procedure', *Peritia*, 5 (1986), 74–106, § 2, at 85.

them, an imitation perhaps made easier because Welsh, like Irish and English, kingship was rooted in Christian and Old Testament models of kings as judges. In tenth-century England, however, that Christian tradition was leading to a presentation of the king as law-maker and a concern with his legal activity which fed the development of royal power.

Church and king

Kings were to some extent sacral, or at least set apart and invested with varying degrees of religious mystique. In early Ireland it is clear that kings were seen as somehow embodying the fertility and good fortune of the land and its inhabitants, and the same notions are present in the consecration rituals of tenth- and eleventh-century English kings. Rituals of inauguration underlined the king's separateness and difference. In these Christian societies, however, kings were not priests. This did not mean that they were divested of all religious significance. Christ himself was one model of a king, a Christ who had himself been remodelled as a king. The Old Testament rulers David and Solomon were ideal types, of the warrior and wise judge respectively. The mid-eleventh-century English king Edward the Confessor was cast as Solomon by his biographer. Where evidence is fullest, in England and Ireland, churchmen had become involved in the inauguration of kings by c.800, specifically in their anointing. Christianity could provide its own validation of kings, and make its own contributions to the ideology of kingship. By and large this worked to strengthen kingship.

Kings were everywhere patrons of churches and often closely linked with individual ones. A mid-ninth-century bishop of Sherborne was a relative of King Æthelwulf; in the late tenth century the abbot of Killaloe was a kinsman of Brian Bóruma; in mid-eleventh-century Scotland the abbot of Dunkeld was a king's son-in-law and father of a king. Such links are one basis for the strong royal ideology in much Christian writing. In Wales there is more criticism of harrying, predatory kings. This may reflect a real difference, though here too kings were patrons of churches and we may be misled by the nature of the evidence which has survived. In both England and

Ireland churchmen could be major propagandists for individual kings. Brian's successful wooing of Armagh is reflected in the insert in the Book of Armagh denominating him as 'ruler/*imperator Scotorum*'. The *Hibernensis*, the influential early Irish canon collection, presents kings who sit in judgment and can order death. Irish ideas were one inspiration of Carolingian (i.e. ninth-century Frankish) thinking on kings, which in turn inspired tenth-century English thinking. These royalist ideas, however, do not merely spring from patronage and kinship connection. Increasing emphasis on celibacy in tenth- and eleventh-century English reform may have been a factor making direct kinship between bishops or abbots and kings rarer here, though that did not apply to abbesses and nunneries. That did not, however, mean a distancing between kings and reforming churchmen. Round about AD 1000 in England Archbishop Wulfstan of York was opening a law of Æthelred with the words 'we shall all love and honour one God and zealously hold one Christian faith and entirely cast off every heathen practice; and we all have confirmed both with word and with pledge that we will hold one Christian faith under the rule of one king', sentiments which linked the unified rule of one king over one people on earth with the one God in heaven.[5]

That an archbishop of York should express such sentiments about a southern English king is especially noteworthy. York was the archbishopric of the old kingdom of the Northumbrians. In the ninth century its archbishops had consecrated Northumbrian kings, and as late as the mid-tenth century an archbishop of York had been involved in accepting a Viking king there. Fifty years later his successor was proclaiming the unity of king and people; now the 'people' were not the Northumbrians but the English. By the later 1060s, in the aftermath of the Norman Conquest, the last native archbishop, Ealdred, transferred that same idea of unity and that same acceptance of a single English king to the Conqueror, William. In spite of northern uprisings after 1066, Ealdred consecrated no rival to William. In the eyes of churchmen like this, England by the eleventh century if not the later tenth was a unified kingdom, the English a single people and ruled by a single king. These same churchmen had developed tenth-century consecration ceremonies in line with a clear idea of kingship as an office with duties. They had been instrumental in

---

[5] V Æthelred § 1, printed Whitelock (ed.), *English Historical Documents*, 442.

extending the king's coronation oath into royally promulgated laws. Wulfstan expressed his sentiments of unity at the beginning of one of them.

The ruthlessness and brute power of West Saxon, Southumbrian overkings was a major factor in subduing Northumbria. The mid-tenth-century archbishop who accepted a Viking king was taken south and imprisoned. The North was harried and the ancient church at Ripon burnt. From now on northern archbishops were southern appointees, their loyalty secured through the joint holding of the rich bishopric of Worcester. But the ideology was not simply a reflection of this, it had its own origins and wielded its own force, binding a Wulfstan or an Ealdred to its ideals.

The basis for such a strong ideological development was present elsewhere, not least in Ireland. Armagh had clear connections with ideas of wider rule, as Brian realized. But development here did not follow the same path or follow at the same pace. Here, for example, the king's law and peace, promulgated at his inauguration, remained limited to that time and place. Irish ideas had fed Carolingian notions of kingship, but the fully-fledged Carolingian royal ideology which played such a role in England was not retransmitted to Ireland. It may be the result of different conjunctions of successful overkingship and ecclesiastical reform. In England the tenth-century dynasty had precisely the profile of success to match reformers' needs for support and their notions of what a king could and should be.

Development of royal resources

In the late ninth and early tenth centuries, a new southern English kingship developed, partly in aggressive expansion against Viking settlements, partly in a union of the Mercian and West Saxon royal dynasties. The latter even more than the former laid the basis, as we have seen, of the extensive and scattered royal lands south of the Thames and in the Midlands. It is arguable that the tenth-century Scottish kingship was itself a product of such a combination of dynastic marriage and battle. If so, Pictish royal lands may similarly have passed to Kenneth MacAlpin's descendants. Neither Welsh nor Irish overkingships appear to have acquired the same wide and permanent landed base.

In addition, the resources of tenth-century English kings included profits from an active trading and monetary economy. Coin was in regular use in England. It was struck in the king's name, and by the late tenth century seems to have been effectively controlled by local royal agents. Dies had to be acquired from royal sources and the coin type was changed regularly. Huge payments were made by English kings to the Vikings who attacked c.1000—peaking in 1018 at £82,000 of silver. The remnants of these enormous sums have been found in the coin hoards of Scandinavia. They are a sign of the monetization of the English economy, or at least the capacity to change bullion quickly into coin. And the king was one beneficiary of this. The only other kings in Britain and Ireland to have this sort of control of coinage were the Irish kings of Dublin, where urban development and trade paralleled that of England, although not in scale. Development here was later, though the attraction of Dublin to Irish kings by the early eleventh century was based in part on this wealth and royal access to it. There is nothing comparable in Wales or Scotland, nor in England north of the Tees or west of the Pennines—Chester and York were the most northerly mints, and both had some of the characteristics of frontier mints. There is undoubtedly a link between the greater wealth of the English kingdom, its more liquid silver form, the ability of English kings to tap it, and the power of tenth- and eleventh-century English kingship.

As a guarantor of the peace and law, Irish and English kings claimed a share of the fines paid in courts. In England, tenth-century laws elaborated this idea, and offered a share to local lords, to nobles sometimes acting as royal agents (ealdormen or reeves), sometimes merely as lords who brought their own men to justice. The nobility, or at least those linked to royal service, thus gained an interest in the extension of royal power. In such partnership of interest, we can begin to see how royal power grows and becomes effective. If the Irish judicial fines were effective, they must have been collected in similar ways. In the Irish case, however, the fines appear to have been restricted in application, linked to the inaugural declaration of law. The differing developments in royal law and ideology here had resource implications.

In the course of the tenth century, English kings also extended their interference into the realm of noble inheritance itself. The king, who had always been a leader of a warband and provided them with weapons and equipment, came to receive a ritual acknowledgement of that in a heriot. This was a payment, in swords, horses, and other equipment, which an heir made to the king when he took over his father's land. Along with forfeiture of land demanded from those who had broken the king's peace in significant ways, this took English kings into the delicate territory of noble family inheritance itself. By the end of the tenth century a great noble like Wulfbold was judged guilty of many crimes and his lands declared forfeit to the king. At a similar date the king, Æthelred, refused to accept the heriot of the widow of Ætheric of Bocking, effectively refusing her right to take over her husband's lands as his widow. In these respects English royal power appears well developed and harsh. There is no apparent parallel in any other British or Irish kingdom—though the difference between the sort of evidence which has survived from England and from everywhere else makes it difficult to be certain.

It is of course possible to overstate English royal power. Wulfbold's lands were declared forfeit three times, and it was only at the point of weakness after his death that intervention was successful. It was at precisely such a moment that Ætheric's widow found herself vulnerable. But such moments of vulnerability occurred. And royal intervention worked here, as elsewhere, in part because it was in others' interests to enforce it. Tenth-century English kings granted forfeit lands to others; it was those others who often pursued the case. One man's loss was another's gain. Once again royal power was as great as that of its local supporters and of the extent of royal aspiration. And ruthlessness if not corruption were almost structural parts of its working. It was a virtuous circle with vicious results. But it was not amoral. What kings aspired to do was to some extent determined by what kingship was seen to be, and by changes in this determined by such developments as tenth-century reform. That also meant that what kings did was judged by what kingship was seen as for. And at moments of crisis, as at the peak of Viking attacks in 1013–17, the oppressions as well as the ideals of kingship could be clearly identified. That very articulation was in turn a proof that the oppressions had been real ones, that royal power had, by whatever means, worked. Tenth-century English kings had been in a virtuous circle of extending power. The more they made their demands work—for fines, for geld, for forfeiture—the more they had to offer. These demands themselves became the stuff of patronage. And few great nobles were anxious to support a claimant to the throne who would have divided the wealthy enlarged kingdom within which this system operated. The North was outside it, in every way. Here royal demands were experienced by the elites as nothing but oppression. The limits of this virtuous circle lay on the Ribble and the Tees, if not the Humber and the Mersey.

External forces—Vikings and Normans

The impact of the Vikings and Normans confirmed some of the developments outlined here, sparked others, and acted as a trace which reveals the patterns emerging. The first Viking attacks and settlements in the late eighth or ninth century turned the Scottish kings of the west eastward; the kingship of Alba was a result of their takeover of Pictish overlordship. The Vikings reinforced Irish Sea links. The Dublin/York Viking kingdom was a threat that brought southern English kings north to try to enforce their rule. Defeat at Viking hands undermined individual kings, like the last native rulers at York and some Mercian kings. Victory against them gave others an edge which they and their descendants could exploit—as in the case of Alfred of Wessex, Kenneth MacAlpin, or Máel Sechnaill. The Irish Sea became a slaving area, and the Welsh were both victims and accomplices. Slaves formed an element in the tributes which drained the resources of tenth-century Welsh kings. The alliance of some Welsh claimants with slaving fleets provided them with support, but perhaps at the expense of the development of deeper links with their own elites. Viking attacks could stimulate kings to ask for gelds, and thus change royal demands and royal aspirations. In England this was especially the case in the Viking attacks c.1000, when the object of Viking activity quickly became a determined milking of the system's capacity to generate liquid silver tribute rapidly, culminating in a takeover of the system itself and the kingship of the English. In Ireland the Viking establishment of Dublin and other eastern towns brought a new source of wealth for which Irish kings fought. Here Viking settlement was never on a scale even temporarily to disrupt native succession to the provincial kingships. As a result Viking Dublin became just another factor in their rivalries.

The arrival of the Normans was more sudden and dramatic. In England south of the Thames and to a lesser extent of the Humber, the Norman takeover was rapid. The loyalties, interests, and habits of the southern English elites and royal servants helped transfer the kingdom. North of the Humber, the uprising which had set in motion the events of 1066 was still in process. As one historian has suggested, the battle at Stamford Bridge, between an English king and a Scandinavian claimant, was arguably as important as that at Hastings between the English Harold and the Norman William.[6] Had the Norwegian king won outside York before William arrived on the south coast, 'England' might have split along the Humber and the still debatable shape of northern Britain been redrawn. Ealdred of York's loyalty to an English king looks all the more significant in this context. In the event, William's ruthless suppression of the North helped complete what tenth-century Southumbrian aggression had begun.

After 1066, as in the tenth century, the problems of controlling the Northumbrians placed a limit on southern royal expansion. The Scottish king Malcolm III treated with William, but accepted Northumbrian exiles. In his view too his southern borders were far from fixed. By 1100 Ireland was still beyond the Norman reach, though Dublin was a refuge for English and Welsh exiles. In Wales the recent collapse of Gruffudd ap Llywelyn's overkingship provided the Normans with the sort of opportunity such collapses had offered to dynastic and other adventurers in the tenth century. Areas whose kings had long had close links with England were most rapidly conquered; the north-west proved resistant. There was to be no takeover of the whole of Wales as occurred in southern England. Overkingship was a personal achievement, not a texture of habits and interests which could be easily transferred.

The Norman Conquest played its own role in the shaping of British if not Irish political geography, but it also serves to reveal its pattern more clearly. That pattern was certainly not as yet fixed and permanent, though it was one within which some significant differences had already emerged. As 1066 itself suggests, it was a pattern which may owe more to accidents and events than the constraints of this brief account has revealed.

[6] G. W. S. Barrow, *Kingship and Unity, Scotland 1000–1306* (London, 1981), 27–8.

Figure 2.0 The Gokstad ship.

The Vikings

Barbara E. Crawford

This is a timely moment to consider the Vikings in the context of Britain, Ireland, and all their surrounding islands. Viking impact has been more usually discussed and analysed from the perspective of individual kingdoms and national entities, such as Anglo-Saxon England, Francia, and recently Scotland (or Alba). However, the Vikings are an international phenomenon; this period of European history is indeed often called the 'Viking Age'. From the point of view of the Vikings, Britain, Ireland, and the islands were regarded as one maritime complex, giving access to different territories available for exploitation. This complex is geographically very much a part of the northern maritime world, and north and east Britain are near neighbours with Scandinavia. Only the historical accident of 1066 turned the kingdom of Anglo-Saxon England into a west European rather than a North Sea country. From the ninth to the mid-eleventh century Britain and Ireland were closely tied into the Scandinavian world—more closely than they would ever be again.

Geographical and maritime factors are very important in understanding the achievements of the Vikings. They were exceedingly mobile seaborne operators who were able to range widely around Britain and Ireland and the range of their operations constantly surprises us. Archaeologists suggest that there may have been contacts between peoples across the North Sea long before the raids are historically attested, as they are from c.790. It is quite likely that ancestors of the Viking seafarers did indeed explore the open seas to the west of Norway and Denmark as they perfected the building of their magnificent sailing vessels in the century before the first raids are recorded. We are able to appreciate the summit of their shipbuilding skills from the superb vessels which have survived from the ninth century in Norway (Oseberg and Gokstad—see Fig. 2.0) and from the eleventh century in Denmark (Roskilde).

Particular circumstances must have stimulated the onset of raiding from all parts of Scandinavia in the early ninth century. Economic conditions at home are likely to have been important, including population pressure (although this is considered a less likely cause nowadays); or political pressures instigated by chieftain rivalry for power; or technological advances in sailing and navigating. Recently it has been suggested that expansion by the Christian Frankish empire may have prompted the Danes into reacting aggressively against the religious bases of north-west Christian Europe as a pagan response to these potent religious symbols of expanding western European society and culture. All of these factors may have played some part in the underlying causes of the Viking expansion movement. More generally we can recognize that piracy is always profitable when the circumstances are right and a victim is waiting to be exploited—as Christian Europe was in the year 800. There was a niche market out there on the islands, headlands, and in the estuaries, and the Vikings took advantage of their newly discovered maritime power, and capitalized on their ability to move swiftly over the seas and fulfil their warrior ethos and their commercial potential.

Celtic Britain and Ireland

Having made the point that it is necessary to understand the Viking impact throughout Britain and Ireland, it must also be recognized that different localities had varying experiences according to the geographical, political, and ecclesiastical circumstances in each kingdom or principality. In north Britain it is highly likely that the Viking impact was a chief causal factor behind dramatic political developments and the creation of the new state of Alba (the term is first used for the northern kingdom c.900), later the medieval kingdom of the Scots.

When the Viking raids started on 'Scotland' (as we saw in the last chapter, the term is anachronistic) in the late eighth century

Figure 2.1 Britain and Ireland during the first Viking Age.

the Pictish hegemony was at its greatest extent. By the year AD 1000 this situation had changed drastically. The Gaels (Scots) had moved eastwards from their west-coast kingdom of Dalriada (Argyll), across the 'dorsum Britanniae' ('Spine of Britain', i.e. the central Highlands) into Pictland, and up the Great Glen into Moray and Ross. They had subsumed the Pictish kingdom and engineered—unwittingly or deliberately—the collapse and disappearance of Pictish language and culture, although the joint kingdom of the Picts and Scots was probably based on remnant Pictish institutions. So the Picto-Scottish kingdom grew into a strong political unit which survived the Viking onslaught, although the outer parts of the Pictish hegemony were subjected to dense Viking settlement.

Sources for the earliest raids

Contemporary written sources from north Britain are almost non-existent, so we have to use a fair degree of hypothesis when trying to reconstruct Viking aims and ambitions in this area. The written sources we have are brief entries in Irish annals and the *Anglo-Saxon Chronicle* (many of which are contemporary) and later saga accounts of the deeds of famous Vikings (most of which have to be treated warily). Archaeological evidence is very important for what it can reveal about Norse settlement and pagan burials, but is incapable of telling us anything about political developments, or who the people were whose remains are uncovered in the sand dunes of northern and western coasts and islands. Nor does it provide incontrovertible evidence for the raiding of monasteries.

As is well known, the main foci of early raids by the Vikings in north Britain were the famous monasteries of Jarrow, Lindisfarne, and Iona. Attacks on these peaceful communities were events which monastic chroniclers were deeply concerned to record, and which literate clerics wrote about (see below). Raids on Iona took place in 795, 802, 806, and 825—when the leader of the monastic community, Bláthmac, was killed for not revealing the shrine of Columba which the monks had hidden. That event was recorded by the famous writer and poet Walafrid Strabo, in his monastery in far-away Reichenau in south Germany. What the Irish chroniclers do not reveal very much about is what was going on in the Hebrides alongside these raids on Iona, but we can be sure that the Viking raiders must have had complete control of the sea lanes around the north and west of Britain. Along with boatloads of family and followings they were establishing bases in the Northern and Western Isles during these decades, from which they were able to launch annual raids further south on Britain, Ireland, and western Europe.

Archaeological evidence, when found, can help to fill out the picture. But such evidence is not always easy to interpret. There is no indication of any destruction on Iona itself, and indeed, the famous Celtic standing crosses were apparently left standing. Iona survived, or recovered, as a spiritual centre—even for the descendants of these early Vikings, once they had been converted or influenced by Christianity. But there is evidence of violence in other places, and it is the Vikings who are usually regarded as the perpetrators of that violence. One can plausibly interpret the hoard of Pictish silver found on St Ninian's Isle in Shetland, hidden underneath a stone slab in the precursor of the twelfth-century church, as the treasure of a community (probably secular) which was threatened by the Vikings, and which did not survive that threat to recover its hidden wealth.

Then there is the recent remarkable discovery at the Pictish monastic site of Tarbat in Easter Ross of fragments of ornamented cross-slabs which had been smashed not very long after they had been carved in the early ninth century. Who was responsible for this? The excavator's current theory is that it was the Vikings; indeed a monastic site in this coastal location, in frontier territory between the Norse settlements of Caithness and Sutherland and the Scottish province of Moray, was very likely to have suffered depredations. A hoard of Norse silver arm-rings dating from the tenth century was found long ago in Tarbat churchyard, and in the eleventh century the famous battle of Torfness took place nearby between Earl Thorfinn of Orkney and a Scottish king (probably Macbeth, mormaer of Moray and king of Scots). So this zone was a flash-point. If it was the Vikings who were responsible for the destruction of the Christian stones at Tarbat, one has to recognize that other remarkable pieces of Pictish Christian sculpture in Easter Ross—at Nigg, Shandwick, and Hilton of Caboll—were left entire. The evidence does not suggest that such monuments were determinedly sought out and destroyed in a fury of pagan zeal. As on Iona in 825 the raiders may have reacted angrily and destructively against the immediate targets when thwarted from obtaining their main objective—gold, silver, and the precious objects of intrinsic value which studded the shrines and liturgical vessels of such holy places.

Evidence for settlement

Archaeological excavations of settlement sites in the Northern and Western Isles reveal another side of the Norse impact in north Britain, and one which has been greatly emphasized since the exposure of remarkable multi-period sites like Jarlshof in Shetland or the Brough of Birsay in Orkney, made decades ago. Many more have been excavated in recent years, but at Pool in Sanday and Scatness in Shetland the Vikings are the least visible of the many prehistoric peoples whose impressive stone structures are revealed at these remarkable sites. Thorny questions are constantly asked of this evidence: what do the sites reveal of the relationship between the natives and the incomers? Was there conflict or assimilation? That the Vikings were settling on the same sites as those used by the Picts before them—and their Iron Age and Stone Age ancestors before *them*—is quite clear. That they were eventually building longhouses in their own style and not roundhouses in the native tradition is also clear. But how did this change occur and in what sort of time-scale? Had they removed the natives in the process of settlement and colonization, suppressed them, marginalized them, or intermarried and adopted their social *mores* and some elements of their material culture? The answer is not an easy one, and recent scientific studies only provide general indicators about the Scandinavian element in the male population of the Isles today. Language and place-names give us further evidence to consider. Here there is a big difference between the Northern Isles, where the removal of the Celtic linguistic strata was total, and where the Gaelic tongue was never heard, and the Western Isles, where the place-names reveal a much more mixed situation and Gaelic probably never died out.

Less controversial is the burial evidence, and the many pagan graves discovered—and to be discovered—on the sandy beaches around the northern and western Scottish coasts dramatically reveal the human element of the incomers, and their way of life. From their burial customs we can glean something about their beliefs and their family relationships; from the boat-graves we can appreciate at first hand their affinity with the sea and their links with the other far-flung communities in the north Atlantic. The family group buried on the very edge of the sea—and nearly washed away by it—at Scar on the island of Sanday in the Orkneys is a recent addition to this body of evidence. An elderly woman, mature male, and child had probably perished in some accident or from disease and had been buried together in a six-oared boat, which may have been brought with them from Norway. Their favourite and symbolic possessions were arrayed round them (those which had survived erosion): the man's weapons, trading weight, and gaming pieces, the woman's weaving equipment, treasured brooch, and remarkably well-preserved whalebone plaque, a household item which probably symbolized her marital status (see Fig. 2.2a). The child's possessions had disappeared, but a young teenage boy buried at Durness on the remotest part of the north-west Scottish coast was accompanied with all the usual warrior equipment of an adult male.

Pagan Norse graves are uniquely recognizable from the burial equipment and the standardized nature of some of the personal objects, such as the gilded bronze 'tortoise' brooches which a Norse woman wore, one on each shoulder, to pin the straps of her kirtle. Such evidence provides material proof of the presence of raiders and colonists of Norse extraction, who had come across the seas to the insular world in search of a better life and rich pickings, bringing their personal possessions and cultural symbols with them. Of equal interest is the building of power structures, apparent from the written sources but visually non-existent, and impressive for what they reveal about the control frameworks established by these incomers.

The 'sea road'

The challenge for historians in this respect is to grapple with the record from many different cultural sources written for disparate purposes about mobile predators with wide-flung interests. Geographical barriers held no Viking warrior band back, for there was usually a waterway which could be sailed along to access the commercial sites and power centres, and especially monasteries—many of which were self-evidently very vulnerable to attack from the sea. The North Sea, the Minch, the Irish Sea, and the English Channel were all routes which were well known and much used by Viking raiders and traders. The route from Norway to Dublin has been called the 'sea road', along which were the archipelagos of Shetland, Orkney, and the outer Hebrides, stepping-stones for the shipborne traveller. Islands like Skye, Mull, Islay, Rathlin, Lambay near Dublin, provided

(a)

(b)

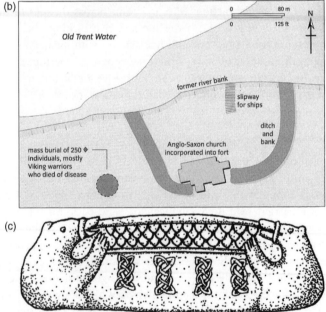

(c)

Figure 2.2 (*a*) Carved whalebone plaque found in the Viking boat burial at Scar, Sanday, Orkney. Reproduced by permission of Historic Scotland; (*b*) Plan of the Viking fort at Repton. From J. Heywood ed., *The Penguin Historical Atlas of the Vikings*. Reproduced by permission; (*c*) A hogback tombstone, Panel type © Oxford University School of Archaeology.

ideal refuges for the early warbands searching out useful pirate lairs for winter bases and summer staging posts. We have later saga sources written in Iceland in the twelfth and thirteenth centuries recording traditions about the ancestors who used this route and made themselves kings in the Hebrides before moving on to Iceland in the late ninth century.

The most famous of these figures is Ketil *flat-nefr* ('Flat-neb' or flat-nose), who appears in *Laxdaela Saga* and *Landnámabók* ('Book of the settlements'), and was believed to have conquered the Hebrides in the mid-ninth century, whose sons and daughter were among the first and most permanent settlers in Iceland. There is difficulty in pinning him down in time and place but no compelling reason to doubt the gist of the saga tradition that such a dynasty existed and provided the ancestors of many families in twelfth-century Iceland. Certainly graves of pagan Norse chieftains have been found on islands of the Inner Hebrides, such as Eigg and Colonsay. Actual historical reality, culled from the contemporary Irish annals, also tells us about warriors with Norse names who terrorized Ireland in the ninth century; one was called Ketil (Caitill *Find*, i.e. 'the White'), who was a leader of the Gall-Gaedhil, or 'foreign Gael', a breed of warrior of mixed Norse-Irish blood. As this name suggests there was interbreeding between the incomers and the native Irish, and the Norse entered with gusto into the complexities of Irish politics, about which much is known because of the literate nature of the monastic communities.

Ireland

The Scandinavian leaders who are named in the Irish annals are rightly regarded as powerful elements in that country's political alliances and inter-tribal wars. The 'Gentiles' who attacked Ireland were referred to as 'men of Lochlann' (*Lochlannaibh*), and Olaf (Amlaíb) was acknowledged as leader by the Norse in Ireland on his arrival in 853 when he took tribute from the Irish.[1] Olaf took control of the new trading place which had been established at Dublin in 841–2, and has

---

[1] Recent focus on the precise connotation of 'Lochlann' by Donnchadh Ó Corráin has revived an interest in the term, which has long been understood to refer to western Scotland in this period, although later coming to mean Norway.

been identified with the king called Olaf 'the White' known from the sagas. During the next decades Olaf and Ivar (Imar) ruled Dublin, along with their brother Auisle (Audgisl), who was murdered by his brothers in 867. These brothers moved their base of operations to Dublin, but their father Godfrey (Gofraidh) 'king of Lochlann' remained in the Western Isles.

This is the background to the desperate situation which compelled the Scots Gaels to move east into Fortriu and Pictland, and during the 850s and 860s there was a combined effort by Olaf and Ivar to take over power in central Pictland. Their operations culminated in the capture of Dumbarton Rock (Alt Cluith) in western Scotland after a four-month siege in 870–1, a severe blow to the independent kingdom of Strathclyde. Complete control of the waterways between the Hebrides and Ireland, with Dublin as the wealthy trading centre of the Irish Sea, made this dynasty exceedingly powerful so long as it could maintain its position in Ireland.

This raises the question of the role of the Isle of Man, a base in the middle of the Irish Sea which must always have been an important control point. The evidence does not suggest that it became particularly significant as a Viking settlement and power base until the tenth century, when it provided a useful offshore refuge for the Dublin Vikings who were expelled. The real 'history' of the Norse kingdom of Man does not start until the next century when the dynasty of Godred Crovan made it a power base for rule over the whole of the Hebrides (in the latter decades of the eleventh century).

Dublin's significance

The recent claim that Dublin was the capital in this period of a sea-kingdom which stretched from Man and throughout the whole of Viking Scotland (including the Orkneys and Ross and Cromarty) may be a realistic reflection of the power of this dynasty. Such an interpretation would certainly help to fill the vacuum in the history of the Northern Isles in the ninth century and lead up to the emergence or creation of the earldom of Orkney in the very decade of Ivar's death (and of that of his father Godfrey, who also died in 873). The unitary framework of control which this dynasty may have established throughout the seaways around and across north Britain must have started to break up into smaller units, and we hear from the

Icelandic sources about Olaf's son, Thorstein 'the Red', warring and conquering in north Scotland in partnership with the first earl of Orkney, Sigurd 'the Mighty'.

This imperial phase of Viking endeavour could not last for ever, and in 902 the Irish reasserted authority and expelled the 'foreigners' of Dublin, while the Picto-Scottish kingdom developed its own strong dynasty which survived the onslaught and remained independent of Viking control. However the fight was long and not easily won, and raids are recorded in central Alba during the early decades of the tenth century. The trading and manufacturing centre, and slave market, at Dublin flourished with its own ruling dynasty, the 'grandsons of Ivar' who reasserted control; they then linked up with the trading centre of York to form one economic and cultural link which spanned the waterways of northern England, and southern Scotland. The dominance of these two industrial and mercantile urban centres may help to explain why early trading bases have never been found in southern Scotland, except for the monastic community at Whithorn near the Galloway coast, where excavation has revealed a trading sector of Hiberno-Norse character.

The Norse were very successful at establishing monopolies, and—apart from any subsidiary exchange markets along the trade routes—rival trading centres would have been firmly disallowed. The excavations at both Dublin and York in the latter decades of the twentieth century have dramatically revealed the wealth of these two urban conglomerations in the tenth century, and later (see Ch. 3 below). They have provided much support for the alternative image of the Viking trader, which is indeed an important counterbalance to the unremitting picture of violence of the age which the monastic annals propagate.

The nature of the impact of these Scandinavian incomers is therefore very varied in the different parts of north Britain and Ireland. We cannot doubt the evidence of the chroniclers (see below), but we now have the material evidence of farming settlements uncovered in the islands and, in Ireland and northern England, of manufacturing and trading urban communities. Toponymic evidence (place-names) is also an unerring guide to the extent of settlement in the islands of the north and west (see Fig. 2.3). But the much sparser toponymic evidence from Ireland tells us that only the place-names in the rural hinterlands of the towns were influenced by those of Scandinavian speech. It was the urban trading communities of Wexford, Waterford, Limerick (all with Norse names) which were established by ruling mercantile elites of Scandinavian origin, which along with the city of Dublin dominated commercial affairs in Ireland.

Raids on north and east England

Moving south to England from the Celtic north we find a more familiar pattern of events, where the monastic record firmly establishes the image of the heathen Vikings' violence against the communities of monks living their peaceful lives on remote Northumbrian shores. Familiarity with these sources does not dull the shocking nature of the message of the record: the events of 793 and 794 presaged the arrival of a new phenomenon in early medieval English history. The apocalyptic entry in the northern version of the *Anglo-Saxon Chronicle* for 793 tells how:

In this year terrible omens appeared over the land of the Northumbrians and miserably distressed the people: these were immense lightning-flashes, and fiery dragons were seen flying in the sky. A great famine immediately followed these portents, and a short while later in the same year, on the 8th of June, the ravaging of heathen men miserably destroyed God's church in Lindisfarne through plundering and slaughter.[2]

War, famine, and portents in the heavens were all signs predicting the end of the world in the Gospels, and this intimation of the advent of some terrible new infliction was also stressed in a letter written about the same attack by Alcuin, a famous cleric at the court of Charlemagne who was himself a Northumbrian and a monk of York. He kept in touch with events in his homeland and wrote to King Æthelred of Northumbria a letter which has miraculously been preserved:

It is now nearly 350 years that we and our fathers have been in this beautiful land, and never before has such terror been seen in Britain as we have suffered from heathen people. Nor indeed was such a voyage thought possible. The church of St Cuthbert is sprinkled with the blood of priests of God, and

---

[2] P. Cavill, *The Vikings: Fear and Faith* (London, 2001), 6.

all the utensils have been plundered: a place more sacred than any in Britain has been given over to the plundering of heathen people.[3]

The sprinkling of the priests' blood over the church of St Cuthbert is an analogy drawn from Old and New Testament example, where the ritual is part of the purification process, but here symptomatic of the defiling of the most sacred place in Britain. As with the attack on Iona, the death and destruction was attendant on the plundering of the 'utensils', liturgical vessels, and the shrines containing the saints' relics. A later account of the attack on Lindisfarne by Simeon of Durham says that the raiders 'dug up the altars and carried off all the treasures of the holy church', which reminds one of the search for Columba's shrine in Walafrid Strabo's poem of the attack on Iona, in 825 (see p. 44 above), which had been buried by the monks 'in the deep bowel of the earth'. In fact the raiders did not get their hands on St Cuthbert's relics—nor the Lindisfarne Gospels (since they survived). Neither did they get hold of Columba's relics, nor the Book of Kells, which was probably kept in Iona at that time. So, the most sacred places of Dalriada (Argyll) and Northumbria suffered very similar raids in successive years, which is unlikely to have been coincidental. These raids may have been launched direct from Norway, or, more likely, from island bases already established in Orkney and Shetland. The Northern Isles provided easy access down both the west and east coasts of north Britain.

Another generation passed before the sources give us information about Danish raiders joining in the Viking exodus from Scandinavia, and these sources are from the Carolingian empire, which began to suffer raids along the North Sea coast, where its trading centres were targets of attack. The Danish dominance of the southern North Sea led inevitably to raids on eastern England at the same time, the first of which, in 834, is recorded simply as 'the heathen devastated Sheppey'. In the 840s and 850s numerous independent flotillas are recorded, from many different sources, as successfully penetrating the rivers and estuaries of north Germany and France. Finally, in 865, several pirate fleets led by the Danish brothers Ivar, Halfdan, and Ubba joined forces, and under the designation of the 'great army' (*micel here*) invaded East Anglia and spent the next ten years as an army of occupation, raiding and conquering throughout England.

There were later explanations of the motivation for this strategic-ally well-planned operation, and legendary elements entered into Scandinavian tradition about this remarkable story of Dark Age enterprise and achievement. Revenge for the death of the brothers' father, Ragnar *lothbrok* ('leather-breeches'), is said to have lain behind the 'great army's' movement north to York in 866–7 and the ritual killing of King Ælla by 'blood-eagling'.[4] There is no doubt about the decisive capture of the city of York and the establishment of Viking forces in Northumbria, which became a Viking kingdom. The army's next move was back to East Anglia in 869–70 when King Edmund was killed at the battle of Hoxne. Although much of the later hagiographical legendary information about his martyrdom can hardly be relied on, there is no doubt about his rapid rise to sainthood. Coins were being minted with the legend 'Saint Edmund' (presumably in Viking-controlled East Anglia) by the end of the century. Then the army moved into Mercia and took over the Mercian dynasty's power base of Repton in 873, as a brief entry in the *Anglo-Saxon Chronicle* tells us. Recent archaeological discoveries have dramatically enhanced this brief historical notice.

Excavations have been conducted both in and near Repton: those around St Wystan's church have demonstrated the size of the forti-fied enclosure which the army threw up to protect its ship base on the River Trent (see Fig. 2.2b). The archaeologists also discovered a mass burial in the vicarage garden, in which the bones of 250 mostly young, male individuals had been placed in a former Mer-cian royal mausoleum. Who these individuals were and what the cause of their death may have been is a real mystery, but the linking of the mass burial with the period of the conquest of Mercia seems incontrovertible. In the nearby countryside, from a cremation burial ground at Ingleby, comes the most solid evidence for the 'commit-ment to paganism' of a group (military or familial) of Scandinavi-ans who must have occupied that territory in 'a war-torn frontier zone' in the 870s. It has been recently argued that this cemetery of fifty-nine barrows on a hill-side was a rather different form of death and burial by incomers from the mass burial down in the Trent

---

[4] There has been much learned controversy about the reliability of the later stories of this method of sacrificing victims to Odin. If legendary, the legend was established already by the early eleventh century when a praise poem of King Cnut tells that 'Ivar, who ruled at York, had an eagle cut on the back of Ælla'.

Valley, which indicates a form of political-military subjugation by an invading force. Both are different aspects of the new element which had arrived in the Anglo-Saxon countryside, and had arrived to stay.

Viking aspirations to control all of Britain and Ireland

Northumbria, East Anglia, East Mercia were all conquered by the 'great army' in the space of eight to nine years (865–74). Bringing Ireland and Pictland into the picture we can speculate that the ambition of Ivar and his brothers was nothing less than the total domination of Britain and Ireland. We have already mentioned the framework of control established by this dynasty in the waterways around north Britain. There must have been justification for the annalist of the Irish *Annals of Ulster* to record the death of Ivar in 873 as *rex Nordmannorum totius Hiberniae et Brittanie* ('king of the Northmen of all Ireland and Britain'). We have to remember the limitations faced by land-based powers, and the potential for success where naval mastery of the coasts and sea lanes is concerned. Capture of Dumbarton Rock (870–1) not only gave access to central Scotland and routes across to the east coast, but also control of Strathclyde and the land routes across the southern uplands of Scotland to Northumbria. A fortified trading base on the east coast of Ireland (Dublin) would provide control of the Irish Sea.

A few years later we read in the Welsh annals of the death (877) of Rhodri, king of Gwynedd, at the hands of Saxons. This may have resulted from a raid into north Wales by Ceolwulf, the puppet king put in charge of Mercia after the Danish conquest of 873–4, and the raid's purpose was perhaps to ensure access from the Irish Sea via north Wales and the Dee to a route across the southern Pennines to York. The interconnection between Viking activity in Wales and Ireland is potentially significant. The idea of a Viking political overlordship of north Wales in the tenth century has been strengthened recently by excavation near Llanbedrgoch in Anglesey of a settlement of the Hiberno-Norse period, which is adding important new evidence for the impact of Scandinavian trading and political connections in the next phase of the Viking Age.

These far-travelled raiders/traders knew every sailing route, waterway, sound, and estuary round Britain and the Irish Sea, and

that is why nearly every island, holm, and skerry has a Norse name—
showing that they were thus designated by Scandinavian speakers.
This is a well-known fact but little attention has been paid to its
significance.

Wessex and King Alfred

Elucidating the strategies of these mobile operators and creating a
plausible political narrative of what the Vikings were up to is exceedingly difficult. Much more straightforward and alarmingly impressive
is the response and success of the sole Anglo-Saxon kingdom not to
be overrun by them. For we have the facts recorded meticulously, and
probably with a deliberate political purpose of impressing the reader
and hearer, in the *Anglo-Saxon Chronicle*. Historians and linguists
have spent much time and thought poring over this record, separating the origins of the different texts and analysing the deliberate
message which they contain. This is a one-sided record, perhaps
indeed intended as propaganda, if it was compiled at the court of
King Alfred, as is most probable. The texts were certainly distributed
around the greater churches of his kingdom *c*.892, at a time when
Viking raiders were still causing trouble. In addition there is the most
remarkable survival of a biography of the king by his Welsh friend
Asser, bishop of Sherborne.

Although this is a one-sided record, there is no strong reason to
treat these sources as unreliable accounts of the war against the
Vikings. The *Chronicle* is concerned to record the final success of the
Anglo-Saxons against the 'great army', and describes the progress of
the late ninth-century raids when they start up again; it is also concerned to record the achievement of King Alfred as the leader and
rallier of the men of Wessex in their darkest hour. The king's attempts
to bring the Viking leader Guthrum into his courtly Christian circle,
and the division of England between them, is described as if it was
some sort of 'gentleman's agreement' (see below).

In one respect Alfred and his brothers were lucky. They all ruled
during the period when the Viking raiders were circling around the
shores of England, but they were not threatened by intensive raiding
during the early decades of the Danish impact. The south-west was

not particularly targeted, and the great army directed its attack first at East Anglia and Northumbria. In 870–1 there was a stand-off situation between Alfred with his brother Æthelred and a number of Danish kings and 'jarls' (earls), on the frontier with Wessex near Reading. The nature of the opposition they met perhaps encouraged the Danes to focus on the softer target of Mercia, which gave Alfred— sole king of Wessex from 871—time to regroup and strengthen his people's resistance to the invader. He also 'made peace', i.e. handed over silver on this occasion and in 875, to pay the Danes to go away. This was no different from the later, despised, payments of Danegeld under his great-grandson Æthelred. Nor was it necessarily successful in winning respite in the ninth century, and in 875 the Danes simply moved on to Exeter. Some circumstance seems to have deterred them, however, and the *Chronicle* records that they there handed over hostages, swore oaths of allegiance, and moved back to Mercia. In 878 they returned and Alfred was forced to retreat to the western marshy parts of Somerset, where however he regrouped his forces, rallying them at 'Ecgberht's stone'. From there he moved out and took the Danes by surprise at Edington, forcing them to retreat to their stronghold where he besieged them for a fortnight. Using guerrilla tactics and subterfuge, Alfred beat the Vikings at their own game. The dramatic turn-around in his fortunes may be exaggerated by the *Chronicle*, and there were no doubt factors which help to explain why, after more than a decade of moving around and fighting and taking tribute, the leaders of the great army decided it was time to capitalize on their gains. Undoubtedly the cohesion of the raiding force was becoming less easy to maintain, and two groups had already split off, one under Halfdan taking land in Northumbria, another section sharing Mercia with the puppet Ceolwulf, so that two-thirds of the original great army were no longer available, and the numbers remaining in the still mobile warband must have been less overwhelming.

The account of the terms between Alfred and Guthrum indicates that the pagan invader was understood to be a permanent element in a newly structured England. The country was effectively divided between Wessex (with west Mercia), and the whole of eastern England, which came under Danish control. The army had promised that their leader would accept Christianity, and three weeks later Guthrum was escorted to Alfred's base at Athelney, where he received baptism and was honourably treated. This was a most crucial aspect of the relationship between the ancient occupiers of the land and the newcomers; if the Danes were there to stay they had to be converted to the religion of the established society for normal relations to function. It was a precondition which the pagan Scandinavians do not seem to have found too difficult to acknowledge wherever they settled. Currently there is much interest in the process of conversion in all the Scandinavian colonial settlements, and historians generally believe that those Danes and Norwegians who moved around the Christian world of western—or eastern—Europe quickly came to recognize the value of accepting the established religions of those societies whose wealth they desired, and whose cultural sophistication they wished to emulate.

The dispersal of the great army

We need to consider the size of the great army in order to estimate the impact that the Danes had on Anglo-Saxon England and the nature of the settlement. This question has greatly exercised historians who are forced to confront the problem of how to estimate the size of a force called a *micel here* (great army). It has been argued that the term *here* was more applicable to a raiding band than an army. Viking warbands were essentially ships' companies (called *lið* in Danish) which combined together, each under its own captain (*styrismaðr*), and which in larger groups were commanded by earls or kings. There was always the potential for splintering, and these forces were never permanently cohesive, but they could easily co-ordinate into a large force for particular campaigns against specific targets. We are only just beginning to appreciate how these forces could combine on either side of the English Channel, in readiness for an attack against the next victim. It is not always evident that chroniclers in England and in Francia are referring to the same warband, unless they name the leader, which they rarely do. A naval force on the Somme in 859 stormed Winchester in 860 and returned to Francia in 861. So the great army which arrived in 865 was a combined force of different ships' companies, and could indeed have included men (like Ivar) who were based in Dublin. It was presumably bigger than any previous raiding force, and the permanence of its presence clearly was a new and significant feature about it. The cohesion of this force for over twelve years was remarkable and tells us that it was firmly led by powerful warriors who had the command of plentiful resources to maintain the loyalty of the men; it also tells us that the advantages to be gained from co-ordination and domination of the Anglo-Saxon kingdoms were attractive enough to keep the force together, or replenished when needed.

This is not to say that the great army was invincible. Viking war-bands were vulnerable if brought to battle, and from the *Chronicle* account it would appear that Alfred brought them to battle over and over again, sometimes successfully. But he was only king of Wessex and had no power in other kingdoms, although close relations were forged with the surviving Mercian dynasty, and Alfred strengthened relations between the two kingdoms by marrying a woman from the Mercian nobility. His main strategy was to expel Guthrum and his army over the Thames, which he succeeded in doing. In the rest of England the Danes were conquerors; they had replaced the political authorities with tributary rulers, and at the end of the day they were able to dominate, to take over authority, and to settle at will.

The phases of settlement are recorded, but nothing more. We are told in the *Chronicle* that 'Halfdan shared out the land of the North-umbrians, and they proceeded to plough and maintain themselves' in 876. The next year, another part of the army 'went to the land of the Mercians, part of which they shared out', and in 880 another army 'went to East Anglia and occupied the land and shared it out'. The scale, the intensity, and the methods of these phases of settlement are quite unrecorded. The only evidence is toponymic, that is, the place-names created by the Danes and imprinted by them throughout eastern England from north Essex to Northumberland. There are thousands of them, the best known and most distinctive being the names ending in -*by* (which is a Danish element meaning 'farm', or an individual landholding). The lesser topographical names like *thorpe*, and in Norwegian-dominated areas *thwaite*, were marginal settlements and clearings. In addition there are the names ending in -*ton* (an English ending) with a Scandinavian name for the specific first element, which suggests that a Dane had taken over an already-existing English settlement. These elements—often represented as dots on a distribution map—give an impressive demonstration of

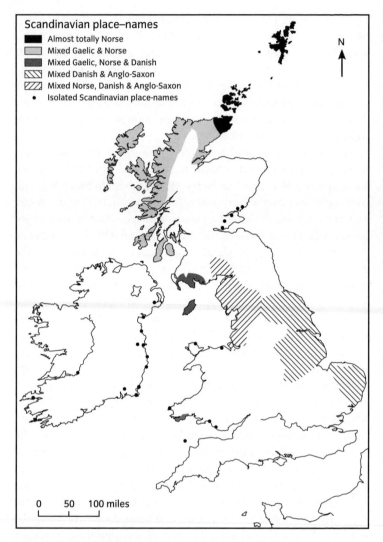

Figure 2.3 Scandinavian place-names in Britain and Ireland.

the overwhelming nature of the Danish settlement on the land (Fig. 2.3). But one has to remember that such maps do not show the Anglo-Saxon place-names, of which there are in general many more in these same areas. Nonetheless the maps serve a purpose in visually imprinting the Danish impact—something which is immediately obvious from the signposts when one drives through the Lincolnshire or east Yorkshire countryside.

Imposition or integration

But impact of what sort? These names do not easily reveal how this settlement took place, or the time-scale in which it happened. Of course it was controlled. It was not the result of a haphazard invasion by thousands of Danish peasants who followed their victorious relations and flooded into eastern England in a colonial movement (although some probably did follow on). It must have been organized by the military leaders, who had exercised discipline over their followings for years, and who would continue to exercise authority in the process of settlement and the awarding of property. It is likely that these leaders maintained a military lifestyle for a generation or so, and there is some evidence that they established themselves in fortified centres in 'D-shaped' enclosures on the important rivers. Such an enclosure has been found on the north bank of the River Fye in Norwich and is thought to represent the Danish fortified base. The Five Boroughs of east Mercia became very important urban centres in the following century (see Ch. 3 below). Each locality with evidence of Danish names has to be studied in its own terms, for there were regional differences, and linguists are continuously developing and refining our understanding of this process of settlement and assimilation with in-depth local studies.

However, this process was hugely important in turning the Viking raiders into neighbours. Even in defeat the Danes could not be contained by moral or commercial sanctions if they were still a mobile, rootless element. But once they were settled, provided with land, and obliged to live according to a political code rather than a military one they were under some legal constraint. Religious sanctions were the most effective of all, and conversion was clearly one of Alfred's chief aims. Once these pagan nuisances had accepted baptism and learned the moral code of Christian behaviour—obedience to God and king and the obligation to love your neighbour—then peaceful coexistence could happen.

We have seen how Alfred required Guthrum to undergo baptism. He tried the same tactic with Haesten a couple of decades later, but with less success, even though Haesten's sons were sponsored at baptism by Alfred and Ealdorman Æthelred. As converts these leaders would be enjoined to enforce their followers to renounce paganism. But did they? And how successful were these evident attempts to pursue a programme of conversion? There is absolutely no evidence from eastern England as to the progress of adoption of Christianity, although there are pointers to the effects of the religion on the incomers. First is the paucity of pagan graves, which, apart from Ingleby and Repton, are very few indeed in the south and east, suggesting that even those who had settled there in the 870s failed to maintain their pagan burial customs. The rapid appearance of the St Edmund coinage, apparently produced by one of the Danish rulers in East Anglia before 900, suggests that his cult was flourishing within a generation of his death, and certainly points to respect and veneration for a Christian martyr among the descendants of the leaders of the great army. By the mid-tenth century it is very likely that the formal structure of a Christian church was once more up and running in the Danelaw, and we can be confident that the conquest of the area in the early decades of the tenth century by Alfred's son, daughter, and grandsons can help to explain the rapid assimilation of the new Danish settlers into a Christian society and their absorption of its established customs and beliefs.

The Danelaw

This very convenient term is commonly used for the area of eastern England settled by pagan Danes in the ninth century, although it is first known in legal compilations of the reign of Æthelred II, over one hundred years after the Danish settlement. It is likely that it came into use when Alfred's descendants made laws which were directed to be applicable to all the parts of England under their authority, for those who lived by Mercian custom as well as Danish. It incidentally tells us that the Danish settlers did establish political and administrative structures which were formulated according to their own social and customary regulations.

A clear factor in the eventual 'reconquest' of this area by the kings of Wessex is the disparity and disunity of the different parts, which indicates an overall lack of political cohesion among the Danish settlers. Once they had abandoned their totally mobile way of life, the underlying secret of their success, they lost their ability, or maybe their will, to co-ordinate any military action in defence of their independence from political authority. This is in some ways not surprising, considering the impetus to settle down and the difficulty of maintaining military preparedness in the face of encroachment from Norsemen in the north. The ambitious Wessex dynasty was committed to conquering the Danish-settled areas, and to bringing them under its own control within a single kingdom of England.

Alfred's son Edward and his daughter Æthelflæd continued their father's policy of fort-building in successful campaigns on the southern frontier with the Danelaw in the early decades of the tenth century, and in western and north Mercia. East Anglia was conquered by 917 and the Five Boroughs had submitted by 920. Moving north into Northumbria brought the battle-front to a completely different cockpit, and tenth-century Viking studies become caught up in a complex pan-British phase.

Northumbria

We left the story in the northern half of Britain at the point where the Dublin Vikings were raiding in central Alba in the early decades of the tenth century, having been expelled from Dublin. The king reigning at the time was Constantín mac Aeda (Constantine II, 900–47), who is one of the few northern kings of this period to emerge into the pages of history, and who can be regarded as the saviour of his kingdom from being overrun by the Vikings. So firmly established was he in the central Scottish Lowlands that he was able and ambitious enough to move south of the Forth into Northumbria in an attempt to fill the power vacuum which existed in Lothian and Bernicia. He fought battles there near the River Tyne with Ragnall, one of the grandsons of Ivar, who was in control of York from c.911. This dynasty which jointly ruled York and Dublin had ambitions to dominate the whole of Northumbria, a situation which both the Wessex and Scottish dynasties were committed to resisting. There were attempts to create alliances in this unstable situation, and peace meetings are recorded as having taken place at frontier locations between all three dynasties, some of which were confirmed by marriages. The alliances fluctuated depending on who appeared to be the greater threat to the independence of the others, and when Athelstan, Alfred's grandson, led an invasion of Constantín's kingdom in 934 then a very remarkable pan-British/Viking alliance against him was forged. Olaf Guthfrithsson, king of York and Dublin, orchestrated the response in 937, along with Constantín, Owain of Strathclyde, and a host of warlords from the Hebrides and the Danelaw, who all combined to penetrate deeply into Athelstan's kingdom and bring him to battle. The encounter took place at *Brunanburh* (perhaps in north-west Mercia), preventing the coalition from penetrating England through that most vulnerable of entry points from the north-west, the Cheshire gap. It was a disaster for the coalition, and although Olaf and Constantín escaped, there was carnage among the Scots and Vikings.

Such decisive military encounters really did establish some sort of political stability, and as far as the Vikings in Britain are concerned they were a spent force in northern England thereafter. After the defeat of Eirik Blood-axe, Norwegian king of York, in 954, the political links between Dublin and York were finished, and the Wessex dynasty was able to dominate York and the surrounding farm settlements of the Vale of York. Northwards was territory disputed between Scots and English for many centuries to come. The Isle of Man, protected by the sea from being overrun by territorial kings, was ruled by an independent dynasty of 'Viking' kings until 1266, but the dynasty was a mixed breed of Gael and Norse, as indeed was the island's population. This mixed culture is well exemplified by the remarkable series of Manx memorial crosses dated to the tenth century, Christian in religion and Celtic in design, but carved with scenes from Norse myths, and with runic inscriptions in the Norse language running up the sides. The patrons who commissioned these memorials, and the dead whom they commemorated, bore both Norse and Celtic names.

Contrasts and conclusions

At the end of this first Viking Age we can see the significance of the impact of these raiders and settlers on the history of Britain and Ireland. They were 'agents of change', in respect of both the ethnic situation and the political pattern of the native societies, especially in England and in north Britain (the Scotto-Pictish kingdom), whereas they instigated significant developments in trading and economic circumstances within Ireland. Increasingly it is being appreciated that the political and ecclesiastical pattern in all areas was greatly affected by the raiding and by the response to that raiding. External threat elicited a response which allowed a ruling dynasty to dominate its rivals and eventually turn the threat into a positive outcome. Such effects are most clearly seen, because we have fuller written information, in England; here the Wessex dynasty was the sole political survivor of the raids and settlement, and yet managed to turn that position of weakness into a source of strength by becoming the church's chosen crusader in the offensive against the pagan invader, eventually defeating the Danish settlers in battle and becoming the figurehead of an all-English unity.

The most permanent effects were brought about by settlement, and to exemplify this one can take two contrasting areas and use very different forms of evidence to illuminate the changed situation wrought by Viking settlement in each. In north England we know from the place-names that many Danes, and some Norsemen from Ireland, settled in the rich arable-growing lands of the plain of York, the upland pastures of the Dales and the Cumbrian fells, as also the Isle of Man. Nothing much is recorded of these warriors-turned-farmers but they left behind some remarkable sculptural memorials and standing crosses, which testify to their mixed cultural backgrounds. Mostly these are rather clumsy and naive monuments, but some, like the Gosforth cross (Cumbria) and the many standing cross-slabs in the Isle of Man, are outstanding pieces of craftsmanship. What is most remarkable is the mixture of Christian imagery and pagan mythology. Even stranger are the recumbent hogback tombstones, house-shaped with shingled roof-ridges, and with muzzled bears, or other animals, supporting the gable ends (see Fig. 2.2c). Variants of these are found throughout midland and north England (the finest at Brompton), and south and central Scotland (with a magnificent collection at Govan on the Clyde). These seem to have been the tombstones of converted Scandinavians of one sort or another, but what the imagery implies or where it originated is obscure. Nonetheless these are powerful relics of a new element in the countryside, commissioned by the new settlers with the wealth to raise such monuments and with pride in their own culture as background to their status in their newly won homelands.

The other surviving evidence is written. It is a saga of a Viking dynasty which came from Norway and established itself in Orkney and Shetland at the end of the ninth century, creating an island empire which was ruled by earls and their successors for six centuries. They perpetuated Norwegian language and culture and expanded on to the Scottish mainland during the first Viking Age, establishing such a reputation as the epitome of the heroic Viking lifestyle that their deeds and doings were written down in Iceland at the end of the twelfth century. We cannot expect this saga of the earls (*Orkneyinga Saga*) to be a sober written record, for it was mostly based on oral tradition, and their story no doubt grew with the telling. Nonetheless it is a written record from the literate north Atlantic world and the first such account from north Britain which tells us about the ambitions, achievements, and rivalries of men who continued to perpetuate the Viking way of life, probably long after the Danish settlers of north Yorkshire had become farmers (and about whom nothing is written). But then the earls of Orkney have left no sculpture behind them, and we have to use the evidence that has survived to help us gain a glimpse of the world of these Scandinavian peoples in such widely different parts of Britain and Ireland in the tenth and eleventh centuries. In fact, the *Orkneyinga Saga* tells us that the Orkney earls, Arnkell and Erlend, were with Eirik Blood-axe when he was ambushed on Stainmore in 954, a location about halfway between Middleton and Gosforth where the stone memorials to farmers of Danish extraction were probably newly raised at that very time!

The second Viking Age

This term is used for another phase of raiding and domination which brought more Scandinavians to the shores of Britain in the late tenth century and first decades of the eleventh, leading to the political conquest of England by the Danes, and the rule of Cnut, son of Swein Forkbeard, and his sons for twenty-six years (1016–42). The Norwegian Olaf Tryggvason also joined in this new phase, which may account for some of the raids on Scotland, but these attacks were very few compared with the regular campaigns conducted against England for the purpose of extorting geld, paid in huge amounts, according to the *Anglo-Saxon Chronicle*.

The traditional explanation for the impetus behind this new phase has been the interruption to the supply of silver from the east on which the Danes had come to rely. The raids were clearly designed with a deliberate purpose of extracting silver coinage from the rulers of England by extortion, and to that end it can be said that there was a greater amount of political control than in the ninth century. There was also less damage to the ecclesiastical infrastructure, for the Danes were theoretically converted by this date—a process which had started with the recorded conversion of King Harald Bluetooth *c.*965—although it is very uncertain how quickly the Christianization of the whole population followed.

It used to be said that Swein's campaign of conquest was of a different order of exploitation from that of the earlier Vikings. He was a king of a unified country with imperial ambitions abroad, leader of a trained naval force under a single command. He had political ambitions to conquer England and take the earlier Danish period of raiding and settlement to its logical conclusion of national conquest. He was Christian and would never sanction the perpetration of atrocities against the monasteries. This made him reputable and his ambitions reputable, and his son achieved those reputable ambitions. However, there is nowadays less certainty about the extent to which some of these beliefs are valid, and Swein and Cnut are regarded as certainly more powerful than their ninth-century predecessors, but still dependent on the support and followings of independent, ambitious jarls (earls) like Thorkell the Tall or Olaf Tryggvason, who defeated the East Anglian levies at the famous battle of Maldon. Their success rested on their ability to attract such men to their side and to keep them there with rich rewards. Certainly the problems which Cnut in particular had with some of his jarls suggests that overriding loyalty to a king was not part of the ethics of the Danish power structure, and that he could not call on the service of such men in any automatic way.

Another factor is clear, and that is that Swein and Cnut could not rely on the population of the Danelaw supporting their campaigns of conquest, although it is noticeable that Swein in particular based himself in Lincolnshire for his final campaign in 1013. We also know that some 'new Danes' took advantage of the confused situation to offer their services to Æthelred in the struggle (as Thorkell the Tall himself did). The *Anglo-Saxon Chronicle* reports disapprovingly that Æthelred lavished patronage on some of these incomers, giving them land and much gold and silver. We really do not know who these people were or what role they played in Æthelred's England, but their wealth and power was eventually resented and feared by the king, who infamously ordered that all Danes within his kingdom were to be killed. The resulting St Brice's Day massacre certainly included Swein's daughter and her husband Pallig, and it was their murder which was said to have determined Swein on his revenge by leading an army of occupation to England in 1004.

The impression that results from this difficult period which spanned the late 990s through to 1013 is that Danes were treating England as a very lucrative field of endeavour, whether it was for regular economic reasons through which they became involved with the king and his court, or whether it was for irregular economic gain as members of very successful raiding parties. The North Sea coasts of north and eastern England were familiar coastal territory, and provided many access points to the trading *burhs* with their mints and markets, many of which were raided at this time, like Ipswich in 991 and Norwich in 1004. Preying upon your neighbours was an activity that was not monopolized by the Scandinavians in the middle ages. The second Viking Age saw that activity focused most especially on England, and it was spectacularly successful because royal leadership within the kingdom was lacking, and loyalties were divided.

Cnut's conquest and the aftermath

The conquest and rule of the kingdom of the Anglo-Saxons was the greatest achievement of the Danish royal dynasty, and foreshadows the more famous conquest by William of Normandy fifty years later. However the Danish conquest did not last as William's did, and the reason seems to lie in the problems of ruling two kingdoms separated by a sea, of having further ambitions within Scandinavia which distracted the Danes from governing their conquered kingdom with the necessary tight grip, and of failing to establish a military aristocracy throughout the shires. There was also the existence of exiled members of the Anglo-Saxon royal house near at hand (in Normandy) and available to return if required.

Were Cnut's ambitions to maintain his North Sea 'empire' for Harthacnut, his chosen son and heir by Emma (Æthelred's widow)? If so, it was an impossible ambition to fulfil, for the distances were too long and the populations of Denmark and Norway not yet fully controlled by a single dynasty. The Vikings had now inherited the Christian world which they had harried for so long, and they had little to bring to their new role as Christian rulers. The best they could do was to sit themselves on the empty throne and submit to churchmen's requirements as the successor to such an ancient and privileged position. Cnut did it quite well and conformed to the demands of the job, issuing privileges to powerful ecclesiastical corporations, issuing laws, to which he seems to have added an extra Danish legal component, and going on pilgrimage to Rome, after which he sent letters to all his people telling them of the privileges he had won for them. He also kept the country peaceful, probably by rather brutal means, and by the appointment of powerful jarls as provincial governors who had royal authority in all but name. He established a dominant position in the north where three kings submitted to him after a military expedition into the heart of the Scottish kingdom in 1031.

It did not last, although it might have done if he had left sons of the right calibre who were able to rule wisely and justly over a long period of stability. What Cnut's assumption of power did do was to give his kindred the claim and the aspirations to get hold of England once more, during the turbulent events which occurred in the 1060s, in an attempt to overturn the situation after William of Normandy had won England for himself and his dynasty. So Harald *hardraði* of Norway, one of the last of the Vikings, intervened in the contest for the Anglo-Saxon throne in 1066, and might have stood a very good chance of achieving his ambition if he had not been killed by Harold Godwinesson at the battle of Stamford Bridge. Then in 1069 Swein Estridsson, son of King Cnut's sister, sent a powerful fleet to Northumbria, led by his brother and three of his sons, to assist an English rebellion against William. It might have undermined the new political situation if it had been better led and with a more strategic purpose. Again, in 1085 Swein's son Cnut planned an invasion, the size of which could very well have threatened the stability of the Norman regime, but it never took place, probably because of domestic tensions at home, which resulted in Cnut's murder the following year. This was the end of the 'Viking' threat, and it was a very different threat from the first raids around the coasts of Britain and Ireland three hundred years before. The sea power was the same but it had become a political weapon in the hands of the medieval kings of Scandinavia, who had learned from the experience of the first Viking Age how to adopt the culture they were threatening, as well as the advantages to be won by conforming to the ecclesiastical establishment they had undermined. They were kings threatening kings and their only link with the past was their ability to transport fighting men over open seas and up estuaries into the heart of a kingdom. Otherwise they had become a part of medieval Europe.

Kings and polities in north Britain

Along the northern periphery the old order was also changing, but the Scandinavian/Norse legacy was firmly embedded in the society which we know about from the *Orkneyinga Saga*. Here we can see the medieval kings of Norway striving to gain authority over the insular polities which were established or just about to be established. Magnus Barelegs, grandson of Harald *hardraði* and king of all Norway from 1095, chose to reassert authority over the old Viking sea route south and west round north Britain, the Hebrides, and Ireland (whereas the campaigns described above had all aimed to penetrate England from the east coast). His court poet celebrated his successful campaign of 1098 in skaldic verse:

> On Sanda's plain our shields they spy:
> From Islay smoke rose heaven-high,
> Whirling up from the flashing blaze
> The King's men o'er the island raise.
> South of Kintyre the people fled
> Scared by our swords in blood dyed red
> And our brave champion onwards goes
> To meet in Man the Norsemen's foes.
> (*Heimskringla*, trans. Samuel Laing)

Magnus yielded control over the Scandinavian settlements on the north and west mainland of Scotland to the king of Scots, but claimed all the islands which he could sail around as his own territory. The saga tells how he had himself drawn across the neck of the peninsula of Kintyre in a boat with rudder set, in order to claim it as part of his island possessions. He then campaigned in Ulster and Gwynedd, fighting a naval battle with the Norman earls of Chester and Shrewsbury off Anglesey. Finally the *Chronicle of Man* tells us that he based himself on the island and built fortresses. This was one of the most ambitious threats from Norway and was aiming to establish maritime control over the western seaways. But Magnus's death in a skirmish in Ulster on his second campaign in 1103 saw the end of this threat, and the consequent flourishing of the independent earldom in the Northern Isles, and the establishment of a powerful kingdom in Man and the Hebrides. It is these insular polities which are the real heirs of the Viking Age in Britain, ruled by sea-lords with maritime power and island bases. They continued to thrive if they could restrict the internecine rivalry within their ruling dynasties, and so long as their sea power was of mercenary value to the kingdoms around them; and they thrived if they could carry on independent trading activity before being curtailed by the centralist ambitions of the medieval states which were in the making.

It has been said that the Viking Age is often perceived as the fulcrum of transformation, or, as mentioned earlier, the Vikings themselves were the agents of change. We cannot doubt that medieval kingdoms were in the process of development before the Vikings arrived off the shores of Britain and Ireland, but there is now a fuller recognition that the arrival of these enemies of civilization was very likely a stimulant to the formulation of unified kingdoms in England and Scotland, and to the urban development of Ireland. Rather than being of 'mere nuisance value' the contribution of the Vikings to the history of this period is profoundly significant.

Figure 3.0 Viking Age buildings during excavation, Fishamble Street, Dublin, 1981. Courtesy Patrick Wallace, National Museum of Ireland.

Exchange, Trade, and Urbanization

David Griffiths

The lives of people in Britain and Ireland between 800 and 1100 continued to depend for the most part on agriculture, and the produce of sea, forest, river, and marsh. Throughout the period, the proportion of people living on the land, as opposed to in towns, monasteries, or palaces, remained well over 90 per cent. The number of people who had specialized roles such as in craft, trade, household retinues, holy orders, administrative offices, and military service remained small, but increased over the period. The demands of conspicuous consumption and piety described in the following chapter grew alongside the needs of an increasing apparatus of state power and defence; the obligations between Irish kings and client lords for the provision of large amounts of military equipment and ships to defend the coast, described in the *Lebor na Cert* (the 'Book of Rights', dating to *c*.1100), are a case in point.

There was a gradual change in the scale and means by which wealth was distributed and accumulated. Traditional reciprocal obligations were at first supplemented and then began to be eclipsed, in England at least, by commercial trade emanating from towns. Commerce, at its simplest meaning buying and selling to an agreed (or predetermined) price without involving any other personal or familial obligation or relationship, was well suited to urban markets where people of widely differing culture and geographical origin were present.

Historians and archaeologists have long debated definitions of towns and town life in medieval Europe. Commerce was certainly an element, although by no means the only one or even the most important. The nineteenth- and early twentieth-century historical tradition in urban studies put legal and administrative status foremost (as exemplified by the English medieval borough or Scottish burgh), thereby introducing a bias towards those places where these aspects were officially regulated and where the associated documents have survived. The later twentieth century saw a greater awareness amongst historians of the social and economic functions of towns. Partly influenced by the expansion of archaeological knowledge in the 1960s and 1970s, there was a recognition that a more flexible approach was appropriate. The definition of a town offered by Susan Reynolds in 1977, a permanent and concentrated non-agricultural settlement, supported by agricultural production located elsewhere, and maintaining a sense of social separateness from the countryside, is still widely accepted. Martin Biddle, a pioneer of English urban archaeology, proposed a series of twelve criteria including legal, topographical, and economic factors, although opinion differs on how many of these would be necessary for a place to 'qualify' as a town. Almost as a by-product of these attempts at definitions has arisen the inelegant (but nevertheless useful) concept of the 'proto-town', meaning a place which represented some urban functions, and potential for further development, but which at the time in question was something less than a full-scale town in terms of size, economic specialization, and separateness from the countryside.

By both institutional and pragmatic definitions, there were hardly any towns in Britain and Ireland in 800 (Fig. 3.1). A handful of former Roman cities in England such as Canterbury, London, and York might qualify on an institutional basis, although the extent of dense inhabitation within the Roman walls is doubtful. A few large monasteries in Britain and Ireland, and the riverside trading zones in southern and eastern England known as the *wics*, had developed proto-urban functions. Of the *wics*, only Ipswich developed *directly* into a significant later town. This should remind us that the development of towns was hardly a smooth evolutionary process, more a complex and often contradictory series of responses to a myriad of local conditions.

By 1100, however, commercial and urban developments added up to a very significant change in Ireland and England especially. The major estuaries of eastern and southern Ireland were dominated by

Figure 3.1 *Wics, civitates,* and proto-towns, *c.*800.

harbour-towns which traded with England, the northern continent, and of course with each other and with the Irish interior. In England, with the exception of the extreme north and south-west, towns, merchants, and money had a significantly more visible and widespread presence than in 800.

The relationship between towns and political power was most marked in Anglo-Saxon and Anglo-Scandinavian England, but elements can be seen in Ireland, where control of Dublin became a powerful objective for high-kings in the eleventh and twelfth centuries. The beginnings of urbanization in England were integral to its political unification. Towns were bastions of legal, military, and fiscal control in a land where many regional disparities and disloyalties remained. Towns became the focus for shire government. By 1086 many English rural landholders, both secular and ecclesiastical, held property in towns. Commercial exchange, conducted at urban markets, was subject to elaborate customs and taxation. The tenth and eleventh centuries saw the spread of trade in bulkier and more numerous commodities, which reflected a greater level of commercialized production and the predominance of fewer but more widely accepted conventions for the measurement of wealth.

Scotland, Wales, the interior of Ireland, and the Isle of Man had yet to experience significant urbanization. Leading families continued to maintain their power through networks of reciprocal obligation. Explanations for this lack of urbanization vary; for example, the Welsh tradition of partible inheritance may have inhibited the production of agricultural surplus, by encouraging a small-scale, dispersed landholding structure, in contrast to England where resources were being gathered towards the larger estates. Fragmented political structures, small populations, large land areas, and poor overland communications also played their part. These areas were, however, within easy reach of maritime trade. The earldom of Orkney and the Norse-dominated isles of western Scotland were key staging posts on the sea routes between the northern seas and Dublin. Silver, including English and other coinages, has been found in hoards across the non-urbanized areas of Britain and Ireland. With trading contacts came cultural and political influence. Growing English power in the north and west of Britain is illustrated by the submission, as described in the *Anglo-Saxon Chronicle*, of several non-English rulers to King Edgar at Chester, the principal English trading town on the Irish Sea, in 973. By 1100, the *awareness* of urbanized life had certainly arrived amongst many of the Scots, Irish, Manx, and Welsh, even if the experience was largely yet to come.

Exchanging and measuring wealth

Tribute, land rents, and renders, and traditional social obligations between lord and client such as hospitality dues, were the means by which the majority of productive surplus had circulated in the kingdoms of Britain and Ireland in the middle centuries of the first millennium. Elements of these survived in some areas well beyond 1100, such as the Welsh food renders *gwestfa* and *dawnbwyd* (land rent from free estates and seasonal food gift from bonded estates, respectively) and the Irish *bés* and *bíathad* (food renders). Royal households rewarded their kinsmen, allies, subjects, and followers within a strict culture of reciprocal bonds and mutual obligations. Itinerancy, feasting, marriage, and inauguration ceremonies, and the public redistribution of wealth, played a significant role in articulating these relationships. The social context of the pre-commercial economy was principally a close-knit network of tribal and kin-based relationships. Historically, these groupings are identifiable in political institutions such as the Irish *tuath*. Inferences may be drawn from mid-Saxon sources such as Bede and the surviving copy of a document known as the *Tribal Hidage* (which records the names of the various petty sub-kingdoms in Mercia), to suggest that a regional structure of traditional social and economic obligations was then still a significant feature in England. Long-distance exchange in high-status goods provided a valuable supplement to the ability of regional rulers to display and distribute symbols of their elevated status. Much of economic value which was collected, held, and distributed by elites, such as large herds of livestock, slaves, land title, and access to mineral resources, has left little by way of tangible remains. We are therefore dependent on tantalizing documentary glimpses of a world where status was defined in terms of the control of land, livestock, and people.

Standard expressions for weight, head of livestock, and areas of land have all left traces in Scottish, Welsh, and English sources, but of the contemporary written traditions, Ireland's have the most extensive coverage of units of value. Many law tracts give us a detailed insight into an elaborate culture of kinship categories and conventions for the measurement of wealth. In the terminology of these

Figure 3.2 Mints in England and Ireland, *c*.1000.

laws, a *míach* was a sack of malted barley, a *sét* a unit of livestock, and a *cumal* a female slave. The latter seems to have been transferred to silver, for as well as *uinge* (ounce) there are references to a *cumal* of silver. A *bó* (cow), according to the *Cáin Aicillne* worth one *uinge*, came in several standard variations depending on whether it was in calf or had recently calved. Apart from reflecting the colour of Irish agricultural life, these conventions show a complex and regulated legal system of value in a pre-monetary economy. Silver, whether in the form of jewellery, foreign coin, or ingots, counted as bullion and enabled wealth to be portable, versatile, and easily protected through hoarding. 'Hacksilver', or cut pieces of ingots and arm-rings, is common to many hoards. This was used in its own right as bullion, but was also liable to be melted down and remade into whole ingots or jewellery.

Vikings introduced an increased silver supply to Ireland and Britain, much of which came from central Asia before the mid-tenth century via contacts in Russia and the Baltic. Some of it was reworked in the west. Tapering arm-rings with stamped decoration are particularly closely identified with Irish hoards (see Frontispiece, p. xviii). Studies of arm-rings and other silver objects in Irish hoards point to the use of a standard unit of weight, which in modern terms is divisible by 26.6 grams, which is therefore very close to the Roman or Carolingian ounce. The 26.6 g unit is given further credence as the primary measure in Ireland, northern England, and possibly also parts of Wales, by studies of lead weights found in market contexts in tenth- and eleventh-century Dublin, York, and recently also at Llanbedrgoch, Anglesey.

Further metrical studies, of silver ingots from large mixed hoards such as the Cuerdale Hoard (Lancashire) of c.905 and the Chester Castle Esplanade Hoard of c.965, have also pointed to use of the 26.6 g unit. A different type of Viking penannular arm-ring, smaller, plainer, and rounder in cross-section than the type found in Ireland, is commonest in hoards in Scotland and the Isle of Man. Known as 'ring-money', these objects conform more convincingly to a 24 g unit, which was used in contemporary Scandinavia.

Coinage was at a very early stage in all parts of Britain and Ireland during the ninth to eleventh centuries. Minting in Anglo-Saxon England had begun in the seventh century on a small scale, initially in gold in imitations of Frankish types. The late seventh and eighth centuries saw further continental influences, as the more numerous cast silver coinage known as *sceattas* circulated in south-eastern Britain. Some of the earliest *sceatta* coinage in use in Britain was Frisian in origin; later types were produced in regional centres such as *Hamwic* (Middle Saxon Southampton), possibly at Thetford, and at York. Offa of Mercia (d. 796) had introduced a fine hammered silver coinage; silver pennies minted at London and in Kent continued to be issued by Offa's successors into the mid-ninth century but ceased as Mercia lost its grip on the south-east of England.

Metallurgical analyses of the silver content of the *styca* coinage (a relatively low-value Northumbrian part-copper coinage of the ninth century) and also of ninth- and tenth-century silver pennies suggests that it was extremely variable; this shows that 'face value' counted for something aside from mere silver content, and the potential for monetary inflation was already present. *Stycas* continued to be issued in desultory fashion until shortly before York fell to the Danes in the 860s, but their low worth (the silver content had been reduced to 2 per cent by the end of the issue) is a testimony to the weakness of the dying Northumbrian kingdom.

The foundation of mints in the *burhs* of Alfred (871–99) and his successors, first in Wessex and shortly afterwards in Mercia, was probably the single most important development in the rise of Anglo-Saxon coinage. The Anglo-Saxon silver coinage of the tenth century reflected idiosyncratic minting practices in the individual *burhs*, and functioned alongside Anglo-Scandinavian coinages such as the St Peter pennies of York and the St Edmund memorial issue of East Anglia. It took until Edgar's standardizing reform of 973 to convert these semi-independent regional coinages into something approaching a national currency. Moneyers worked under strict regulation; the rewards in wealth and status could be great but transgressions were brutally punished. Control of the distribution of coin dies, and the frequent changes of issue (from every six years under Edgar down to two in the eleventh century), offered maximum opportunities for royal profit. The number of mints increased from twenty-six under Athelstan (924–39) to over sixty under Æthelred II (978–1016) (Fig. 3.2).

The silver penny represented a significant unit of wealth throughout the period to 1100. Henry Loyn remarked in 1986: 'We might not be far wrong if we thought in terms of silver pennies in the eleventh century being carried about in the possession of ordinary non-official people as frequently, say, as gold sovereigns in the pre-1914 period and £50 notes today.' A continuing trickle of excavated and metal-detected discoveries since Loyn's comment shows that silver coinage was more common than previously suspected. Pennies were cut in half and quartered into farthings, but were never to become numerous enough or of low enough value to function as 'small change' during this period. Large areas of the English economy remained unmonetized; barter and reciprocal exchange in kind remained a feature of much trading activity, especially in the countryside.

Anglo-Saxon hoards show a steady decline in mixed hoards (including both coins and hacksilver) and a rise in coin-only hoards, together with a gradual disappearance of foreign coin during the tenth century, indicating that the English currency gradually eclipsed the earlier and more eclectic methods of standardizing wealth. Silver hoards in Ireland and northern Britain were predominantly coinless or mixed until the end of the tenth century. In the mixed hoards, the coins were frequently a combination of Kufic (Arabic) *dirhems* and Anglo-Saxon and Frankish coins, all of which would have acted as bullion. Production of regional English-imitative Hiberno-Norse coins began at Dublin in *c.*995, and in the eleventh century extended to minting on the Isle of Man. This is a sign that issuing coinage had become an attractive policy for rulers in these areas too (perhaps influenced by the perceived fiscal success of their English counterparts). However, the extent to which the Hiberno-Norse coinages permeated trade is debatable. Most known examples are from hoards, and surprisingly few have been found at Irish Sea market sites (under fifty at Dublin and as few as two or three at Whithorn and Meols). Minting began to peter out again later on in the eleventh century, and it seems that the success of the Anglo-Saxon coinage in supplanting bullion and foreign coin was not repeated in the Hiberno-Norse areas.

Surviving Anglo-Saxon coins in hoards and single finds dated to between 973 and 1066 have been ranked by Michael Metcalf. The six best-represented mints are those of London, York, Lincoln, Winchester, Stamford, and Chester. The amount of currency in circulation in England between 973 and 1059 has recently been estimated as £25,000, rising to £37,500 by 1086. These figures are comparatively small, even allowing for later inflation (the same source—N. J. Mayhew, summarized by Richard Britnell in the *Cambridge Urban History*[1]—estimates currency circulation in 1205 as £250,000 and 1311 as £1,100,000). Hoards in Scandinavia indicate the exceptional production of Anglo-Saxon mints during the reign of Æthelred II (978–1016), which is partly explained by an increased European supply of silver from the Harz Mountains in Germany. Not all of this production simply bypassed the internal English economy by going directly to geld payments to the Danes, and Metcalf has stressed that the numismatic picture reflects the growing prosperity of England at this time. It would be easy to minimize and underestimate the importance of money in later Anglo-Saxon England. Although its official function was still primarily as a means of taxation, money permeated the urban commercial economy by the eleventh century. It

---

[1] D. M. Palliser (ed.), *The Cambridge Urban History*, i (Cambridge, 2000), 119.

was still far from a universal medium of exchange, and coin was still restricted to larger transactions, but it was fast gaining importance as a part of everyday life.

The ninth century: upheaval and change

The year 800 marked the latter days of a period of prosperity for the kingdoms of Britain and Ireland. The eighth century had seen the regional kingdoms and larger monasteries of Britain and Ireland became major landowners and economic powers. In many ways, the church led these developments. In the seventh century, Cogitosus's *Life of St Brigit* described the monastery of Kildare as a 'city' (*civitas*) with *suburbana*. Armagh, and perhaps Bangor, Clonfert, and Clonmacnoise, must have been as impressive and equally dominant in their regions of Ireland. In Britain too, there can be no doubt that the major religious houses were the focus of much landed wealth, munificence, and pilgrimage. In the wake of these came people and goods in pursuit of opportunities for trade, craft production, and artistic endeavour. The monastery of Whithorn in south-west Scotland, for example, attracted a growing settlement of traders and artisans from the eighth century onwards. Southern English religious houses such as those in St Albans and Canterbury, and St Frideswide's, Oxford, formed a nucleus for urbanization. The permanency of the ecclesiastical presence has been remarked upon by John Blair as a factor in early urbanization, in an age when secular power as represented by royal households was still itinerant.

The role of the English church in attracting markets and traders was at least as important as its secular counterparts. Continental and Anglo-Saxon coins including *sceattas, stycas*, and silver pennies, together with large numbers of seventh- to eleventh-century metal objects such as pins, brooches, strap ends, and styli, have been discovered in recent years, largely by metal detector users, at places in the rural landscape of eastern and southern England. The locations of these finds have been grouped by archaeologists under the general heading of 'productive sites'. They seem to reflect non-urban and perhaps seasonal markets which served minsters or secular estates, or were on the borders of territories. The relationship of productive sites to the settlement pattern is still unclear, and it seems that these markets were not officially regulated in the same way as town markets and therefore went historically unrecorded. The phenomenon was almost certainly extremely varied across the country, ranging from important regional centres to remote boundary points. Local exchange also took place at hundred meeting places, often at moot-mounds, where small-scale barter in agricultural produce went on alongside the settling of local disputes and the occasional criminal execution.

One of the functions (and possibly the earliest one) of the *wics* was to provide the regional Anglo-Saxon secular and ecclesiastical elites with manufactured and imported goods, including fine pottery, wine, and foodstuffs. In *Hamwic* (Southampton) and *Lundenwic* (London) there were regular streets with an apparent element of planning. Their populations, although not large by later standards, were dense and their occupations became increasingly specialized in craft and trade. (Derek Keene has recently estimated *Lundenwic*'s population in 800 as between 5,000 and 10,000; *Hamwic*'s was probably between 3,500 and 5,000.)

By 800, most of the English *wics* had already seen their best days as centres of overseas trade. They represent a largely temporary phenomenon which arguably depended too heavily on external trading systems and vulnerable long-distance contacts, and on the patronage of too few people who were too near the top of the social hierarchy, and too little on well-founded economic predominance in their own agricultural hinterlands. Excavations in the 1980s showed that *Eoforwic* (York) was partly demolished around 800 and a less intensive presence remained on the site. *Hamwic* survived into the ninth century, but did not expand after 800, and by 850 decline and depopulation had set in. Excavations in the later 1990s on the Royal Opera House site at Covent Garden (in the centre of *Lundenwic*) have confirmed that the trading settlement was in decline in the first half of the ninth century. Ipswich, by contrast, continued to expand in the ninth century, which is possibly a reflection of a greater level of integration into the rural economy of its region and a correspondingly lesser dependence on North Sea trade, which was in difficulties by the mid-ninth century as the Viking raids increased.

Vikings first settled on some of the islands off the north and west coasts of Scotland around the beginning of the ninth century, and

Viking groups began overwintering in Ireland in the later 830s. In 840–2 they had established *longphorts* ('ship fortresses') on Lough Neagh in the north, Linn Dúachaill on the coast of Co. Louth, and on the River Liffey near Dublin. Others may have existed at places along the River Barrow in south-east Ireland, together with Clondalkin, near Dublin, and Youghal in Co. Cork. Little is yet known about the *longphorts*, but a banked or palisaded riverside enclosure with temporary dwellings and safe moorings for ships is probable. Large Viking cemeteries, probably those of the Dublin *longphort*, at Island-bridge and Kilmainham, a short distance west of the later town, show the sustained ninth-century Viking presence and are a demonstration of its cultural roots.

The deposition of silver hoards in Ireland, which in the ninth century largely consisted of jewellery and bullion rather than coins, shows a short-lived peak in the 850s, suggesting that more silver was in circulation but also possibly that the political climate was more threatening (increased warfare is one explanation for people concealing their silver in holes in the ground, and of course failing to come back and retrieve the deposit). A. T. Lucas, in a study of Viking involvement in Irish secular and ecclesiastical rivalries, demonstrated that the indigenous political climate was already turbulent enough to make the Viking contribution seem hardly more disruptive than 'normal' events. The Vikings deployed their consummate opportunism to great effect in ninth-century Ireland. Raiders here, allies there, traders somewhere else, they were drawn into the patchwork of Irish power structures and rivalries. The Vikings brought silver, goods, and mercenaries from overseas and probably took at least as much away in Irish slaves, fine metalwork, and the products of the countryside. The Irish were as yet, however, unwilling to yield a permanent role to the foreigners in their midst and expelled them.

The *Annals of Ulster* record that the Dublin *longphort* was brought to an end by concerted Irish attacks in 902, but within it had begun the process of creating a mixed Viking-Irish population, which was to prove a significant factor in the growth of an urban culture in Ireland after the refoundation of the Viking settlements in 917. The tenth century was to see the Irish Sea Vikings take on an influential and innovative trading role, in which their habit of military opportunism was more than matched in the commercial sphere. There are hints of the beginnings of this at the turn of the ninth and tenth centuries on the British side of the Irish Sea. The ancient beach market site of Meols, Wirral, on the coast of north-west England (a place which goes back to the Iron Age as a location for maritime trade), was revitalized during the Viking period. Finds of Hiberno-Norse ringed pins, decorative metalwork, and Anglo-Saxon coins (mostly discovered on the eroding coastline during the nineteenth century) indicate an upsurge in trading activity during the tenth century after the settlement of the surrounding area by fugitive Irish Vikings. Their presence is documented by our only detailed historical account of this migration: the story of the chieftain Ingimund and his followers, who first attempted to seize land in Wales but were expelled, and then settled in Wirral, whereupon they (unsuccessfully) besieged Chester but were allowed to stay permanently.

The Ingimund episode is largely detailed in an Irish annalistic source, but Welsh annals mention a battle on Anglesey in 903 where 'Ogmundr' was defeated by the Welsh. Until archaeological discoveries in the 1990s, there were few indications of Welsh participation in the Viking trading networks of the Irish Sea. However, near the village of Llanbedrgoch, a short distance inland from the east coast of Anglesey, recent excavations have revealed the presence of a small late ninth- and tenth-century trading and manufacturing settlement. A defensive ditch and impressive stone wall enclose a one-hectare area centred on a spring. Middens, paved areas, and a small number of metalworking hearths surround up to six buildings, at least two of which were of the longhouse type often associated with Viking settlement (elongated rectilinear dwelling houses with internal roof supports, a central open hearth, raised side benches, and space for animals in one end). Finds of Frankish and Anglo-Saxon coins, Viking-style hacksilver, lead weights, and jewellery suggest that the settlement participated in the growing trading network in the Irish Sea. Rotary querns, quantities of cattle bone, shellfish, and carbonized barley grains show the agricultural aspects of everyday life in the settlement. The rulers of Gwynedd, who developed dynastic links with Dublin in the eleventh century, may have fostered this settlement as a means of obtaining goods for themselves.

The movements of Viking armies, gradually establishing a semi-permanent presence in Ireland in the mid-ninth century, were closely followed by similar exploits in England. The *Anglo-Saxon Chronicle* records the first Viking overwintering on the Isle of Sheppey in the

Thames estuary in 850, and a short cessation in coin minting together with a subsequent decline in silver content suggests that raiding in 851 adversely affected the economic well-being of London and Canterbury. From then on, in both Ireland and England, a core of Scandinavians recruited followers whose earlier political loyalties and obligations had lost their force or had disappeared altogether. Many of these recruits adopted some elements of Scandinavian language and culture, just as their leaders simultaneously began to involve themselves in the religious, economic, and political culture of their adopted lands. This growing ethnic mix of followers presaged the emergence of towns in the tenth and eleventh centuries as centres of Anglo-Scandinavian and Hiberno-Scandinavian acculturation. Despite this, the vindictive massacre of the small community of Danes in Oxford on St Brice's Day in 1002 shows that ethnic differences persisted, even in settled populations far away from the vulnerable east coast.

Towns as centres of power, 876–1016

Scandinavian towns in Britain and Ireland

The transfer in 876, recorded in the *Anglo-Saxon Chronicle*, of conquered Northumbrian lands to his own followers by the Viking leader Halfdan established a permanent Scandinavian presence in the landscape and revitalized the link between the newly acquired stronghold of York and the estates outside the city. York's Roman walls were partly refortified and a defensive bank was constructed alongside the River Foss in the late ninth century (Fig. 3.3). Excavations between 1976 and 1981 at 16–22 Coppergate, south of the legionary fortress above the Foss–Ouse confluence, have shown that property boundaries were laid out by the early tenth century. This central zone between the two rivers was to become densely occupied by industrial and commercial tenements. Within these plot boundaries, marked by successive fences, stake-and-wattle-built buildings were created and then replaced later in the tenth century by plank-built structures. Such tenements were not restricted to this area, as demonstrated by other excavations at Skeldergate, in the former Roman *colonia* southwest of the Ouse, and at Walmgate, on the east bank of the Foss.

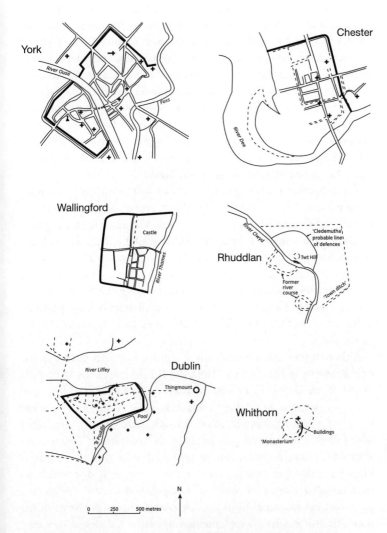

Figure 3.3 Comparative plans (to scale): York, Chester, Wallingford, Rhuddlan, Dublin, Whithorn, *c.*1000. Sources: Map of York, from Richard Hall, The *Book of Viking York* (English Heritage/Batsford, 1996). Map of Dublin, from *Viking and Medieval Dublin* (O'Brien, Dublin, 1988). Map of Wallingford, from M. Biddle and D. Hill, *Antiquaries Journal,* 1971 (vol. LI, pt 1).

The rich environmental evidence from the large number of water-logged archaeological deposits in York has given an unparalleled insight into the diversity of diet, leather-working, metalworking, bone-working, and carpentry in a tenth-century town. The range of material preserved, from fish and bird bones and worked antler to textiles and oak planks, presents a picture of vibrant urban–rural interdependence. Intestinal parasites found in the remains of human faeces, the remains of insect species which thrive on rotting matter, and overflowing cess-pits dug next to wells reveal the effects of overcrowding and haphazard refuse disposal in the closely packed tenements, which were also vulnerable to fire. That these factors contributed to a high early mortality rate is suggested by analyses of the earliest inhumations excavated from the graveyard of St Helen on the Walls.

The transition from pagan to Christian burial customs in Anglo-Scandinavian York is marked by the presence of grave goods in burials at St Mary Bishophill Junior, and Viking-style stone grave-markers in a cemetery beneath York Minster. There is evidence of continuity of ecclesiastical use from Anglian times at St Mary Bishophill Junior, whereas churches such as St Helen on the Walls and St Andrew, Fishergate, were founded during the Viking period. The townscape became a network of small interlocking parishes, a feature also characteristic of Dublin, as well as many Anglo-Saxon *burhs*.

Although they are not explicitly mentioned as such until 954, the establishment in the eastern Midlands of England of the 'Five Boroughs of the Danelaw', Lincoln, Stamford, Nottingham, Derby, and Leicester, together with the Viking takeovers of the East Anglian towns of Thetford, Norwich, and Ipswich, must shortly afterwards have followed the general pattern set by the conquest of York. Excavations at Flaxengate in Lincoln in 1972–6, despite lacking the water-logged organic preservation which made the York discoveries so rich, revealed a series of wooden buildings which were constructed on two street frontages from the late ninth century onwards. Initial domestic use was later supplemented by glass- and bronze-working workshops. The Flaxengate excavations have given the most detailed picture of occupation within any of the five Scandinavian boroughs of the Danelaw, our knowledge of which is otherwise disappointingly sparse as yet. Historical and topographical analysis of their medieval and modern townscapes has identified the probable sites of the Anglo-Scandinavian borough enclosures, but with the exception of possible domestic or industrial structures of only approximately contemporary date at High Street/Maiden Lane in Stamford, archaeological excavation has so far contributed few revealing insights. The pottery industries centred on Stamford, York, and Torksey near Lincoln (which may have been a small borough in its own right), however, became highly productive and influential in eastern England during the eleventh century (Fig. 3.4). Their early development (at Stamford in particular, where ironworking was also important) probably arose from demand created in the Five Boroughs.

The East Anglian towns already had a lineage going back to the time of the *wics* and were to become some of the most advanced urban centres in England before the Norman Conquest. Norwich was resited to the south bank of the River Wensum, opposite the site of a probable earlier proto-urban enclave. Ipswich was revitalized, as almost certainly was Dunwich, although the subsequent loss by coastal erosion of the site of Dunwich has limited the possibilities for

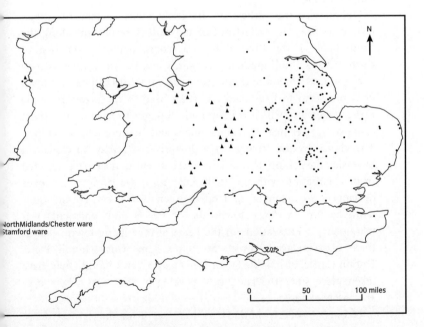

NorthMidlands/Chester ware
Stamford ware

Figure 3.4 Distribution of Stamford ware and North Midlands ware, c.1000.

archaeological investigation. Thetford was one of the largest towns in England in 1066, but failed to sustain its urban importance after the upheavals of the Conquest and later declined to a remnant of its pre-Norman status.

The Viking hold on the five Danelaw boroughs and the East Anglian towns, which extended to Colchester and London for a brief period in the 870s and early 880s, did not last long. They were all back in English hands by 917–20. By contrast, the foundation of new Scandinavian-dominated towns in Ireland was to prove a more lasting episode. In 902 the Vikings had been expelled from Ireland, but in 917, partly prompted by the growing power of York, the 'foreigners' returned. The initial incentive may have been to trade in slaves. By this time having a yet more heterogeneous admixture of people and cultural influences gained in Britain and elsewhere over the previous fifteen years, the Scandinavians re-established a presence on the river estuaries at Dublin, Wexford, Waterford, Cork, and Limerick. The Viking rulers of Dublin kept a dynastic link with York until the latter kingdom was conquered by the English in 954.

Dublin was the earliest of the Irish towns to take on urban characteristics. The waterfront of the earliest settlement along the south bank of the River Liffey was consolidated by the first of thirteen banks built gradually outwards into the tidal inner estuary over the next three hundred years. The siting of the post-917 town does not seem to have paid any great heed to the position of the earlier *longphort*, which is commonly thought to have been a short distance upriver near the Kilmainham and Islandbridge cemeteries. The choice by the Vikings of a downriver site may be explained by easier navigation to the sea; alternatively it may have resulted from negotiation with the Irish. Like York, the commercial focus developed on a tongue of land between two rivers. By the mid-tenth century, a dense townscape of streets and tenements was taking shape. Excavations in the heart of the Viking town, such as those at Winetavern Street, St John's Lane, Christchurch Place, Dublin Castle, Fishamble Street (see Fig. 3.0), and Wood Quay, have taken place since the late 1950s, peaking in the 1970s when large areas were exposed.

Dublin's property boundaries were set from the earliest dense occupation, and wattle fences were replicated numerous times in the same positions. The majority of the buildings were post and wattle constructed with internal roof supports. Discarded objects bearing trial attempts at decorative motifs, manufacturing debris, and finished objects in leather, bone and antler, wood, and mostly inexpensive metalwork such as ringed pins characterize the industry and crafts going on in the town. The outstanding state of wood preservation, especially at Fishamble Street/Wood Quay, allowed detailed study of both carved objects and building construction techniques on a scale unprecedented in Ireland or Britain. The Dublin tenements, in their structure and in their material culture, were a genuinely cross-cultural urban environment. Scandinavian-style building and decorative traits were expressed in wood, bone, and metal, and yet were also influenced in numerous and fundamental ways by existing Irish practices. The mixed and acculturated Hiberno-Norse population became more culturally diverse as the town grew and Dublin began to dominate economically the eastern midlands of Ireland.

Archaeological excavations at Wexford, Waterford, and (as yet to a lesser extent) Limerick and Cork have revealed evidence of diverse and growing urban communities developing in the eleventh and twelfth centuries (although tenth-century evidence is still rare). At Waterford in particular, evidence for urban building types and industry is extensive. At Wexford, the buildings excavated at Bride Street are closely comparable to Dublin wattle types, whereas Waterford (where cellared buildings became more common) shows a stronger Anglo-Saxon influence in its urban architecture. Lacking Dublin's tenth-century connections with Chester and York, the southern towns depended more on trade with northern France and the Bristol Channel area, which is also reflected in the contemporary rise of the port of Bristol. The importance of the role of English merchants has been acknowledged by Patrick Wallace, the leading archaeological excavator of Dublin, and by the twelfth century a culturally distinct merchant class known as the 'Ostmen' had emerged. The Irish annals point to the establishment of rural hinterlands by 'foreigners' around the five towns, such as the territory known as the *Dyflinarskiri* around Dublin; the likely extent of these territories has been traced in later documents by John Bradley. In fact, the Scandinavian towns in Ireland became less and less 'Viking' and more and more Irish as they increasingly came under the political control of Irish kings and magnates before the Anglo-Norman invasion of 1169.

Anglo-Saxon towns

The classical concept of a 'city' (*civitas*) had at least persisted in the cultural memory of some western Europeans (if only a literate minority) since the Roman period. Pope Gregory's instruction of 597 to St Augustine to found dioceses in the former Roman cities may have failed to appreciate their decrepitude, but is evidence that they had not been altogether forgotten. The list of subscriptions to the episcopal council held in 803 at *Clofesho* (the exact location of which is uncertain) uses the word *civitas* only for former Roman towns; others mentioned such as Hereford and Sherborne were simply described as *ecclesiae* ('churches'). There is certainly no doubt that within many former Roman towns and fortresses in England, there still remained many impressive, if ruinous, standing defences and buildings in the ninth century.

Charters issued in Canterbury in the period before 870 mention the regulation of town land, suggesting the development of burgage plots. The Mercian centres at Hereford and Worcester were probably approaching urban status in the later ninth century and foreshadowed the subsequent spread of *burh* (borough) towns. At Hereford and Tamworth, and also at Winchcombe, archaeological evidence points to the construction of defences by the early ninth century, and a charter refers to a market at Worcester. An intriguing charter reference of 857 to the bishop of Worcester holding an important property in London suggests that a commercial hierarchy of towns was already operating.

The *burhs* of Wessex are documented in the source, dating to the turn of the ninth and tenth centuries, known as the *Burghal Hidage*. This merely lists the names of the places endowed with the political status of a *burh* with their 'hidage': the number of household-based units of land in their surrounding territory or shire which were required to provide resources for their construction and maintenance. Wallingford and Winchester had the largest number (2,400 hides each), whereas Lydford and Lyng in the south-west had as few as 140 and 100. Strategic places were adopted in order to establish a network of secure fortified enclaves across the kingdom. Some of these were at existing settlements; others were on long-deserted or new sites.

It would be unwise to interpret the information in the *Burghal Hidage* as demonstrative of a preconceived strategy for urbanization dating to Alfred's reign. At their earliest stage, the *burhs* were merely a response to a military emergency. The construction, reconstruction, and consolidation of the physical fabric of many of the *burhs*, and the confirmation in law of increasingly 'urban' functions in the shire centres, continued for decades under Alfred's successors. Many of the places mentioned in the *Burghal Hidage* were clearly intended to be temporary defensive expedients and never developed into towns. Former Iron Age hillforts such as Chisbury (Wiltshire) and strategic points on rivers such as 'Sashes', an island on the middle Thames near Cookham (Berkshire), were probably only maintained for a few seasons. Some places in the list include former Roman sites such as Winchester, Exeter, Portchester, and Chichester. Some, such as Oxford and Malmesbury, had an existing monastic presence, whereas others, such as Wallingford and Cricklade, were constructed on new sites. The *Burghal Hidage* is an impressive survival and is a useful historical document, but like the Domesday Book, it must be interpreted with care. It can give an impression of systematic urban innovation in the last quarter of the ninth century, perhaps leading to a corresponding lack of recognition of developments outside its (relatively limited) coverage. If a general point can be made about the *burhs*, it may well be that those which developed into enduring towns were sited in places which already had a proto-urban presence such as a significant minster, or had such advantageous positions within the network of routeways, river crossings, and emerging shire territories that they functioned as a regional nucleus or 'central place'.

From the Wessex heartland in Somerset, Dorset, Wiltshire, and Hampshire, Alfred's forces moved east towards Kent, and took London in 886. The creation of *Lundenburh* is now regarded as the time at which the former Roman walled city was reoccupied, whereas for the two previous centuries activity was focused in *Lundenwic*, west of the city walls (which became known as the old *wic* or 'Aldwych'). London, despite its economic and strategic importance, remained a border town for as long as Mercia and the Danelaw retained any independence of Wessex, and only became the location of the main royal household under Edward the Confessor in the mid-eleventh century. Until then, Wessex remained the centre of the English monarchy; Winchester, with its important religious houses and royal connections, was its principal town. Excavations in Winchester by Martin Biddle between 1961 and 1971 were among the first to give a substantial insight into the topography of an Anglo-Saxon town. The street system was shown to have been a completely new imposition over the long-disused Roman street plan, with an intra-mural street to create easy access around the restored Roman defences (a common feature of *burh* topography elsewhere), street frontages, burgage plots, and lanes.

The complete reordering of Winchester's street plan may indicate that it was seen from the beginning as a special case amongst burghal towns. Elsewhere, the typical Roman cruciform plan of main streets was retained, or even introduced from new as in Oxford, Wallingford, and Cricklade. Analysis of the width of plots and lengths of defensive walls suggests that the pole (equivalent to 5.03 metres) and its subdivision, the perch, were the principal units of measurement. David Hill worked out that the lengths of some of the *burh* defences, measured in poles, appear to bear a close relationship to their *Burghal Hidage* value (where four hides were required to maintain a pole's length of defences). Although not a universal rule (it does not apply to Chichester or Exeter where the walls are much longer than their listed hidage suggests), there seems to be more significance to this calculation than mere coincidence; it seems to give us a glimpse of the methodology of Anglo-Saxon design and construction.

Excavations at St Michael's Street, Oxford, indicate that the earliest defences of the Late Saxon town were a simple earthen ditch and bank topped by a wooden palisade, with an intra-mural street behind. These were renewed, extended, and the wooden structures were replaced in stone during the tenth century. In the mid-eleventh century, the defences were extended and made more elaborate (the stone tower of St Michael at the Northgate, which was constructed at this time, may be one of the last surviving gate towers from an Anglo-Saxon *burh*).

Along with the attention given to constructing the defences and street systems, property boundaries within the burghal towns became subject to official regulation. Initially, officialdom was concerned with military requirements, but as populations grew and pressure on land provoked boundary disputes, the role of regulation increased. Excavated evidence suggests that domestic and commercial occupation in many of the burghal towns did not become dense until well into the tenth century. The principal streets were probably amongst the earliest topographical features, and the blocks of land between them gradually became filled with long and narrow burgage plots of regular width stretching back from the street frontages, divided by town lanes. Not all intra-mural land was divided; some was initially left open for temporary dwellings, future development, cultivation, animal herding, or markets and fairs. At Cricklade and Wallingford, neither of which happened to grow very much in later centuries, this is still a visible feature of the town topography.

Apart from churches and defensive works, the buildings within English towns were largely of timber until well after the Norman Conquest. Excavations in London, Chester (see Fig. 3.3), Canterbury, Oxford, and Wallingford have indicated that the initial ninth- and tenth-century buildings were simple rectangular sunken-featured structures (similar in some respects to earlier Anglo-Saxon *Grubenhäuser*). These buildings were in many cases upgraded later in the tenth century to cellared buildings which for the most part served both domestic and industrial/commercial purposes. The latter type, with its post-and-plank-built ground-level storey over an earth-cut or even rock-cut cellar (sometimes with a separate sloping or stepped entrance way), was a utilitarian structure which appears to have carried few overt cultural or ethnic associations. Buildings of this type also became a feature of Anglo-Scandinavian towns such as Thetford and York; in Ireland they were prominent at Waterford but less so at Dublin.

The period 900–24 saw a significant extension of the *burh* and shire system into Mercia, as documented in the *Mercian Register*, an addendum to the *Anglo-Saxon Chronicle*. The transfer of existing Mercian saints' relics into newly endowed churches in Chester and Gloucester was perhaps an attempt to reinforce the symbols of traditional Mercian legitimacy in areas where the kingdom's authority had been eroded. Worcester, Warwick, Stafford, Tamworth, and Bridgnorth were also fortified. Edward the Elder of Wessex (899–924) recaptured large areas of the Danelaw, and in 918 annexed English

Mercia. New *burhs* from Hertford and Colchester in the south-east to Bakewell and Nottingham in the north Midlands consolidated his advance. In north-west Mercia, the completion under Edward of a string of small *burhs* on strategic sites in the Dee and Mersey basin around Chester, including Thelwall, Manchester, and *Cledemutha*, seems to have had the effect of antagonizing the local Mercian population, the Welsh, and the recently settled Vikings. A revolt in Chester in 924 was defeated by Edward, but he died shortly afterwards at his estate at Farndon, outside the city.

Cledemutha was founded in 921. The only convincing location for it (otherwise unspecified in the *Mercian Register*) is Rhuddlan, which was at that time the lowest fording point before the mouth of the River Clwyd in north-east Wales (see Fig. 3.3). Rhuddlan, recorded in the Domesday Survey as having eighteen burgesses, ironworks, and a mint, changed hands between the English and Welsh several times in the eleventh century, most notably when it was held by Llywelyn ap Seisyll and Llywelyn ap Gruffudd of Gwynedd between 1015 and 1063. Rhuddlan was the closest approximation to a town in pre-Norman Wales during its brief periods under Welsh rule. Excavations have revealed some evidence of pre-Norman occupation in the area of the later Norman borough, in the form of a handful of simple sunken-featured structures comparable to examples in Chester and possibly Manchester. The Norman castle motte known as Twt Hill probably overlies the site of the palace constructed by Llywelyn ap Seisyll in 1015. The large defensive earthwork system surrounding the town is more likely to date from the campaigns of Edward I in the 1270s than from the pre-Conquest period, despite various archaeological and historical attempts to prove it was associated with *Cledemutha*.

Many of the Anglo-Saxon diocesan centres such as Sherborne and Elmham were small-scale settlements outside the *burh* system. In the later tenth and eleventh centuries, proto-towns, with concentrated settlement areas and some market functions, began to form around monasteries, such as St Albans, Abingdon, Pershore, and Bury St Edmunds. The powerful Northumbrian monastery at Durham became an important border fortress in the eleventh century, and excavations beneath the edge of the Norman castle motte have revealed evidence for tenements of contemporary urban type. The transition from 'rural' to 'urban' forms of building and settlement organization is illustrated by excavations at Steyning (Sussex), a small market town which was characterized by widely spaced post-built buildings of a sort more usually found at agricultural settlements.

The shires, initially tied into the burghal towns for defensive purposes, evolved in the tenth and eleventh centuries into complex legal and commercial provinces, and began increasingly to function as urban hinterlands. Laws of Edward the Elder, Athelstan, Edgar, and Cnut regulated markets in towns (which were termed 'ports') and set up administrative supervision of town life. Trade was restricted to ports and transactions were subject to the authority of the port-reeves, although this was later limited to transactions over twenty shillings. Mints were created, facilitating the standardization of the taxation of both commercial activity and also tribute derived from the Welsh and the Vikings. By the 920s, foundations of new *burhs* had virtually ceased, but urban growth continued in the existing centres. Only during the turbulent reign of Æthelred II was the practice of creating royal *burhs* briefly revived, when strongholds and mints were removed from lowland towns at Ilchester and Wilton to long-abandoned hilltop strongholds at South Cadbury and Old Sarum.

The rise of commerce, 917–1100

Statistics on climate in northern Europe for the ninth to eleventh centuries are virtually non-existent. Archaeological evidence suggests that settlement was extending further into marginal land in northern Britain and Scandinavia, and this contributes to a general impression that the climatic improvement which characterized the twelfth and thirteenth centuries had already begun to take effect in the ninth and tenth centuries. Population figures are similarly hard to define. Even our only substantial contemporary source in this respect, the Domesday survey of England, completed in 1086, omits significant elements, such as the number of properties and people in London and Winchester. The density of the population figures by county shows a decided bias in favour of East Anglia. The Domesday population of Norwich has been suggested as around 5,000, and London probably at least twice as much, but the wider treatment of population in Domesday is regarded by many historians as a significant underestimate. The total population of England has been variously estimated by historians as between two and three million at the time of the Norman Conquest, with Ireland probably just under a million and Scotland and Wales each substantially below that (perhaps little over half a million). It is impossible to give definitive numbers, but even with these difficulties it is hard not to perceive a general sense of growth and expansion in population and economic activity which was quickening in the eleventh century.

Without Domesday our perception of urbanization in England in the later eleventh century would be altogether less detailed and systematic, and perhaps therefore would contrast less with our view of contemporary Ireland, Scotland, and Wales. In Ireland, there were the five Hiberno-Norse towns, of which Dublin was the only one of a size rivalling the larger English towns. In Scotland, Edinburgh, Stirling, Dunfermline, and Perth were all to develop into towns in the twelfth century but it is doubtful whether they were functioning as such before 1100. Apart from the occasional possession by the kings of Gwynedd of the English *burh* of Rhuddlan, and the creation by English lords in the march (border zone) of tiny fortified enclaves such as Brecon and Ewyas Harold, Wales was not urbanized. The western Mercian towns of Gloucester, Hereford, Shrewsbury, Worcester, and Chester served some market (and thereby 'urban') functions for parts of eastern Wales as well as their own counties.

Up to 112 places in the Domesday Book have been identified as towns, based on indicators such as their population and the use of the descriptive terms *civitas* or *burgus*. The distribution of towns shows a marked difference between eastern and western England (Fig. 3.5). In the east, fewer and larger towns contrast with a denser distribution of mostly smaller towns in the west and south. It is difficult to see any explanation for this other than as a distant reflection of the geopolitical differences of the late ninth and tenth centuries. In Wessex and western Mercia, the pattern of *burhs* seems to have institutionalized a pattern of smaller shire and market zones, in contrast to the former Danelaw area where larger hinterlands (including more non-urban markets as possibly indicated by 'productive sites') were present. Some places such as Tewkesbury and Evesham had developed as proto-towns in the eleventh century and had only acquired the right to operate a market and port a few years before the Norman Conquest.

By 1100 in England, urban self-confidence brought about by increased urban commercial and economic power had begun to erode the earlier monopolistic links between towns and the rural estates in their own hinterlands. Citizens and merchants began to assert some signs of independence, as marked by the emergence of guilds in Canterbury, Cambridge, and Lincoln. The emergence of guilds in the eleventh century is a sign that a feeling of commonality and even separateness from rural life had begun to pervade townspeople's view of themselves.

Harbours, wharves, and hithes represented a focus for markets, mints, and customs. The *burh* of Exeter was fostered as a port for the tin trade during Alfred's reign, and Queenhithe in London was developed shortly after the establishment of *Lundenburh* in 886. The Graveney Boat, a remarkable surviving example of contemporary shipping, was preserved by the estuary mud of north Kent until it was excavated in the 1970s. The felling of strakes used in its clinker-built hull has been dated by dendrochronology to the 880s. The Thames estuary and Kent, through seaports such as Fordwich, Dover, and Sandwich, was the focus of a growing trade with the continent which had surpassed that of eighth-century *Lundenwic* by 1000. Several specialized markets in fish, meat, and manufactured objects operated in different zones of the city including Newgate, Billingsgate, and Cheapside. The opportunities for revenue were substantial: a record of the tolls imposed in London during the reign of Æthelred II refers to cloth, timber, fish, wine, eggs, cheese, and butter. Wine, wool, metalwork, silks, and spices were arriving at London from Rouen, Flanders, the Meuse, and the Rhine, and in an arrangement which foreshadowed London's participation in North Sea trading leagues in later centuries, German merchants were allowed the same privileges as the English. The presence of such a growing mixture of *people*, notwithstanding the goods they brought, must surely be a defining factor in the development of urban culture.

The Hiberno-Norse towns were all located at trans-shipment points on the upper tidal estuaries of the larger Irish river systems. Riverine transport connected with maritime shipping at these

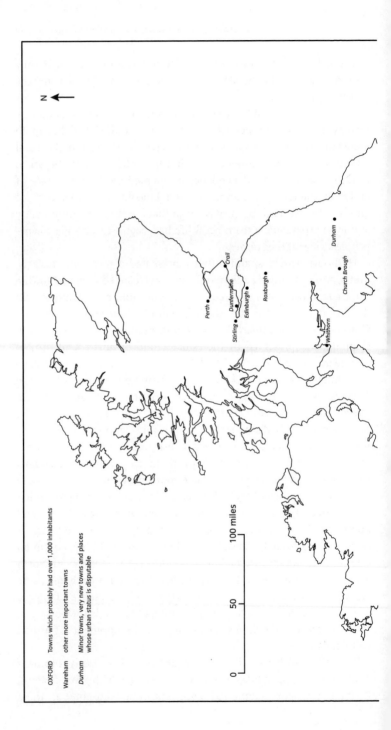

N ←

OXFORD   Towns which probably had over 1,000 inhabitants

Wareham   other more important towns

Durham   Minor towns, very new towns and places
           whose urban status is disputable

Perth •

Stirling •   Dunfermline •

Edinburgh •   *Crail*

          Roxburgh •

Whithorn •

          Church Brough •

          Durham •

0   50   100 miles

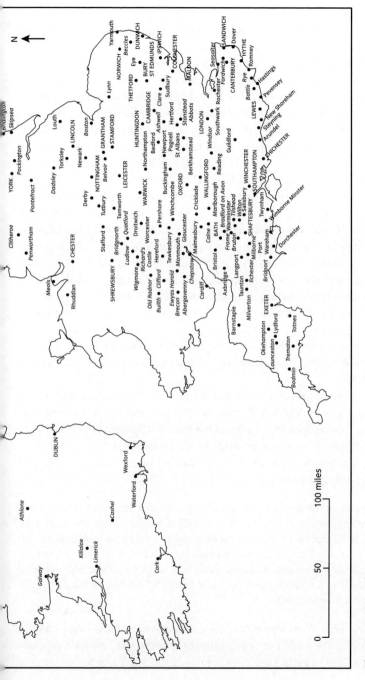

Figure 3.5 Towns in 1100.

centres of market activity. The Dublin excavations are amongst the most informative in Europe for the development of successive water-front quays and revetments. In England, even the towns located well inland had river frontages and wharves allowing access for com-mercial water transport. The spread of pottery from regional produc-tion centres such as Stafford and Stamford points to trade along river routes, in the former case the Dee/Severn network and in the latter, the Nene, Trent, Witham, and Ouse. Southampton, Exeter, Chester, York, Lincoln, Dunwich, Ipswich, and Norwich became the largest seaports in England outside London during the tenth and eleventh centuries. Chester experienced a steep rise in importance from the 920s. The output of the Chester mint, as measured in contemporary hoards, was larger than any other in England during the reign of Athelstan. Rather than any dramatic economic take-off in its north-west Mercian hinterland, this is probably explained by Welsh pro-duce and slaves passing through the town (which are likely to have been extorted by the English) and the rich trading opportunities which this English foothold on the Irish Sea offered. The growing dominance of Chester-minted coins in Irish hoards, which radiate westwards into the interior from Dublin, is evidence that Chester, ahead of York, was the principal trading partner for tenth-century Dublin.

Although the rise of Bristol, Waterford, and Wexford had drawn the focus of Anglo-Irish trade southwards during the eleventh cen-tury, the continuing vitality of the port of Chester at the time of the Norman Conquest is indicated by the unusually detailed description in Domesday Book of the tolls charged on shipping arriving and departing from its port:

If without the licence of the king ships arrived at or departed from the port of the city, the king and the earl had 40 shillings from each man who was on the ships. If against the peace of the king and in spite of his prohibition a ship arrived, the king and the earl had both the ship and all the men that were in it. But if it came with the peace and licence of the king, those who were in it quietly sold what they had; but when it departed the king and the earl had 4 pence from each last.

The same Domesday entry recorded the powers of the king's reeve to inspect the quality of goods brought into the port, mentioning mar-ten skins in particular. Strict regulation did not just apply to imports, but also to goods produced by the citizens; the punishment for brewers of bad beer was to be put in an apparatus called the *cathedra stercoris* ('dung chair').

Trade between Mercia and Dublin is confirmed by the numerous finds in the Dublin excavations of Chester or Stafford ware (also known as North Midlands ware) (see Fig. 3.4). It has been suggested that these pottery jars contained exported Cheshire salt, although this is perhaps more likely to have been exported in wooden containers. A reference to 'Salann Saxannach' in the Irish source *Aislinge Meic Conglinne* confirms that English salt was present in Ireland. Exotica of cultural importance to the partly Viking-descended Dublin population, such as soapstone, Viking-style metalwork, amber, walrus ivory, and Norwegian hones, continued to come in from Scandinavia, but archaeological and historical evidence for the eleventh and twelfth centuries points to bulkier staple cargoes, such as salt, grain, horses, and preserved fish, crossing between Dublin, Mercia, and Wessex. Much of this passed through the waterfront markets and industrial tenements of Dublin into the Irish interior.

Dublin's probable role as a major shipbuilding centre, which is implied historically by several Irish sources, is supported by dendro-chronological analysis of the timbers of one of the ships sunk as a blockade at Skuldelev in Roskilde Fjord, Denmark. Skuldelev 2, a large warship, recently was shown to have been constructed of oak matching the known Irish tree-ring pattern. The Hiberno-Norse were also active in the slave trade, the presence of which in the Irish Sea in the eleventh century is confirmed by the denunciation at Bristol by Bishop Wulfstan II of Worcester of the slave trade with Ireland. Further evidence of increased Irish Sea trade centred on Dublin was demonstrated in the 1980s by excavations of a settlement with Dublin-style wattle buildings which developed close to the monastery of Whithorn in the late tenth and eleventh centuries (see Fig. 3.3).

In the eleventh century, York, Lincoln, Norwich, Thetford, and Ipswich, all of which had seen periods of Viking rule in the ninth and early tenth centuries, had like their Irish counterparts retained some long-distance trading contacts in the Scandinavian world. But these had increasingly become incidental to their roles as regional centres, trading in bulkier staples such as meat, wool, pottery, and iron with other English towns and regions, and the nearby coast of the European continent, particularly the area from the Rhine to Normandy. London became the undisputed commercial and political focus of the English kingdom in the eleventh century, and it was to London that Duke William of Normandy came (by a circuitous route via Wallingford) in the closing weeks of 1066.

The temporary dip in English urban fortunes caused by the immediate aftermath of the Norman Conquest itself was less marked in the south than in the Midlands, East Anglia, and the North. Over half of Ipswich and Oxford tenements were destroyed or deserted between 1066 and 1086. These places recovered, but Thetford's losses led to a precipitous decline and abandonment. Further north, Chester, York, and Durham suffered disproportionately from the Conqueror's harsh treatment (Chester lost over 40 per cent of its houses between 1066 and 1086). The decision by the Normans to build their greatest castles in towns (the greatest of all being the White Tower at London) and to impose castles over existing urban streetscapes, as happened in Lincoln, Norwich, Canterbury, Huntingdon, Cambridge, Shrewsbury, Warwick, Chester, Gloucester, Oxford, and Wallingford, is a confirmation that possession of the towns was the key to both political and economic power in the land. The pressure points for the control and subjugation of the landscape and population lay within town walls. Nor was this lesson forgotten in the following centuries, as the reign of David I in Scotland, the Anglo-Norman invasion of Ireland under Henry II, and the Welsh campaigns of Edward I were to show.

Figure 4.0 The eleventh-century shrine of the Stowe Missal, with an Irish inscription, asking the viewer to pray for Donnchadh son of Brian Bóruma. In the eleventh century a number of great men in Ireland commissioned elaborate precious-metal objects for religious communities. Many of these pieces were inscribed with the names of their donors. Courtesy the National Museum of Ireland.

4

Lords and Labour

Robin Fleming

Landscape and lordship in Britain

Extraordinary transformations were taking place in Britain between the ninth century and the eleventh, which were changing the lives of both lords and their low-status dependants. At the beginning of the ninth century, before the transformations had begun in earnest, parts of England and Wales alike were places in which kings, great lords, and powerful religious communities often controlled very large territories. These territories were comprised not of single villages, but rather of scatters of small hamlets and farmsteads, and they often encompassed not only multiple settlements, but thousands of acres of fields, woodlands, and moors (Fig. 4.1). The people who lived in outlying hamlets within these territories were organized to provide their lords—who had large, leisured retinues—with food, livestock, and labour. Lords exploited little if any of their own holdings directly; but they did develop estate centres, which acted as collection points for all that was owed to them by their agricultural dependants and slaves. Sometimes, especially in Wales, but also perhaps in Mercia by the late eighth century, these centres were fortified. More often, however, they were undefended compounds comprised of elaborate wooden halls and outbuildings, courts where lords, in the company of their womenfolk, their military retainers, and their clients, could reside until they had eaten up all the tribute that the locals had supplied. They would then move on to other estates and other halls. In Scotland, too, where we know almost nothing about the organization of early estates, there is, nonetheless, evidence for similar centres, such as Forteviot in Strathearn (Perthshire) and Burghead on the coast of the Moray Firth. Similar levies of tribute from the

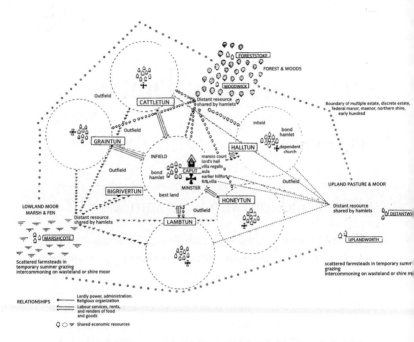

Figure 4.1 A hypothetical multiple estate, illustrating the relationship between an estate centre, with its aristocratic hall, and its dependent settlements, woodland, and marsh. Source: Michael Aston, *Interpreting the Landscape* (Routledge, London, 1985).

countryside doubtless supported the great men who controlled these sites.

The laws of an English king, written in the last decade of the seventh century, give some indication of the kinds and amounts of tribute people living within such territories rendered to their social betters. Every ten hides, so we are told (and large estates in England during this period could be 300 hides or more), were to provide the king with:

ten vats of honey, three hundred loaves, twelve ambers of Welsh ale, thirty of clear ale, two full-grown cows or ten wethers, ten geese, twenty hens, ten cheeses, an amber of butter, five salmon, twenty pounds of fodder and one hundred eels.[1]

Welsh descriptions of renders, too, list beer and bread, meat and

---

[1] Laws of Ine, 70, printed in D. Whitelock (ed.), *English Historical Documents*, i, 2nd edn. (Oxford, 1979), 398–407, at 406.

honey. Such renders allowed elite households to live well and never labour. Still, in good years this level of tribute was far from onerous: but there was little point in squeezing peasants harder. The largely perishable renders needed to be used in fairly short order; and since they were consumed by lords, rather than sold on the market, there was little purpose in demanding more. The lordship most men practised, therefore, in the early ninth century, was extensive rather than intensive. A tiny minority controlled vast tracts of land, but their agricultural subordinates were rarely pushed to create larger surpluses.

Britain was a world, then, of small, scattered settlements, and powerful, but often quite distant landlords. Although nucleated settlements and demesne farming belonged to the future, there were, nonetheless, a few places that were quite populous and permanent, places that were organized to meet the special needs of the privileged few. The sites of important religious communities, for example, such as Llancarfan and Caerwent in Wales, Inkberrow in England, or Iona in Scotland, had dozens of year-round residents as well as stone or timber churches, saints' shrines that attracted pilgrims, barns to store renders, and craftsmen and slaves housed to service the praying professionals.

Sometime in the ninth century these estates and this landscape, particularly in England, began to evolve. Around the middle of the ninth century some large, complex territories began to come apart. It appears that the great men and religious communities who controlled them were dismantling some of their estates, alienating modest parcels of five or ten hides, and granting them out to elite followers. This was happening in south Wales as well; indeed, the process may have begun there a century earlier. But it is in England that we have the sources to witness this fragmentation best, and in England that this development was most advanced by the end of the eleventh century. Thousands of English thegns, between the mid-ninth and the mid-eleventh centuries, came into possession of their own small estates. Because these new estates were more compact and had fewer resources than the old-style, loose-jointed territories, special care was sometimes taken in creating them, and there is evidence that when a number of thegnly retainers were granted pieces of one of these great estates, the land was systematically reorganized to create viable, self-sustaining holdings for each new proprietor (Fig. 4.2). Oftentimes older territories were divided by kings or ecclesiastical communities into a number of long, thin, five-hide estates, narrow to ensure that each holding had a share of river bank, some woodland, some access to nearby trackways or roads. When an older territory was split between a number of men, the new estates were sometimes rechristened, and called after their thegnly proprietors—Woolstone for 'Wulfric's estate', or Alerton for 'Algar's estate'.

By the middle of the eleventh century thousands of such small, prosperous manors had come into being, presided over not by great and distant lords, but by country gentlemen. These more modest landlords were obliged to manage their resources directly and carefully if they wished to live like lords, and they were more rooted on their lands than earlier great men, since they resided year round in single neighbourhoods. As thegnly families established themselves on their lands, they began transforming the landscape and re-engineering rural society. Many thegns seem to have laid out

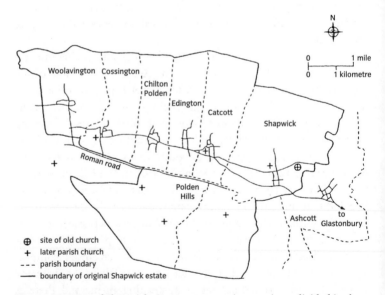

Figure 4.2 Map of Shapwick, Somerset, an ancient territory divided in the century or so before the Norman Conquest into a number of small, thin, thegnly estates. Source: Michael Costen, *The Origins of Somerset* (Manchester University Press, 2002).

planned villages after they had been granted their estates, and local peasants who farmed there moved from older scattered hamlets into these nucleated sites, often building their houses on equitably measured plots radiating out from a central road or path. Extensive open field-systems were laid out around many of the new villages; thegnly estates, as a whole, fell under more organized agricultural regimens, and the new villages became places where pools of labour could both be found and organized, and where stock and agricultural equipment could more readily be shared by those who laboured in the fields. Low-status peasants and slaves were doubtless herded into these villages, but other men and women, who had more choice and freedom, probably came of their own accord for the advantages village-living afforded them. Many new lords, for example, built water-driven mills on the streams running near their manors, and these must have acted as powerful incentives for peasant resettlement. They allowed the processing of grain, everyone's staple, to move from hands and households to machines and specialists, and they freed female labour for other tasks. Village communities were being founded across north-western Europe during these centuries, in part at the instigation of landlords, but also, one suspects, because many in Europe now felt that village life was proper life. So, this phenomenon is very widespread, and it was probably driven both by lordly intervention and by the shifting social preferences of rural workers.

In a large swathe of England—a long, south–north zone running from the Hampshire and Dorset coasts up through the Midlands and into Northumberland—thousands of communities and landscapes were remade in this way, and in the process patterns of work, the look of lordship, and, indeed, the very appearance of the countryside were transformed. Nonetheless, in 1086, the year of the Domesday inquest, King William's commissioners found hundreds of outsized manors, mostly in the hands of the king or the church, and thousands of small farmers not yet enmeshed in village life and demesne farming. Still, by the Norman Conquest the move towards villages and common fields was well advanced.

The transformations just outlined led to the extension of arable, to greater cereal yields and to the more efficient disciplining of labour. These three developments, in turn, contributed to the well-being of the landed elite. Rights to an increasing share of other people's labour were critical in the success of England's emerging country gentlemen, and many worked hard to increase their grip on rural workers. In one eleventh-century tract on estate management, for example, we are told that the *gebur*, one of the lord's demesne labourers, and a person now likely to be housed with his family on a crowded little lane in the shadow of the lord's own residence,

must perform week-work for two days each week of the year . . . and for three days from the feast of the Purification to Easter . . . And from when the ploughing is first done until Martinmas, he must plough one acre each week [for his lord], and he himself must present the seed to the lord's barn . . . When death befalls him, let the lord take charge of whatever he leaves.[2]

And in Ælfric's *Colloquy*, the ploughman, when describing his work, laments:

Oh, I work very hard. I go out at daybreak driving the oxen to the field, and yoke them to the plough. Because I fear my lord, there is no winter so severe that I dare hide at home. Each day I must yoke the oxen and fasten the ploughshare to the plough. Then I must plough a full acre or more every day . . . I have a lad driving the oxen with a goad, who is now hoarse because of the cold and from shouting.[3]

The hard labour of the many contributed to the astonishing prosperity of the few. The rise of thegnly compounds, which were coming to be a standard feature of England's new, more nucleated settlements, is evidence of this. The typical late Anglo-Saxon thegnly establishment is famously described in a text known as *Geþyncðo* as an estate of five hides, centred on a compound with a church and a bell-cote, a kitchen, and a gatehouse. This text is in remarkably close agreement with the archaeology. Again and again excavations have uncovered late Anglo-Saxon high-status sites created *de novo* in the decades when these estates were first forming, and then rebuilt and elaborated in the eleventh century. By the time of the Norman

---

[2] *Rectitudines Singularum Personarum*, printed in Dr. C. Douglas and G. W. Greenaway (eds.), *English Historical Documents*, ii, 2nd edn. (Oxford, 1981), 875–9, at 876.

[3] Ælfric's *Colloquy*, printed in M. Swanton (ed. and trans.), *Anglo-Saxon Prose* (London, 1975), 107–15, at 108.

Conquest, thegnly compounds often had large, aisled halls built alongside separate structures, which provided private accommodations for thegns and their intimates. These sites always had separate kitchens as well, housed in their own buildings. Some even had elaborate latrines. This assemblage of buildings was usually set within an enclosed site of an acre or more, and they were often marked off, along with a new timber or stone church, from the altogether different houses of the peasantry, by ditches, fences, or hedges.

The upgrading of thegnly residences was going on at breakneck pace in the eleventh century and represents massive expenditures of labour and resources. But the lives lived in these compounds were not simply about the exploitation of peasant labour or the squandering of prime timber and stone: they were about cash. One of the clear differences between ninth- and early tenth-century thegnly establishments and late tenth-/early eleventh-century ones is that the latter appear to have been much less involved in craft activity—iron smithing, jewellery-making, potting, bone-working, and the like— and yet later sites are littered with manufactured goods. These things must now have been purchased from itinerant traders or urban merchants, in whose towns all of these crafts had become established, and which had become places where agricultural surplus could be sold.

Hints of similar transformations can be found in Wales, although the scope and scale of both the landscape's and lordship's remaking were more muted there. There is good evidence for the fragmentation of some large, complex estates in south Wales. Grants to monasteries, for example, given by laymen after the late eighth century, were modest in comparison to earlier gifts—measuring in the dozens of acres rather than the hundreds—and these later parcels may represent holdings carved out from larger and older territories. It seems that some estates were being broken into their component *trefi* or *villae*, as they are called in the charters, and alienated to form single-settlement holdings typically comprised of about 125 acres. Sometimes, as in England, these smaller holdings were named after their new proprietors with appellations like *Tref Ili* or *Villa Conuc*. There is also some evidence for the growth of low-status dependants—servants rather than clients—from the eighth century on. By the eleventh century a few lords were even practising demesne farming. Still, there is nothing to suggest that Welsh lords during this period had systematically taken hold of the labour of agricultural workers settled on their estates, the way thegns in England had done; and there is no evidence for the widespread laying out of planned villages and common fields or the building of gentrified residences.

In Scotland there is evidence that a handful of the most powerful members of the local Norse elite were building lavish residences in the second half of the eleventh century. At Birsay, for example, the seat of the earls of Orkney, an impressive domestic complex was carefully constructed by skilled masons and included a long hall, workshops and other outbuildings, a church, and a stone-built sauna. Elsewhere, at sites like Jarlshof, Shetland, earlier houses were enlarged in the eleventh century, and their proprietors for the first time had access to a few modest luxury imports. But because the evidence for Scotland is so slight, we will probably never know how widespread the upgrading of domestic sites was among the landed classes, and whether changes in agricultural exploitation and lordship stood behind the elaboration of some high-status accommodations. Still there is slight evidence—in Orkney, for example—that infield and outfield systems may have been developing at the very end of the eleventh century.

Landscape and lordship in Ireland

Ireland at the beginning of the ninth century, like early ninth-century England and Wales, was a place with a long-settled landscape and tens of thousands of settlement sites. Like the vast majority of people living in north-western Europe, most Irish in the year 800 did not reside in village communities. Instead, they lived, as their grandparents and great-grandparents had done, on dispersed farmsteads and in tiny hamlets, often within sight of other kinsmen and neighbours, and close enough to co-operate during ploughing or harvesting or when herds needed moving. The clearest manifestation of this settlement form is the ringfort (sometimes called a rath), a site marked out by impressive earthen or drystone walls 2 metres high or more. Ringforts were built for and resided in by a whole spectrum of prosperous people—well-to-do free farmers who nonetheless owed labour services, food renders, and a portion of their herds to more powerful men; little chieftains with a couple of followers of their own; and noblemen and kings with aristocratic retinues and a crowd of lesser clients. Some 45,000 ringforts were built between the beginning of the seventh century and the end of the ninth, and many thousands still stand (Fig. 4.3).

Within the circular confines of a ringfort, a single family would reside, usually in two or three houses, with an extended household of relatives, retainers, and slaves. In spite of their name, the stone or earthen walls which defined the vast majority of these enclosures were hardly strategic: they could keep livestock and children in, and they would have discouraged casual thievery and wild animals, but they could not have withstood much greater trouble. They could, however, be seen from afar, and because of this they announced the prestige of their proprietors to all those residing in or riding through the neighbourhood. It is clear from early legal tracts that the size of a ringfort and the number of its banks and ditches helped to define its owner's social status. Men from the higher ranks of society owned slaves, and they were owed fixed amounts of labour from their free dependants, including help with the construction of ringforts. Thus, the more substantial the ringfort or the more circles of banks and ditches it had, the more clients and human property under its owner's control. This correlation between ringfort size and social importance, remarked upon by early medieval legal theorists, is born out by modern archaeological excavations. The vast majority of ringforts—about 80 per cent—are somewhere between 20 and 50 metres in diameter, and they have a single bank and ditch. When excavated, ringforts of this size have produced a limited range of finds—modest jewellery, like ringed pins and jet bracelets, tilling and milling equipment, textile and leather-working implements, and some evidence for bone-, antler- and ironworking. But the most extensive ringforts—places with enclosures of between 90 and 110 metres in diameter or sites that are double or triple ditched—have not only preserved similar artefacts, but have produced finds which suggest that luxury craftsmen and even scribes were working at these sites, fashioning fancy millefiori and enamelled jewellery, and leaving behind evidence of

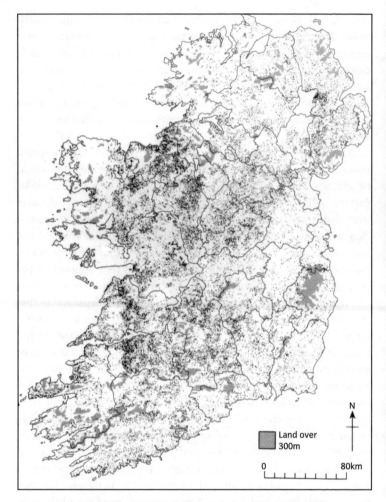

Figure 4.3 Map showing the distribution of surviving Irish ringforts.
Source: Matthew Stout, *The Irish Ring Fort* (Four Courts Press, 2000).

bronze-casting, motif-pieces, and styli. Sites like these were clearly the residences of nobles or kings.

Crannógs, artificial islands built near lakeshores as platforms for settlements, served the same powerful strata of society as the grandest ringforts, although crannógs were defensible in a way that only the most elaborate ringforts could be. Because of the huge amounts of timber, stone, and labour involved, the two thousand or so crannógs built by AD 800 seem to have been universally very high status, and some, we know from written sources, were, indeed, royal.

The houses built in both ringforts and crannógs up through the ninth century were exceptionally conservative in form. They were roundhouses, a domestic architectural style ubiquitous in Iron Age Britain and Ireland, and a form absolutely dominant in Ireland at the beginning of the ninth century. These roundhouses were generally fashioned from double-walled, woven wicker or from posts and wattle. As far as we can tell the roundhouses of kings and great lords were larger than those of other men, but they were not better constructed than the houses of people of lower social standing; thus, Irish elites seem to have had a lack of interest in expressing their status through their houses. Rather it was with cattle herds, crowds of clients, extraordinary brooches, and the banks, ditches, and walls of their ringforts that they asserted their prestige.

Cattle farming and dairying dominated the agricultural practices of ringfort and crannóg dwellers. The size of a man's herd, like the size of his ringfort, was a measure of his status. Nonetheless, crop husbandry was crucial. Corn-drying kilns and horizontal water mills were common, suggesting that crop cultivation was a conspicuous component of the period's economy. Indeed, Ireland has the largest corpus of early medieval water mill sites in the world. Through the evidence of dendrochronology we know that the vast majority were built between 581 and 843, the heyday of ringfort and crannóg construction. Kings and nobles, presiding over some 150 circumscribed little territories known as *tuatha* and living in this world of cultivated fields and dairy herds, received tribute from their clients, carefully calibrated to the particular social ranks of the parties involved. Clients contracted with nobles, who furnished them with set amounts of land, livestock, and/or other material goods, and a promise of legal and military support. Clients, in turn, provided set labour services and entertainment. More important, they gave large annual renders of milk cows, dairy products, meat, malt, grain, and other foodstuffs, and it was these renders that fed great men and their retainers.

This settlement pattern, these settlement sites, and the social structures and agricultural regimens that supported them were long-standing, well-entrenched complexes in the ninth century. But over the next hundred years or so the Irish landscape would begin to be remade as social relations were restructured, and as the long-dominant territorial unit, the *tuath*, eroded in the face of larger political entities: under these circumstances novel kinds of communities began to form.

The clearest evidence for all of this is the waning of the ringfort. Ringforts ceased to be built over the course of a single century, and not one can be shown to have been put up after the year 1000. The sites around many ringforts during this period of transition remained occupied, but the ringforts themselves were abandoned. The enclosed space within them apparently ceased to be considered an appropriate dwelling space for all but the most powerful kings and nobles, so houses were increasingly put up just outside the walls of more middling ringforts. These new houses, moreover, were built in a novel fashion: they were rectangular, generally built with dry-stone or turf walls, and their interiors were now paved with stone. The reasons behind this dramatic shift from round to rectangular and wicker to stone cannot be explained as technological or practical improvements, since hazel-rod construction is remarkably strong and cheap, and since unmortared stone walls do not make for the most comfortable of dwellings. Nonetheless, it seems that the millennia-old roundhouse, within the course of a single century, came to be seen as socially unfitting, and that everyone who could, rebuilt their houses in an altogether new way. Irish houses, moreover, were now often built in close association with souterrains, stone-lined, underground passages, sometimes as much as 100 metres in length. Souterrains, like the ringforts built before them, required skill and large amounts of labour to construct and, like ringforts, they are very impressive monuments. But the several thousand that were built functioned differently, since their underground locations meant that they could not operate as display structures. They could, however, act as bolt holes when gangs of slavers raided, a growing menace from the ninth century on. Perhaps the ability to protect was the new social marker *par excellence*. Whatever the reasons behind these dramatic changes, *c*.1000 the abandonment of the interiors of the smaller ringforts along with the construction of rectangular houses and souterrains were the new order of the day.

A small number of ringforts, however, places like Gransha, Lismahon, and Rathmullen, evolved in a different way. Their enclosed interiors were deliberately raised with dumps of stone and clay, heightened for greater visibility and security and to set them apart from old-fashioned ringforts. In Ireland sites like these are known as raised raths, but in any other European setting they would be called mottes. At the same time many of the great crannógs continued to be occupied. Strategic forts, too, some strongly fortified, like the one at Beal Boru in Co. Clare, were being thrown up from scratch by kings who wished to extend or hold on to their territories.

More or less contemporary with these changes in high-status sites are hints that relatively large, undefended proto-villages were beginning to coalesce, and the centuries-old pattern of dispersed settlements was starting to evolve towards nucleation. A number of low-status cluster settlements have been found through aerial photography. Most lie along deserted hillsides in the uplands, just beyond the margins of modern agriculture. One such settlement is Ballyutoag, in Co. Antrim. Here settlement was much more extensive and peopled than at earlier ringfort sites. There were at least twenty-three houses here, which would have accommodated 100 people or more. Finds were numerous, but limited to coarse pottery and the most basic jewellery. This may have been a transhumance village occupied seasonally, when those who worked the land moved their cattle to upland summer pastures: if so, Ballyutoag would have had a twinned settlement at some lower elevation. Nonetheless, cultivation ridges show that crops were grown here, and the site is very substantial for a seasonal camp; thus, it may well have been occupied year round. A similar clustering of people can be seen at the prehistoric tomb at Knowth, in Co. Meath, which served as a royal residence from c.800 on. A zone outside the royal compound became the focus of an extensive, unenclosed settlement consisting of thirteen houses and nine souterrains. Concentrations of undefended houses can also be found near some Irish monasteries, which were beginning, during this period, to take on quasi-urban features. Thus religious communities, as well as secular nobles, may have been pioneering new social arrangements with a crowd of people now housed outside their enclosures.

Knowth, Ballyutoag, and a number of monastic sites hint, then, that clustered, open, secular settlements were developing around the same time that ringforts were transforming. Social, political, and economic changes must in some ways have been driving these transformations. The intensification of agriculture and the pressures of growing population during the seventh, eighth, and ninth centuries probably meant that the number of base clients grew by the ninth century to the point where some men's holdings no longer produced the tributes they needed to give over to their lords in order to meet their social obligations. Failed client families, dislodged from their former homes, may under these circumstances have gravitated into larger settlements around the compounds of the powerful. Beyond this was the coming of the Vikings, whose initial terrifying period of raids (795–840) provided great men with a bona fide emergency and a useful pretext to better their positions at the expense of their neighbours, their clients, and their more distant kin. The changing landscape, then, hints that formerly free farmers were being pressed downwards by the hard circumstances of debt, political disruption, and ruthlessly bargained relationships with their betters, and the death of the ringfort alongside the simultaneous rise of nucleated settlement suggests that thousands of families were giving up prior independence and freedom for a kind of servile security. Under these circumstances, those with power—the families settled in raised raths or grand crannógs—may no longer have been satisfied with free-farmer clients, traditional annual food renders, and a share of their followers' calves. Instead, they may have sought a more subjugated group of underlings, over whose labour, harvests, and herds they had more direct control.

The dramatic changes just outlined were far from complete at the end of the eleventh century, and dispersed settlements and old client relationships persisted into the twelfth century and beyond. Nonetheless, the evolution of the Irish landscape and Irish lordship were moving in the same general directions as changes that could be found across a large swathe of central England and parts of Wales.

Aristocratic consumption

It was against this backdrop of evolving landscape and lordship that the social and economic differences between lords and the people who laboured in their fields came to be expressed in new ways across Britain and Ireland, as families on the winning side of these transformations pioneered new forms of aristocratic life. Although social differentiation and conspicuous consumption were hoary traditions by the year 1000, some of the ways in which lords now chose to expend their resources and underscore their august positions were, nonetheless, novel. In England and Ireland especially, the powerful now had more and different kinds of wealth to devote to the good life than had their ancestors in the early ninth century. These were boom years for English and Irish lords alike, and years in which silver was flowing into their coffers. English thegns and Irish lords, moreover, were striving to acquire similar possessions in their pursuit of the good life. Yet Ireland and England inhabited different economic universes, and the ways in which trade and towns developed and functioned in each of these places came to shape the ways their elites lived status.

In England the centuries of agrarian reorganization were also centuries in which English kings developed a full-blown minting system, with a centrally produced and carefully regulated coinage and an extraordinarily sophisticated monetary system, which allowed for short-cycle remintings and periodic weight-standard reforms. Kings during this period also refined the system of land tax. This tax, which came by custom to demand twenty-four pennies from every hide of land, forced thegnly landlords to organize each of their estates in such a way that cash was one of its products. The need for cash and the intensification of agricultural exploitation together, over the course of the ninth and tenth centuries, increased the demand for traders and regulated markets. Under these circumstances, it is not surprising that by the late tenth century *burhs* had grown into full-blown market towns, and by 1066 something like 100,000 burgesses lived within them. Thegnly landholders thrived within this monetizing and commercializing economy, and the general impression one gets is that they were growing steadily richer.

Indeed, the Old English word *rice*, from which we get our word 'rich', was changing its meaning during this period. In its earlier incarnation *rice* could be translated by the Latin *potens*, 'powerful'; but by the third quarter of the tenth century *rice* was coming to describe not just powerful people, but powerful people who were rich, as if *the* distinguishing characteristic of those with authority was now their conspicuous wealth.

In Ireland, too, elites seem to have had greater access to wealth. Although the state was less developed and no state-backed currency emerged there, from *c*.850 on Ireland was awash with silver. Hack silver and coins brought into Ireland by Vikings rapidly fell into Irish hands. Indeed, most of the Viking Age hoards discovered in Ireland have been recovered from areas that were controlled not by Scandinavians, but by the Irish. A number of silver hoards, for example, have been recovered around Lough Ennell, the centre of the territory controlled by the powerful Clann Cholmáin branch of the Uí Néill family. This silver must have come to them through some combination of raiding, slave trading, tribute, and gift exchange. Hoards found in Irish territory, moreover, are comprised primarily of coins, suggesting that elites in regions rich in hoards, in particular Meath and northern Leinster, were participating in some way in a coin-using economy, and that wealthy Irishmen were using silver money to purchase luxuries in the new Hiberno-Norse towns established in the first decades of the tenth century along the east coast of Ireland. Goods acquired there—items of long-distance trade as well as objects crafted by Hiberno-Norse townsmen—no doubt betokened the prestige of individuals and families who were profiting from the demise of free farmers.

Wearing status

So what were elites consuming in the tenth and eleventh centuries, and how were they consuming in new ways? Apparel is one interesting arena of aristocratic consumption. It is difficult to know how exactly English aristocrats dressed in our period, but there are indications that some, by the tenth century, were wearing very elaborate costumes. Manuscript illustrations from the period, in particular the highly idiosyncratic vignettes found in the Old English Hexateuch, suggest that great men in the eleventh century often wore tunics and robes edged with broad bands of embroidery or brocade (Fig. 4.4). Cloth-of-gold and gold embroidery were also worn by the rich and powerful, and some of their clothes were so thickly embroidered with precious-metal thread that we are told they looked like chain-mail hauberks.

Acquisition of the most spectacular textiles and clothing would

Figure 4.4 An illustration from the Old English Hexateuch, BL MS Cotton Claudius Biv, fo. 13ʳ. This scene, a depiction of Genesis 6: 4 ('There were giants in the earth in those days . . .'), shows clothes embellished with broad bands of luxury textiles.

have been limited to those who received diplomatic gifts or who had womenfolk whose time was free for fancy needlework. But although some luxury textiles would have been acquired through gift exchange, England was awash with deluxe fabrics in the late Anglo-Saxon period, and this suggests that they were the subject of a large and important international trade. Indeed, it was the merchant in Ælfric's *Colloquy* who supplied the wealthy with 'purple cloth and silks, precious jewels and gold, unusual clothes ... ivory and bronze'.[4] The ability to procure luxury textiles was trickling down the social hierarchy in the century or so between *c.*950 and 1066. The most elaborate secular clothing, for example, seems to have been adopted by the king in the mid-tenth century, and probably followed Ottonian and Byzantine styles. But by the mid-eleventh century some of these ostensibly royal fashions had been co-opted by powerful courtiers. Thus long robes, first adopted by King Edgar, were being sported at court on the eve of the Norman Conquest by earls. And great rectangular brooches, which seem to have begun their lives as royal cloak-fasteners in the tenth century, ended up, in the eleventh, worn by other great men. But it was not just the earls dressing in this manner. One thegn, for example, 'wearing garments suited to his noble rank', was mistaken by Italian bandits for an earl because of the splendour of his attire.[5] In the late tenth and eleventh centuries gold embroidery and silk were also being acquired by people outside the charmed circle of the royal court. Archaeologists have uncovered the remains of some gold braid and gold-thread embroidery used on secular garments dating from the ninth and tenth centuries, but the number of such examples increases dramatically for the eleventh century. Indeed, it was in the eleventh century that silver gilt began to be employed in the making of gold thread, which made it much less expensive and must have put it, for the first time, within the reach of thegns-on-the-make. And although silk robes and tunics probably continued to be monopolized by the very top strata of society, silk caps, ribbons, and bags have been found in York, London, Lincoln, and Winchester, and were doubtless sold there.

Irish elites from the tenth century on also had access to luxury

---

[4] Ælfric's *Colloquy*, 112.
[5] *The Life of King Edward*, ed. and trans. F. Barlow, 2nd edn. (Oxford, 1997), 54–5.

apparel. When Brian Bóruma (Brian Boru) attacked Dublin, one of the things he seized was luxury textiles. Excavations of later tenth- and eleventh-century levels of Dublin have revealed that the Hiberno-Norse settled there were producing garments made from specially woven diamond twills imported from England, and that they were using silk tabbies from Byzantium and Persia and gold braids that may have come from central Asia. Tenth- and eleventh-century descriptions of Irish clothing are few and far between, but high-status fashions there may well have resembled those found in England, with an emphasis on clothes bordered with bands of luxury fabric. One tenth-century woman, for example, was described as wearing 'a fair cloak, which was shining and beautiful, surrounded by a hem of red gold'.[6] The author of the early twelfth-century *Wars of the Gaedhill with the Gaill*, however, had a passionate interest in aristocratic clothing, and this may reflect a growing sartorial obsession among the audience of such tales. Although it is impossible to determine with any precision who exactly among the Irish elite had access to such clothing, it is clear that some in Ireland were successful in acquiring it via long-distance traders operating out of the Hiberno-Norse towns.

Simultaneously, Irish high-status jewellery exhibited a marked change in sensibilities. The brooches of the great, which had been very large, spectacularly ornate, and highly coloured early in our period, gave way in the later ninth century to smaller, monochromatic silver and black niello pieces. This aesthetic mirrored fashions outside Ireland, particularly those found in the south of England, but display jewellery was also growing more restrained on the European continent. As in England, then, there seems to have been a growing emphasis in Ireland on fabric and clothes and a scaling back of jewellery. This suggests that displays of exotica from abroad purchased with silver were being used in the tenth and eleventh centuries to reinforce social status, the way domestically produced craft items, such as brooches, had earlier been deployed.

In Wales high-status dress is much more difficult to track. Welsh kings and noblemen did wear luxury apparel. According to his

---

[6] Áed Finn, in G. Murphy (ed. and trans.), *Early Irish Lyrics: Eighth to Twelfth Century* (Dublin, 1998), 101–5, at 101.

eleventh-century biographer, St Cadog as a boy, in spite of his royal birth, despised 'the pomp of royal apparel',[7] and he wore meaner clothes when he went to church. Perhaps he was objecting to the same cloth-of-gold clothes that one king stripped off and gave the saint, when seeking his forgiveness. One man, speaking in a tenth-century text, admonished his servants not only to mind his gold and silver while he was away, but to 'stay behind and guard my clothes',[8] so clearly exotic apparel was highly prized. Indeed, a queen's cloak, red linen, and entire sets of garb were traded for land. The giving of purple mantles, moreover, is a common poetic trope in this period. Fine clothing, then, was available in Wales, but it is impossible to determine how far its wearing had descended the social ladder. It seems unlikely, however, that it was often found on the backs of local landowners. Beyond this, there is no evidence that this kind of clothing was regularly available for purchase in Wales, and its exchange appears for the most part to have remained embedded in social relations. As a result, an article of clothing seems to have been as much an object of patronage and gift exchange as a form of social display.

Eating status

Feasting was an important component of the high living and hospitality practised by aristocrats across the whole of the middle ages and across all of Europe. Lavish meals with large numbers of guests must have been one of the most visible and envy-inducing of all the early middle ages' elite social practices, separating the lives of the rich and well-fed from those of the labouring and the hungry. High-status deployment of food, however, changed quite dramatically in the latter part of our period, but in different ways and at different rates across Britain and Ireland.

It is in England that aristocratic eating practices were most clearly following continental fashions. Feasts in England like the

---

[7] *Life of St Cadog*, in A. W. Wade-Evans (ed. and trans.), *Vitae Sanctorum Britanniae et Genealogiae* (Cardiff, 1944), 25–141, cap. 5.

[8] *De Raris Fabulis*, printed in W. Stevenson (ed.), *Early Scholastic Colloquies* (Oxford, 1929), 1–11, cap. 4.

ones described in *Beowulf*—long on mead and joints of meat, but short on culinary pyrotechnics—were giving way in the late tenth and early eleventh centuries to celebrations of fine dining. There is clear evidence that the landowning elite in England by the eleventh century were eating more elegant dishes in a more elegant manner (Fig. 4.5). Sauces, spicing, wheat bread, a choice of dishes at every meal, cooks, even serving boys were all part of English aristocratic dining on the eve of the Norman Conquest, and what all these things represent is not just food, but cuisine, a development that anthropologists see as a tell-tale sign of growing social stratification.

Part and parcel of this development was the fact that English thegns and earls were coming to eat an ever-expanding group of animals. By the year 1000 English elites were consuming more beef and pork (especially young beef and pork) than did their ancestors or their peasants, and they were eating noticeably less mutton. This suggests that unlike the eighth and ninth centuries, when many animals were simply butchered and eaten after they had outlived their usefulness, some were now being bred specially for the tables of the well-to-do. Beyond this, new animals were being introduced into the thegnly diet. In late Anglo-Saxon England the rich began to eat fish,

Figure 4.5 An eleventh-century illustration of a feast, replete with tablecloth, servant boys, and decorated tableware (BL MS Cotton Tiberius Cvi, fo. 5ᵛ).

in particular sea fish. Marine species begin to appear in great numbers in the archaeological record only decades before the Norman Conquest, and they are closely associated with high-status sites. The most interesting of the choice marine species, ubiquitous in both the written accounts and the archaeology, are porpoises and herring. Porpoise is not so surprising in high-status contexts, given that it was still a luxury food in the thirteenth century and that it must have been impressive when brought to the table; but herring, which was the cheapest fish by far in the later middle ages, is a surprise. The herring industry was becoming organized along the south and east coasts of Britain around the year 1000, yet herring fishermen and herring renders are found in the Domesday survey only in association with the most powerful men and institutions of the realm— important courtiers, powerful thegns, and the most important monks and bishops—and these men received thousands, sometimes tens of thousands, of herring each year from their men. Thus, it seems that herring was served at the finest tables in England, and that the very great went to some effort to secure it. They were also doing what they could to acquire freshwater fish. Behind fish on the table lay considerable outlays of resources for those who caught fish with their own fleets or raised or caught them in their own stews and fisheries; but there is also evidence that fish could be bought for cash, and that the fishing industry was beginning to commercialize. Indeed, at the very end of the eleventh century there is some indication that as far north as Scotland a few coastal sites were becoming involved in deepwater fishing, fish curing, and exporting, and that this activity in turn led to those profiting from the fishing industry having access to more import goods. Nonetheless, there was not a widespread move from subsistence fishing to fishing for exchange in Scotland until the twelfth and thirteenth centuries.

Food in Ireland operated differently. Aristocratic feasting was important—as important in the year 800 as it was in the year 1100— but cuisine was slow to take hold, and the Irish evidence gives the impression that the quantity and variety of the food provided to guests rather than its rarity was the mark of a great feast. So far as we can tell, most food in Ireland between 800 and 1100 was consumed within the households in which it was produced or to which it had been rendered because of the customary obligations of clients and tenants. Furthermore, how much one had to share with guests and followers seems to have been a function of the number of social inferiors within one's orbit. Thus, there was a close link between great feasts and great lords of men. At the same time, however, only very limited amounts of food in the countryside seem to have been obtained through commercial transactions, even in the eleventh century. The exception to this general rule was wine, a high-status import drink of long standing; indeed, there is ample evidence that Merovingian and even eastern Mediterranean wine was occasionally drunk at the feasts of the wealthy as early as the fifth and sixth centuries. The development of Dublin and other Viking towns over the course of the tenth and eleventh centuries and the large amounts of silver in Irish hands improved the Irish elite's access to import goods, and this no doubt facilitated and enlarged the wine trade. Certainly, Brian Bóruma received regular tributes of wine from the Scandinavians in Dublin and Limerick, suggesting both that wine was one of these communities' staple imports and that it was one of striving Irish noblemen's most sought after comestibles.

With this notable exception, however, the bulk of the Irish diet during these centuries, high status and low, would have been comprised of locally grown grain, dairy products, and meat. The Irish, according to Finbar McCormick, were 'extremely conservative eaters', and the diet of most, so far as it is reflected in the archaeological record, seems to have changed little from the ninth century to the twelfth. Diet, in Ireland as in England, was related to social status, but the more extravagant forms of newfangled culinary display, so prevalent in England on the eve of the Norman Conquest, seem not to have established themselves in the upper reaches of Irish society. Nonetheless, there are hints of some sumptuary food. Eighth-century Irish legal tracts speak of a hierarchy of grain, with wheat and rye characterized as proper food for great men, and oats and barley portrayed as better suited for people of less dignified stations. Cereal remains from excavated sites around Ireland more than support the evidence of the legal treatises, and show that wheat and rye were, indeed, as rare as oats and barley were common. The economics behind these tastes and levels of use are straightforward. Wheat and rye were cultivated almost exclusively for human consumption, but because oats and barley were grown for fodder as well as human food, and barley could be malted, they were better crops for most farmers. Prior to a well-developed, structured market economy, few farmers in wheat-growing regions could have afforded to specialize in the production of wheat strictly for elite consumption at the expense of cereal crops more suitable for broad-based, local use. And judging from excavated cereal remains from high-status sites, even the richest tables would have had their share of barley bread and porridge. The eating of wheat, however, appears to have been much more widespread in England among the thegnage, and there is evidence for its refining and trading in urban communities during this period. Thus, it seems that wealthy Irish and English elites shared similar grain preferences, but the better developed markets and more highly commercialized economy of late tenth- and eleventh-century England facilitated the supply of wheat to wealthy tables and made it widely available to large numbers of the well-to-do. So, the difference between English and Irish high-status eating habits here was not determined by taste, but rather by economics. Long-distance luxury items like wine were increasingly available in Dublin, but there was no network of little inland trading communities in Ireland closely tied to rural hinterlands, as there was in England, which would have allowed elites to consume Irish-grown products more selectively.

The meat Irish elites consumed during this same 300-year period was comprised almost entirely of four-legged domesticates, primarily cattle, but also pigs. There is some evidence that royal sites enjoyed the eating of more and larger cattle, carefully fed, but there is little to suggest that the balance between species or the age of the animals eaten changed markedly during these centuries the way they had done in England. Only minuscule numbers of fish bones have been excavated from high-status sites. Beyond this, there is no evidence to suggest that freshwater fish were being raised or bought by middling Irish lords, nor is there evidence that marine fish were being rendered to great men or purchased by them. Indeed, the Irish words for cod and ling were adopted from Old Norse, and the Irish word for herring is probably an English loanword, suggesting that open-sea fishing and sea-fish eating were introduced to the Irish by foreigners and adopted late. Again, different market structures and perhaps different levels of dependence on renders of tribute from clients or peasants were coming into play here. English lords were able to trade surplus and then purchase special food if they wished, while Irish lords were more likely to consume, rather than trade or sell, what was grown for them.

The great in England by the early eleventh century, unlike others, were also eating what they hunted. At the end of the Anglo-Saxon period they were pursuing red deer and roe deer, animals which are all but absent in earlier bone assemblages. We can also see landlords on the eve of the Norman Conquest beginning to engage in deer husbandry and establishing deer parks, and we find even exceptionally modest thegns beginning to employ huntsmen and dog-keepers. It seems that the hunting and consumption of venison were becoming socially necessary for the well-to-do. English thegns were also increasingly taken with game birds. Their bones are found in astounding numbers and stunning variety in the excavated remains gathered from high-status sites, and many of them would have been caught for sport by thegns with their goshawks or falcons. Fowl also loomed large in contemporary descriptions of dining. One pampered community of canons on the eve of the Norman Conquest, for example, dined on blackbirds, plovers, partridges, and pheasants from Michaelmas to Lent. But even domestic birds, in particular geese, were increasingly eaten by the well-to-do in the tenth and eleventh centuries.

The bones of fowl, both wild and domestic, like those of fish, make up only a tiny percentage of the animal bones found on most high-status Irish sites, and there is little evidence that birds during this period were seen as special food. The same is true for deer. Although early Irish status tracts insist that important nobles would have owned deerhounds and that royal households would have employed huntsmen, deer bones are hardly present on settlement sites, and hunting as a social practice among lower rungs of the elite seems not to have been established. Certainly, there is no evidence for deer parks in Ireland during this period, nor for hawking. So the social activities of hunting, hawking, and venison eating, common among English thegns by the eleventh century, were late in establishing themselves among well-to-do landholders in Ireland.

Aristocratic hunting, of course, requires leisure, something that Irish grandees valued as much as any English thegn. According to an eighth-century Irish tract on status, if a king was found working with a mallet, an axe, or a spade, his honour-price was lessened, underscoring the shame of physical labour. This attitude was as true in 1100 as it had been in 800. In *The War of the Gaedhil with the Gaill*, one of the triumphs of Brian Bóruma was that he captured so many Norse in Dublin that

no son of a soldier or of an officer of the *Gaedhil* deigned to put his hand to a flail, or any other labour on earth; nor did a woman deign to put her hands to the grinding of a quern, or to knead a cake or wash her clothes, but had a foreign man or a foreign woman to work for them.[9]

Clearly, idleness was an aristocratic virtue of long standing in Ireland, but it does not seem to have been diverted in the eleventh century into hunting, hawking, and deer-park making the way it had been in England. Perhaps this is the result of England's relative peace and Ireland's fractious politics and militarized culture. Ireland's political circumstances may have channelled aristocratic leisure into fighting rather than blood sports.

Food also conferred status in Wales, and feasting was an important high-status activity there. Monastic households had cooks, butchers, bakers, and officers who oversaw their kitchens and bakeries, and this may reflect the practice of important secular households as well. There are also hints that great lords ate special food. St Cadog as a boy rejected the more sumptuous food of his father's household for bread and water. We also hear about loaves of wheat bread, although Cadog, as a boy, sometimes ate oats. At the same time, it is clear that fishing rights and weirs constituted important appurtenances for landlords. Hawking rights, like fishing rights, were things given in charters, and we can catch glimpses of aristocratic retinues hawking and kings catching ducks with the help of their favourite raptors. Some hawks were highly prized: in a mid-eighth-century Llandaff charter, for example, a single hawk was valued at twelve cows. Thus, Welsh noblemen participated in some of the same social practices related to food as the neighbouring English and shared similar tastes for fish and game birds. Nonetheless, there is no indication that they ate food that had not been raised by their dependants or that they had not caught themselves; and they drank mead, rather than imported wine.

---

[9] *War of the Gaedhil with the Gaill*, ed. and trans. J. H. Todd, Rolls Series (London, 1867), 117.

Conspicuous piety

In England well-to-do landlords on the eve of the Norman Conquest were also constructing new churches or refurbishing old ones. The most powerful secular landlords in England founded new communities for canons and built outsized churches for them. In the eleventh century Earl Leofric and his wife Lady 'Godiva', for example, helped build a church for the community at Stow in Lincolnshire. Stow's transepts, which still stand, are 85 feet in length, and the arches of its central crossing are 33 feet high. In short, the church is the size of an Anglo-Saxon cathedral. Thegns with fewer resources also established churches, often next to their own halls; and increasingly they were made from stone. These structures memorialized their proprietors' piety, but they also advertised their social standing. The small church excavated at Rauds Furnells in Northamptonshire certainly did. Enlarged in the early eleventh century, the church was transformed from a one- to a two-cell structure. This rebuilding, however, provided no more room for villagers than the old church had; instead the solemnity of the service was improved with the addition of a new, roomy chancel and the installation of a clergy bench. Rauds's graveyard had a plot apparently restricted to its proprietor and his family, and unlike the village dead, they were interred beneath elegantly carved grave-covers. A priest in tow could also add to a thegn's *gravitas*. When the Hampshire thegn Ælfric built his church just after the Norman Conquest, the priest provided to him by the local minster had to dine with him on Sundays and could never start mass before Ælfric himself had arrived, 'Ælfric being the greater man'.[10]

Elsewhere in Britain there are few indications that middling lords were building churches, proprietary or otherwise. An elaborately carved arch at Forteviot indicates that important royal sites in Scotland had mortared stone churches as early as the mid-ninth century, and a chapel excavated on the Brough of Deerness, Orkney, suggests that some small timber churches were being replaced in the eleventh

---

[10] Christ Church Cartulary (British Library, MS Cotton Tiberius D vi B), trans. T. H. Hase, 'The Mother Churches of Hampshire', in J. Blair (ed.), *Minsters and Parish Churches: The Local Church in Transition 950–1200* (Oxford, 1988), 45–66, at 60.

century with small stone ones. Beyond this, very great men in eleventh-century Scotland, men like Thorfinn, earl of Orkney, probably built churches near their residences. In Wales, until the turn of the tenth century, churches had often been granted to religious communities. There was some attempt in the middle of the ninth century to ban laymen's holding of churches, and this may account for the disappearance of grants of churches after *c*.910. This may also provide a partial explanation for elite Welshmen's lack of interest in building churches on their own estates. Beyond this, most churches in Wales before 1100, even those of important religious communities, were wooden rather than stone. Master craftsmen built some Welsh churches, and these may well have been adorned with ornate wooden carvings. Still, even the most important ecclesiastical institutions had churches that were modest in comparison to England's. We know, for example, that Llandaff's stone cathedral church, probably built just before the end of the eleventh century, had a nave 28 feet long, that is, 22 feet shorter than the church at Raunds, which by English standards was exceptionally small. Thus, it appears that few in Wales had the wherewithal to build great stone edifices, but it is also likely that Welsh elites did not think of architectural patronage as a particularly pious act, nor, apparently, did they believe they would accrue the admiration of their competitors or their social inferiors if they undertook such work.

In Ireland, on the other hand, stone churches were being put up in the tenth and eleventh centuries. Four, for example, survive in Co. Down, and they may have been built with the aid of pious laymen. Still, before *c*.1100 Ireland's churches were small. Nonetheless, from the mid-tenth century to the end of our period, impressive round towers made of stone became characteristic features of major ecclesiastical sites, and some were built with the aid of secular patrons. A tenth-century king of Connacht, for example, paid for one of Clonmacnoise's round towers. The same man also provided funds for the construction of a causeway to the site, which crossed over a nearby bog. Other great men were similarly the patrons of pious building works. Máel Ciaráin Mac Conn na mBocht built a stone road between two pilgrimage sites, and other important lords constructed causeways across rivers. Thus, from the tenth century on in England and Ireland alike the very great were patrons of major pious building works. Nonetheless, it was only in England that the lower reaches of the landed elite were caught up in the frenzy of church-building, and it was only in England that the look of the rural landscape was thoroughly altered by their conspicuous displays of piety.

Another form of religious benefaction practised across Britain and Ireland was the giving of manuscripts, money, and precious-metal objects. The gifts of one of England's greatest men, Earl Harold, to his own foundation at Waltham Holy Cross testify to the extraordinary generosity of some English patrons. The most impressive of Harold's gifts were three large gospel books bound in gold covers and five other books bound in gilt silver. Illuminated and jewel-bound codices were considerably more valuable than estates, and wealthy Englishmen were commissioning and giving them to religious communities with impressive regularity by the later tenth century. Harold also gave Waltham a collection of gold and silver crosses. We have evidence from half a dozen English communities that similar groups of man-sized crosses were cluttering the interiors of their churches. We know that they were not only provided by Harold, but by a number of other courtiers, noblewomen, and bishops, indicating the prevalence of collections of large, precious-metal crosses in the eleventh century as overt symbols of pious giving. Another extraordinary set of gifts bestowed by Harold on Waltham was a collection of life-size statues of the twelve apostles and two lion-sized lions, all covered in or cast from gold. The life-size crosses and figures of saints were one of the great forms of benefaction in the eleventh century and are described in churches across England. They must have been wildly expensive, and their commissioning seems to have been *de rigueur* for comital families. Such objects were rare before the mid-tenth century and seem to constitute a new form of conspicuous piety. Less is known about thegnly gifts of chattels, but they, too, gave crosses, books, and luxury textiles.

Great men in Ireland gave similar gifts to religious communities from the tenth century onwards. The career of Brian Bóruma coincided with a revival of the production of high-status ecclesiastical objects in Ireland, and great monastic centres like Armagh, Clonmacnoise, Kildare, and Lismore prospered mightily in the eleventh century because of the generosity of powerful secular patrons. About a dozen extraordinary pieces of ecclesiastical Irish metalwork survive from this period in the form of croziers, bell shrines, and book shrines, and there are also descriptions in Irish annals of other gifts that have long since disappeared. Kings and abbots gave most of the known objects, suggesting that the fanciest pieces were granted by an exclusive little circle at the pinnacle of Irish society. We know, for example, that the church of Clonmacnoise was in possession of a number of treasures given to it by tenth- and eleventh-century kings, including a model of Solomon's temple. As in England, the number and magnificence of lay gifts in the tenth and eleventh centuries are breathtaking.

Although Welsh churches, like English and Irish ones, had gospel books, book and bell shrines, croziers, and reliquaries, church treasuries were much barer there. There are few descriptions of gold and silver ecclesiastical paraphernalia: St David's shrine, stolen in the late eleventh century, for example, was gold and silver, and St Cadog's similarly purloined reliquary was gilded. Nonetheless, the only Welsh ecclesiastical metalwork that survives from the ninth, tenth, and eleventh centuries is seven hand bells made from iron and copper alloy. At the same time, there are less than a dozen extant early medieval Welsh manuscripts, and only three are illuminated. Beyond this, notices of lay donations of precious objects are few and far between. But Welsh kings and lesser lords did participate in an expensive and conspicuously pious practice: they employed what wealth they had on extravagant almsgiving. The eleventh-century *Life of Cadog* pointedly describes the saint's feeding of hundreds of paupers and widows at Easter, and a common refrain in the *Brut y Tywysogyon*'s obituaries is the high praise for dead men who had been 'generous towards the poor and merciful towards pilgrims and orphans and widows'.[11] Gerald of Wales, describing Welsh openhandedness in the twelfth century, wrote:

No one begs in Wales . . . for the Welsh generosity and hospitality are the greatest of all virtues. They very much enjoy welcoming others to their homes. When you travel there is no question of your asking for accommodation or of their offering it: you just march into a house and hand over your weapons to the person in charge.[12]

Largesse to the poor, to pilgrims, and to strangers was costly in the early middle ages, and its practice was as conspicuous as the bestowing of precious objects. Given the constraints imposed on Welsh lords

[11] *Brut y Twysogyon or The Chronicle of the Princes*, trans. T. Jones (Cardiff, 1952), 17.
[12] Gerald of Wales, *Journey through Wales, The Description of Wales*, trans. L. Thorpe (Harmondsworth, 1978), 236.

by Wales's lack of towns and its dearth of silver, it is of little surprise that almsgiving was such a dominant feature of Welsh high-status piety.

The landscape across much of Britain and Ireland, then, was remade between the ninth century and the eleventh, transformed under the twin pressures of shifting settlement patterns and new-style lordship. Nonetheless, these changes played out differently in different parts of Britain and Ireland because of their diverse economic and political histories. As a result, the look and feel of lordship in Ireland, England, Scotland, and Wales, the wealth of landlords, and their command over the labour of others remained distinct. When Irish, English, and Welsh aristocrats encountered one another, which they often did in the tenth and eleventh centuries, they would have recognized each other as lords, but one imagines that the Welsh would have seemed poorer and somehow more old-fashioned, that the English and Irish would have seemed rich, that the Irish and the Welsh would have appeared the more experienced warriors, and the English the keenest managers of estates and the most enthusiastic connoisseurs of architecture.

Figure 5.0 The east face of Muiredach's Cross, Monasterboice, Co. Louth, datable to the early tenth century, illustrates a fundamental aspect of Christian belief in the context of biblical history. The cross-head contains the most impressive depiction of the Last Judgment on the early medieval Irish crosses: Christ stands in the centre, with the saved to his right and the damned, herded by a devil with a trident, to his left; St Michael weighs souls below Christ's feet. The bottom three panels on the shaft portray Old Testament scenes, beginning with Eve's temptation of Adam, and above these the Magi are shown adoring the infant Christ. Courtesy Duchas, The Heritage Service of the Departments of Art, Heritage, Gaeltacht and the Islands.

5

The Christianization of Society

Huw Pryce

A church triumphant?

By the early ninth century the Christianization of society was complete. So, at least, is the impression given by the *Martyrology of Óengus*, a calendar of saints' days written *c*.830 in Irish verse at the monastery of Tallaght near Dublin. The prologue to this work celebrates the triumph of Christianity: whereas the pagan rulers of Ireland and their fortresses had passed away, the renown of saints such as Patrick, Ciarán, and Brigit was greater than ever, reflected in powerful churches that resembled flourishing cities.

> The little places that were settled
> by twos and threes
> are Romes, with assemblies
> of hundreds and thousands.
>
> Though it was far-flung and splendid,
> paganism has been destroyed:
> the kingdom of God the Father
> has filled heaven, earth, and sea.[1]

The *Martyrology of Óengus* gives no hint of the new pagan threat to churches in Ireland and Britain that had emerged in the previous generation or so: the Vikings. One of the earliest recorded Viking

---

[1] J. Carey, *King of Mysteries: Early Irish Religious Writings* (revised paperback edn.; Dublin, 2000), 191.

attacks, on the monastery of Lindisfarne in Northumbria in 793, led the English churchman and scholar Alcuin, resident in Charlemagne's court at Aachen, to adopt a very different tone from that of Óengus. In a letter to the bishop and community of Lindisfarne, Alcuin interpreted the attack as God's punishment for sins and urged repentance and reform: 'Do not go out after the indulgences of the flesh and the greed of the world, but stand firm in the service of God and the discipline of the monastic life, that the holy fathers whose sons you are may not cease to protect you.'[2]

In different ways, both Óengus and Alcuin reveal that the Christianization of society—the full absorption of Christian beliefs and practices as distinct from the initial step of conversion—was both less complete and more complicated at the beginning of this period than the former's *Martyrology* might suggest at first sight. Certainly, by 800 paganism was no longer an organized form of religion, with its own priests (known in Ireland as druids), supported by kings. Conversion had been consolidated by the establishment of structures of ecclesiastical organization, under the authority of bishops, with the result that the church had become a powerful and wealthy institution, backed by Christian kings whose subjects were expected to adhere to the Christian faith, notably through the sacrament of baptism. But the break with the pagan past was by no means total. Alcuin complained about the enthusiasm of monks in an English community for pagan Danish legend: 'What has Ingeld to do with Christ?' he famously asked.[3] Likewise, Óengus was clearly familiar with figures of pagan Irish legend and history. In both Anglo-Saxon England and Ireland, it was churchmen who wrote down the traditional tales and lore that were so central to the culture of the aristocracies from which many of them were drawn; the same was true of Wales, to judge by the 'History of the Britons' (*Historia Brittonum*), composed in 829/ 30. Admittedly, as the *Martyrology of Óengus* stressed, paganism belonged to the past, vanquished by Christianity. Its deities had only been human beings after all: when the genealogy of the West Saxon kings was expanded in the mid-ninth century, their ancestor Woden

[2] S. Allott, *Alcuin of York c. A.D. 723 to 804: His Life and Letters* (York, 1974), 37.
[3] Quoted in R. Frank, 'Germanic Legend in Old English Literature', in M. Godden and M. Lapidge (eds.), *The Cambridge Companion to Old English Literature* (Cambridge, 1991), 91.

was made a descendant of Noah and thus ultimately of Adam. But the legacy of paganism remained potent, not only in the realm of culture and legend but also as a continuing influence on popular religious practices.

The interest of educated churchmen in pagan culture was but one expression of the links binding them to lay society. For Alcuin and many other ecclesiastical writers in this period, these links carried with them the danger of secularization: an excessive identification with secular values and interests at the expense of the distinctively Christian life and mission which churches were intended to exemplify and promote. Viking attacks made matters worse, for they threatened the very survival of churches and thus of the institutions designed to ensure a continuing Christian mission. As Alcuin also made explicit, the antidote to secularization—which he saw as the root cause of Viking violence—was reform. For all his triumphalism, Óengus like-wise subscribed to an ideology of reform, since Tallaght had been founded by Máel Ruain (d. 792), one of the leaders of the reform movement of the *Céli Dé* (culdees). This movement espoused a life of extreme austerity and asceticism, and spread from Ireland to Scotland and almost certainly also to Wales. In England, too, attempts were made to revive monasticism by King Alfred (871–99), and a major programme of monastic reform was undertaken in the reign of Edgar (959–75). From the mid-eleventh century an increasingly inter-ventionist papacy extended and intensified demands for reform: in 1070 papal legates issued canons for the reform of the English church and deposed Archbishop Stigand of Canterbury together with other prelates.

The dynamic between the twin processes of secularization, includ-ing attacks on churches by both native Christian rulers and pagan Vikings, and of ecclesiastical renewal, reflected especially in monastic reform, is a dominant theme in interpretations of the ecclesiastical history of Britain and Ireland from the ninth to the eleventh centur-ies. Another important topic in much recent work is the nature of ecclesiastical organization. These themes will help to inform the fol-lowing discussion. However, the overriding emphasis will be on the significance of Christianity in society as a whole. Of course, the development of ecclesiastical institutions, including efforts by reforming churchmen to uphold Christian values and behaviour, is highly relevant to such an enquiry, as these were vital elements in the transmission and maintenance of Christian belief and practice. But such a focus is insufficient if we wish to assess the nature and extent of Christianization in societies where the church was thought to comprise all baptized Christians, not just the clergy and their churches. We also need, for example, to try to distinguish between prescriptive norms set out in laws, synods, or sermons and religion as it was actually lived and practised.

Dioceses and monasteries

As elsewhere in western Europe in this period, ecclesiastical organization was largely decentralized, effective authority residing with individual bishops and abbots. Though the authority of the papacy was recognized, it was not yet the coping stone of a coherent institutional structure: papal intervention was rare before the late eleventh century, and Rome was revered above all as the burial place of St Peter and numerous other early Christian saints. Within Britain and Ireland some bishops enjoyed special pre-eminence. This was especially so in England, where the archbishops of Canterbury and, to a lesser extent, York exercised metropolitan authority over other bishops, while in Ireland the claims to superiority of the archbishops of Armagh were increasingly recognized from the mid-ninth century. In Wales, by contrast, the designation of Elfoddw (d. 809) and Nobis (d. 873) as 'archbishops' of Gwynedd and St Davids respectively was probably a mark of personal distinction rather than metropolitan authority. The same may also be true of the description of Tuathal, abbot of Dunkeld, as 'chief bishop of Fortriu', a region in central Scotland, on his death in 865.

Bishops played an essential role in ensuring the continuity of the church through their ordination of clergy, consecration of churches, confirmation of the baptized, and other pastoral duties within the dioceses which formed their spheres of authority. Though the concept of territorial dioceses was well established, diocesan organization was more fluid than it became from the twelfth century onwards. Firm evidence for bishoprics in Scotland is scarce before 1100. It is uncertain whether the Anglian bishopric of Whithorn in Galloway continued to function after c.900; no bishop is attested on Iona after the late tenth century, and the jurisdiction of the bishop established at Orkney c.1050 may have extended as far south as Man, which only seems to have had a bishop of its own from the late eleventh century. Though the see of Glasgow was founded only in the early twelfth century, this does not preclude the possibility that Strathclyde had its own bishop earlier in the middle ages, perhaps based at Govan, a major ecclesiastical site in the tenth and eleventh centuries. The pattern north of the Forth is also obscure. St Andrews appears to have been the most important episcopal centre by the tenth century; it has also been suggested that Dunkeld, Brechin, Muthill (later Dunblane), and Mortlach in the north-east may have been sees, but these identifications are far from certain. In Wales the number of bishoprics declined over this period. In the ninth century bishops are attested at Bangor, St Davids, Llandeilo Fawr, and at least one site in the south-east; by the eleventh century Llandeilo Fawr had lost its episcopal status, and its lands appear to have been appropriated by a new south-eastern see fixed at Llandaff under Bishop Joseph (c.1022–1045), which also possibly took over small territorial dioceses with sees at Glasbury near Brecon and Dewstow near Caldicot.

Recent work has shown that, in Ireland, territorial dioceses, far from falling victim by the eighth century to powerful monastic federations as was previously thought, survived at least into the eleventh century and probably beyond. The scale of these dioceses is admittedly difficult to determine. It is pretty certain, though, that the pattern revealed by earlier Irish sources, whereby each diocese corresponded to a small kingdom or lordship (*tuath*), of which there may have been as many as 150, no longer obtained from the ninth century onwards. Instead, tenth-century annals associate bishops with larger areas, in several cases corresponding broadly with modern counties and in a few instances with the provinces of Munster or Leinster, although this does not rule out the possibility, suggested by other evidence, that the authority of some bishops was restricted to a single *tuath*. The number of dioceses is likewise uncertain, although some indication is provided by the annals, which associate forty-eight churches with bishops in the tenth century. Unless most of these churches enjoyed episcopal status only briefly, this would suggest that bishops were significantly more numerous in Ireland than in Britain in this period.

By contrast, English dioceses mostly followed the boundaries of

seventh-century kingdoms, making their bishops both more powerful and remoter figures than their Irish counterparts. Admittedly the
division *c.*910 of the dioceses of Winchester and Sherborne, together
with Athelstan's creation of a Cornish diocese with its see at St Ger-
mans, increased the number of bishops in Wessex to six. On the other
hand, Viking settlement and subsequent West Saxon conquest had
the opposite effect in areas of the Danelaw. Both bishoprics of East
Anglia, together with those of Hexham and Lindsey, collapsed in the
late ninth century, while the see of Leicester was relocated south to
Dorchester-on-Thames by 971. Moreover, even after dioceses were
revived, the numbers of bishops were fewer than in the pre-Viking
period: the East Anglian bishoprics were eventually replaced by a
single diocese in the mid-tenth century; after being temporarily
restored twice, the bishopric of Lindsey was incorporated into the
vast diocese of Dorchester at the same time (though the see was
moved to Lincoln in 1072); and for substantial periods following the
final conquest of Northumbria by Eadred in 954 the archbishopric of
York was held in plurality with a southern English see, notably with
Worcester from 971 to 1016.

Bishops' sees were often located in churches described as 'monasteries' in the sources. Canterbury, Lindisfarne, St Davids, and Armagh
are all cases in point. Monasteries—or minsters as they are often
called by historians of Anglo-Saxon England—were essential components of ecclesiastical organization in early medieval Britain and
Ireland. In England before the mid-tenth century the terms monastery or minster are applied indiscriminately to any community
staffed by a group of clergy, possibly but not necessarily comprising
or including monks, without implying adherence to any specific rule
or liturgical routine. Alcuin, like Bede before him, was highly unusual
in criticizing some of these establishments for their allegedly excessive identification with the secular world, and it was only under King
Edgar that a major effort was made to impose a new, uniform model
of monasticism. The tenth-century monastic reformers believed that
religious life had declined in England because monasteries had been
taken over by secular clerks whose behaviour fell far short of the
standards expected of true monks, not least in their disregard for
celibacy. Measured by the yardstick of reformed monasticism, what
had hitherto passed as monasteries in England were no longer
deemed worthy of the name. Though the speed and thoroughness

with which reform was implemented varied—Bishop Æthelwold's expulsion in 964 of married clerks from the Old and New Minsters, Winchester, as well as from Milton Abbas and Chertsey and their replacement by professed monks from Abingdon was not only dramatic but exceptional—there can be no doubt that the foundation or refoundation by 1000 of about forty monasteries and nunneries marked a radical change.

The character of this change is pointed up by comparison with the earlier *Céli Dé* reform in Ireland, originating in Munster in the second half of the eighth century. Whereas the *Céli Dé* drew their authority from the example and prescriptions of individual Irish monks such as Máel Ruain of Tallaght, and aimed at extreme asceticism, tenth-century reformers in England such as Bishop Æthelwold of Winchester (d. 984) and Bishop Oswald of Worcester (d. 992) drew their inspiration from continental reform movements in Lotharingia and France, and aspired to a uniform religious practice based on the sixth-century Rule of St Benedict, a practice which they codified *c.*973 with Edgar's approval under the title of the 'Monastic agreement' (*Regularis Concordia*). While, like the *Céli Dé*, the English reformers gave priority to the regular observance of the liturgy, they differed from the Irish movement both in prescribing a single template for the religious life and in avoiding extremes of self-denial: monks were expected to be celibate without also starving themselves. How far opportunities for female participation differed between the two movements is difficult to assess. Some abbesses and female communities were associated with the *Céli Dé*, whose rules include references to nuns and the proper conduct of their relations with monks. Yet there is nothing comparable to the *Regularis Concordia's* formal recognition of communities of nuns, placed by Edgar under the protection of Queen Ælfthryth. Although these female communities—of which there were about nine in later Anglo-Saxon England—were fewer and generally poorer than their male counterparts, and clearly lacked the status enjoyed by the double houses of nuns and monks headed by abbesses that were such a notable aspect of seventh- and eighth-century Anglo-Saxon monasticism, the support they received from both monastic reformers and the royal family helped to uphold their institutional identity and independence. In addition, however, other late Anglo-Saxon women, both virgins and chaste widows, vowed themselves to lives of religion outside the cloister, either alone on their estates or in small communities, and similar vocations seem to have been followed by some women in Ireland.

The extent to which the tenth-century monastic reformation in England transformed the church should not be exaggerated. Geographically, its reach was limited to areas south of the River Trent, especially greater Wessex, the Severn Valley in Mercia, and East Anglia; Cornwall and Northumbria were unaffected. The influence of the *Céli Dé* was considerably more extensive, spreading not only to many major monasteries in Ireland, including Armagh and Clonmacnoise, but also to Scotland, probably through Abbot Diarmait of Iona (d. in or after 831), where communities of *Céli Dé* are attested later in the middle ages at, for example, Iona, St Andrews, Brechin, and Lochleven. There are hints, too, that the movement reached Wales. Admittedly we can only guess how closely these communities adhered to the ascetic practices of the movement's founders, and for how long. Certainly no monastery in Celtic Britain or Ireland conformed to the Benedictine ideal before the late eleventh century. But in this they were no different from the majority of minsters in late Anglo-Saxon England. Although some of the latter were re-established as colleges of secular canons, such as Harold Godwinesson's foundation of Waltham Holy Cross (1060), the important point is that many minsters survived without being turned into Benedictine monasteries. Moreover, such unreformed establishments continued to attract patronage alongside the new reformed monasteries: reform was less of an issue for the pious laity than for the reforming monks whose views have tended to distort our picture of the church through their prominence in the surviving written record. Thus, while the tenth-century monastic reformation in England introduced new distinctions between different types of ecclesiastical communities, it by no means swept all before it. Across Britain and Ireland as a whole, moreover, it was the types of monasteries or minsters considered decadent by reformers that were in fact the norm.

Ecclesiastical organization and pastoral care

Ministry to the laity was ultimately the responsibility of bishops who alone could ordain priests and deacons. The mechanisms for delivering this ministry have received close scrutiny from historians in recent years. As a result, there is now a strong case for concluding that, contrary to previous assumptions, the structures for organizing pastoral care were basically similar in Anglo-Saxon England and in Celtic Britain and Ireland. At their heart lay monastic communities, in the broad sense outlined above, which served as mother-churches for proto-parishes or *parochiae* that corresponded to secular administrative units such as the small kingdom or *tuath* in Ireland or the subdivisions of Anglo-Saxon kingdoms sometimes referred to as *regiones*. In Ireland, and possibly also in parts of south Wales, these units may in some cases have also been coterminous with dioceses, whereas the large dioceses of England were divided into minster *parochiae*. According to one estimate, by 800 most settlements in lowland England probably lay within five or six miles of a minster. Admittedly, the patchiness of the evidence for all parts of Britain and Ireland makes it impossible to prove conclusively that a comprehensive network of pastoral care based on monasteries or minsters had been established by the beginning of our period. But the model does help to make sense of the evidence which has survived and explain how ministry to the laity was organized in a world without parishes of the kind established from the twelfth century onwards.

A central assumption of this model is that bishops, priests, and deacons based in monasteries were actively engaged in pastoral work among the surrounding population, rather than simply serving the monks, nuns, and other clergy of the monastic community itself. The obligation to provide pastoral services to the laity is made explicit in a (probably eighth-century) Irish text, *The Rule of Patrick*, a version of which was incorporated in the early ninth-century *Rule of the Céli Dé*. This opens by stressing the bishop's duty to ordain clergy, consecrate churches, and provide spiritual direction for the heads of all churches and all secular lords, as well as the necessity of baptism, communion, confirmation, and confession for the spiritual well-being of families and kindreds. Admittedly other sections of the text refer specifically to monastic tenants (*manaig*) as the recipients of such pastoral care, possibly suggesting that in practice ministry was often limited to a church's immediate dependants. Yet even if this was so, the explicit recognition of at least some lay people's rights to communion, requiem masses, and other pastoral services is notable. Bishops in England were likewise expected to fulfil a pastoral role. Since dioceses were large, this could require extensive travel, as vividly depicted in the Life of Bishop Wulfstan II of Worcester (d. 1095), who celebrated communion, preached, and performed mass confirmations during journeys round his diocese. Before his election as bishop in 1062 Wulfstan had been a monk at Worcester cathedral priory. In this respect, he represents a wider trend: nine out of ten English bishops between 970 and 1066 were drawn from reformed monastic communities, some of whose members also wrote texts for the instruction of the secular clergy. Moreover, although the reformers' emphasis on maintaining a cloistered life prevented monks who were priests from active ministry in the localities around their monasteries, the reformed houses of late Anglo-Saxon England also contributed directly to pastoral work. The *Regularis Concordia* not only stresses the monks' duty to feed poor strangers but assumes the regular attendance of a lay congregation at mass, while Ælfric (d. *c*.1010) seems to have aimed his *Catholic Homilies* at a mixed audience of monks and laity in a monastic church, perhaps at Winchester or Cerne Abbas.

The centrally organized ministry provided by bishops and monasteries or minsters was supplemented by that of local churches. Typically staffed by a single priest, these constituted a further crucial component of pastoral care, and one which became increasingly widespread as the period progressed. Comparison of the provision of local churches in this period across Britain and Ireland reveals more contrasts than similarities. Some Celtic areas were provided with numerous local churches by 800. This is especially true of Ireland, where each small kingdom (*tuath*) was provided with its principal church—and thus by implication lesser churches too, a conclusion arguably supported by the archaeological remains of very substantial numbers of early medieval ecclesiastical sites in Cos. Cork and Kerry. Likewise remains of numerous small chapels on Man and Islay may date from the tenth century onwards, following the conversion of the Norse settlers. To judge by charter evidence, south-east Wales was provided with a dense concentration of local churches in our period, and a network of local churches seems to have existed in Cornwall by the early tenth century. On the other hand, while the quite extensive territories dependent on mother-churches, including bishoprics, in most of Wales had cult sites such as holy wells and cemeteries, it is uncertain when local daughter-churches started to be founded in significant numbers.

It has been suggested that local churches, comparable to the small ecclesiastical sites of Ireland and subject to minsters, may also have existed in England before the tenth century. This view should not be dismissed out of hand, given the patchy nature of the surviving evidence. However, even if it is correct, it was only in the tenth and eleventh centuries that the pattern of ecclesiastical provision was radically altered in England, with the establishment of thousands of local churches, most of which went on to become parish churches. These churches were mainly founded by thegns on their estates, sometimes originally within the manor-house enclosure, though town-dwellers also contributed to the process: by 1086 Norwich had at least forty-nine churches and chapels. This privatization of ecclesiastical provision belonged to the wider process whereby large estates fragmented into individual manors that supported a new gentry class, for whom the ownership of a church was as much an emblem of social prestige as an expression of piety. The process started earlier and went further in the Danelaw, especially in Lincolnshire and East Anglia with their booming populations, than in other areas of England where the privileged status of the old minsters was more effectively protected by kings and indeed often preserved in varying degrees after local churches gained parochial rights in the twelfth century. For example, mother-churches in Kent and Herefordshire reserved the right in the eleventh and twelfth centuries to distribute chrism—holy oil received from the bishop which was used for baptism and extreme unction for the dying—to their daughter-churches. Nevertheless, there can be no doubt that the multiplication of manorial churches diminished the role of minsters as providers of pastoral care.

The clergy: a caste apart?

The effectiveness of pastoral care depended ultimately on the capacity and commitment of the clergy. Reform-minded kings, monks, and bishops in England, influenced by norms promoted on the continent in the late eighth and ninth centuries by Carolingian rulers and ecclesiastics, drew up demanding blueprints for the clerical life. These stressed that a priest should teach through personal example, so that, as Ælfric put it, 'his life shall not be like that of laymen'.[4] A crucial means to this end was celibacy. An ecclesiastical council convened by King Edmund (939–46) declared that all in holy orders 'are to maintain their chastity according to their orders', on pain of forfeiting their property and the right to burial in consecrated ground.[5] By contrast, Wulfstan, archbishop of York (1002–23), held out the carrot of social advancement, laying down that any priest who remained chaste would be entitled to the wergeld (life-price) of a thegn. Clergy were also urged to avoid drunkenness, showy dress, hunting, and participation in secular lawsuits. A further requirement was the ability to read service books and other works needed for the celebration of mass and other pastoral duties such as preaching, administering penance, or anointing the sick with holy oil.

The ambitious prescriptions of moralizing, usually monastic, authors in late Anglo-Saxon England are important evidence for attempts to impose a wide-ranging programme of ecclesiastical reform. A central aim of these attempts was to draw a firmer line between the clergy and lay society. The emphasis on chastity, education, and other virtues was intended to monasticize the clergy in order to enhance their status and thus their authority over the laity— for, as Ælfric emphasized, in line with earlier Carolingian precepts, one of the duties of a priest was the correction of his people. Yet arguably the greatest significance of such prescriptions was their assumption that in reality clerical standards fell far short of the ideals to which reformers aspired. The educational failings of clergy in

---

[4] D. Whitelock, M. Brett, and C. N. L. Brooke (eds.), *Councils and Synods with Other Documents Relating to the English Church*, i: *A.D. 871–1204* (Oxford, 1981), i. 205.

[5] Ibid. 61–2.

England were grist to the mill of moralizing writers from King Alfred to monastic authors after the Norman Conquest. Likewise demands for celibacy continued to be voiced long after 1100. The impracticability of enforcing these demands, at least in one English region, was acknowledged in the early eleventh-century *Northumbrian Priests' Law*, which merely insists that a priest should not leave his wife for another woman. The same text acknowledges the enduring ties between a priest and his kin by stipulating the right of the latter to receive a priest's wergeld if he were killed, though a fine was payable to the bishop too.

Moreover, while in England reforming ideals had powerful support from prelates and kings, the picture was different elsewhere in Britain as well as in Ireland. True, individual Irish monks took part in the reform of monasteries in tenth-century Lotharingia, while by the later eleventh century Ireland and, perhaps, south-east Wales were exposed to the norms of the English Benedictine reform through contacts with Worcester cathedral priory, where Patrick, bishop of Dublin (1074–84) had been a monk. However, notwithstanding such contacts or the reforming endeavours of Queen Margaret (d. 1093) in Scotland, there is little to suggest that comprehensive efforts, comparable to those of Ælfric or Wulfstan, were made before 1100 to improve clerical standards in Celtic Britain or Ireland. Although the *Céli Dé* saw celibacy as an essential part of the religious life, the prevalence of hereditary clerical dynasties at the highest levels of the church in Ireland and Wales implies that marriage remained entirely acceptable. The ideals promoted by reformers in late Anglo-Saxon and Norman England were a world apart from those of the family of Sulien, bishop of St Davids (d. 1091), one of whose four sons—all of whom also became clerics—wrote a Latin poem praising his father's learning and devotion to Christ (Fig. 5.1). There were doubtless many others in Britain and Ireland who believed that marriage was no bar to exemplary clerical behaviour.

More generally, the goal of defining clerical status more rigorously was difficult to achieve because, far from being sharply distinct from lay society, the clergy were in important respects a microcosm of it. As elsewhere in Europe, great bishops or abbots often belonged to royal or aristocratic families. Indeed, in Ireland the boundaries were blurred to the extent that some kings themselves held episcopal or abbatial office: Cormac mac Cuilennáin, king-bishop of Munster (d.

Figure 5.1 The opening of Psalm 1 in the Psalter and Martyrology of Rhigyfarch (Trinity College Dublin MS 50, fo. 35ʳ). The manuscript, written for Sulien's son Rhigyfarch at Llanbadarn Fawr *c*.1079 by a scribe called Ithael and illuminated by Rhigyfarch's brother Ieuan, is important evidence for the devotion and culture of this notable Welsh ecclesiastical family. By permission of Trinity College Library, Dublin.

908), is a case in point. A vast social distance separated figures such as Bishop Theodred of London (d. *c.*951)—who in his will bequeathed almost thirty estates as well as substantial sums of gold—from ordinary rural clergy, usually drawn from the ranks of the peasantry. The manorial churches that mushroomed in tenth- and eleventh-century England were served by a new clerical proletariat, dependent on their lords for their livings. It is also possible that, as later in the middle ages, the numbers of deacons and priests ordained outstripped the availability of benefices. Prohibitions on clergy working as reeves, traders, or entertainers in taverns may indicate that some had difficulty in making ends meet, a conclusion supported by Wulfstan of York's recommendation that each priest should learn a handicraft. Of course, some priests were nobler and wealthier than others. Wulfstan insisted that no highborn priest should despise one more lowly born: ordination did not efface all distinctions of social rank.

Wealth and power

The wealth of the greatest churches both reflected and reinforced the ties binding clergy to the secular world. One consequence of Christianization was the transfer to churches, by kings and other benefactors, of substantial resources, principally land and its surplus produce but also precious metals. According to one estimate, the church held a quarter of the wealth of England by the end of William the Conqueror's reign. Some churches were major landholders. Thus by the early eleventh century the community of St Cuthbert, relocated from Chester-le-Street to Durham in 995, owned extensive estates in northern Britain between the Tweed and the Tees, while by 1066 Glastonbury, the richest monastery in England, possessed over seventy-seven estates in seven counties which brought in an annual income of almost £700 (the value of about 80,000 young sheep to judge by one eleventh-century source). Glastonbury was one of the beneficiaries of the monastic reformation supported by Edgar which resulted in the transfer of huge resources to the new foundations. Some of these endowments came from the king, but the establishment of reformed houses in East Anglia by Bishop Æthelwold of Winchester seems to have been financed out of the bishop's ample pockets. Throughout Britain and Ireland, as on the continent, the fundamental source of ecclesiastical wealth was the labour of dependants settled on churches' lands; for example, in Ireland the major monasteries were supported by tenants known as *manaig*, a term that had originally meant 'monks'. In addition, the most powerful Irish churches levied tributes by promulgating the 'laws' (*cána*) of their patron saints—Armagh imposed the 'law of Patrick' on wide areas in the northern half of Ireland in the second half of the ninth and in the tenth century as well as in Munster in 972—while tenth-century English kings augmented the resources of major churches or minsters by enforcing the payment of tithes.

The wealth accrued by some churches made them powerful institutions and thus important political players. However much they may have been intended to provide oases of sacred space, they were connected by multiple ties—of patronage, kinship, and lordship—with the world outside. In part, these ties derived from churches' religious functions. One of King Athelstan's laws stipulated that the clergy of each minster should sing fifty psalms for the king every Friday, while later in the tenth century the reformed monasteries were expected to offer a psalm and prayers daily for the king and queen. Churches also served as royal mausolea. Kings number among those commemorated on ninth-century disk-headed crosses at Llanilltud Fawr (Llantwit Major) in Glamorgan; Clonmacnoise (Co. Offaly) is referred to as a royal graveyard in 935; and one of the functions of both St Oswald's, Gloucester, founded by Ealdorman Æthelred of Mercia and his wife Æthelflæd *c*.900, and the New Minster, Winchester, founded by Edward the Elder in 901, was to provide burial places for their respective dynasties. King Constantine II of the Scots retired to become abbot of the *Céli Dé* community at St Andrews, where he died and was buried in 952. But major churches also provided material support for rulers and lords. For one thing, such churches sustained members of dynasties who resided in them as monks, clerics, or nuns; these in turn supplied their secular kinsfolk with hospitality and sometimes more. In Ireland, Armagh collaborated with the powerful Uí Néill kings, while Kildare was in effect the royal capital of Leinster, its abbesses being drawn from the royal dynasty or prominent aristocratic families in the kingdom. Moreover, if, as occurred in some cases in ninth-century England, a community was dispersed or destroyed, its land could be reappropriated by the royal or aristocratic dynasty that had originally endowed it.

Of course, their links with the powerful in secular society did not prevent churches from developing their own sense of corporate identity, expressed in a determination to promote their independent interests. Rulers who sought their support had to recognize this. Thus King Giric (*fl.* 878) was remembered as having been the first to grant freedom to the church in Scotland, while in the early tenth century preservation of the rights of Scottish churches featured among the pledges allegedly made by King Constantine II (900–43). The mutual self-interest underlying such concessions is illustrated by Brian Bóruma (Brian Boru), who, in his bid for domination over Ireland in 1005, wooed Armagh not only with 20 ounces of gold but also with a recognition of the church's claims to superiority over all the Irish churches. In England, the staunch royalism of the reformed monasteries was reciprocated by King Edgar's support for the enhancement of clerical status through adherence to the ideals of Benedictine monasticism. Royal grants may also explain why some churches in Cornwall, northern England, Scotland, Wales, and Ireland enjoyed unusually extensive rights of sanctuary which developed into privileged zones immune from secular authority.

However, secular potentates did not always treat churches with respect. The wealth bestowed by an earlier generation or a different dynasty could later become an all too tempting target for a Christian ruler or lord, eager to enrich himself or weaken his enemies at a church's expense. Thus in Northumbria both Osberht and his victorious rival Ælla, who deposed him in 862, seized estates from the community of St Cuthbert during their struggle for the throne, while King Alfred was remembered as a second Judas by the monks of Abingdon for having seized the vill on which the minster had stood. Likewise in Wales, Hyfaidd, king of Dyfed, plundered the lands of St Davids in the late ninth century, while attacks by both Welsh rulers and Norman lords probably help to explain the vengeful ferocity with which St Cadog, patron saint of Llancarfan (Glamorgan), was depicted by his hagiographer, Lifris, *c.*1100. Moreover, churches could get drawn into wider struggles for power. This was especially true of ninth-century Ireland. In 833, for example, Feidlimid mac Crimthainn, king of Munster (820–47), attacked the monasteries of Clonmacnoise and Durrow, and Cellach mac Brain, king of Leinster, defeated Kildare in battle. Nor were such incidents exceptional, for battles between Irish monasteries and their dynastic associates are recorded from the second half of the eighth century onwards: Óengus's Tallaght was plundered by Kildare in 824. Churches were occasionally caught up in political violence in tenth-century England too. King Eadred burned Ripon minster in 948, in retaliation for the archbishop of York's support for the Scandinavian rulers of York against whom he was campaigning, and the short-lived wave of attacks on reformed monasteries in East Anglia and the Midlands that followed King Edgar's death in 975 was probably driven to a large extent by rivalries between the ealdormen Æthelwine of East Anglia and Ælfhere of Mercia. Churches also suffered in conflicts between England and its neighbours: Gruffudd ap Llywelyn burned Hereford in 1055 and killed its bishop the following year, while Lindisfarne was ravaged by Malcolm III of Scotland in 1061.

From pagans to Christians: the Vikings and the church

Violence against the church is often associated above all with the Vikings. Alcuin's response to the raid on Lindisfarne in 793 is but one testimony among many that Vikings killed clerics and plundered churches in the late eighth and ninth centuries. At Iona, sixty-eight of the community were slaughtered in 806 and Bláthmac was killed on the island in 825 when he refused to divulge the whereabouts of the shrine of St Columba. Though apparently less intense, attacks continued in both Scotland and Ireland in the tenth and eleventh centuries: Iona was plundered on Christmas night in 986 and members of its community killed, and Hiberno-Scandinavians from Dublin plundered Kells and captured and killed many men there in 1019. Hiberno-Scandinavians also ravaged churches in Wales: St Davids was attacked at least eleven times between 907 and 1091 (Fig. 5.2). The second wave of Danish attacks on England in the late tenth and early eleventh centuries claimed more ecclesiastical victims, most notably Archbishop Ælfheah of Canterbury, murdered in 1012 after refusing to have a ransom paid on his behalf. Churches were targeted as

Figure 5.2 A late eleventh- or early twelfth-century cross-carved grave-marker from St Davids, commemorating Hedd and Isaac, the sons of Bishop Abraham of St Davids (1078–80). According to one set of Welsh annals, Abraham was killed in a Viking attack on his church. Crown Copyright. Royal Commission on the Ancient and Historical Monuments of Wales.

sources of treasure, tribute, and, especially in Ireland, slaves. It is likely that Insular metalwork found in ninth- and tenth-century Norwegian graves derived from churches in Ireland and Britain. One example of the recovery of such plunder, dating from the latter part of the ninth century, is the purchase from a Viking army and subsequent donation to Christ Church, Canterbury, of a fine illuminated gospel book, the Codex Aureus, by Alfred, ealdorman of Surrey, and his wife Werburg.

Were such raids essentially irritants, causing temporary losses and disruption, or did they result in a substantial erosion of the material base of the church and a severe reduction of its institutional capacity to continue the Christianization of society through the provision of pastoral care? The short answer to this question is both 'yes' and 'no', as the extent and permanence of damage varied both within and between different regions of Britain and Ireland. Admittedly, any assessment is hampered by the gaps in our evidence. This is particularly true of Scotland. Though Iona survived, despite several attacks, its community may well have been reduced, and its abbot's establishment of a new monastery at Kells in Ireland in 807 was probably intended to provide a safe haven; the fate of monasteries and hermitages in the Hebrides associated with Iona is unknown. The same is true of Pictish churches in the regions of northern Scotland and the Northern Isles settled by the Norse. By contrast, the position in Ireland is fairly clear. There the great monasteries seem largely to have weathered the storm, a reflection, perhaps, of their considerable landed resources as well as of the limited scope of Viking settlement on the island. Thus repeated raids on Armagh in the ninth century— as on St Davids in the tenth and eleventh centuries—imply considerable powers of recovery, although the loss of treasures and dependent labourers together with payments of tribute probably took their toll, to judge by the declining quality of Irish ecclesiastical metalwork and manuscript illumination.

Northumbria presents a bleaker picture. Major monasteries of the pre-Viking era such as Wearmouth, Jarrow, and Whitby vanish from the records in the ninth century, and were only refounded after the Norman Conquest by monks seeking to restore the golden age of monasticism they had read about in Bede's *Ecclesiastical History* (731). The lack of surviving authentic pre-Viking charters from Northumbria, and their virtual absence from the other English regions settled by the Vikings, likewise points to substantial destruction. On the other hand, one Northumbrian ecclesiastical community not only survived but apparently prospered in the era of Scandinavian raids and settlement. Although the community of St Cuthbert abandoned its home of Lindisfarne in 875 and eventually settled at Chester-le-Street in c.883, it seems to have come to terms with the new Scandinavian rulers of York for it not only retained most of its lands but also attracted new benefactions.

The experience of St Cuthbert's community illustrates the dangers of making broad generalizations about the Viking impact on the church. Yet the exceptional character of that experience should also warn us not to underestimate the damaging consequences of Viking raids and conquests. In Kent, for example, coastal minsters such as Folkestone, Lyminge, Minster-in-Thanet, and Reculver were abandoned in the mid-ninth century, their lands being seized by the West Saxon dynasty. This may have been part of a wider process whereby ecclesiastical lands in England were taken over by kings as part of their defensive strategies against the Vikings. Like Whitby in Northumbria, several of the Kentish minsters had been double houses, comprising communities of nuns and monks ruled by an abbess. These had been among the most important monasteries of the seventh and eighth centuries. That they largely disappear from view by the tenth century cannot be attributed solely to the Vikings: their decline resulted above all from the absorption of their lands by the nuns' male kin (a process which affected entirely male monasteries too). Nevertheless, women's communities probably suffered disproportionately from the Viking wars, as their lands were either abandoned or taken over for military defence. In addition, as mentioned earlier, diocesan organization in the Danelaw was severely disrupted. Admittedly, this disruption was quite possibly prolonged by the political opportunism of the West Saxon kings, determined to prevent the archbishop of Canterbury from consecrating bishops in eastern Mercia and East Anglia before the final conquest of York in 954 in case this strengthened the Danes or fostered Mercian separatism. Yet the abandonment of sees in the first place surely resulted from the crisis caused by Viking conquest and settlement.

In assessing the impact of Scandinavian settlement on ecclesiastical structures and the progress of Christianization it is also important to consider the settlers' adoption of Christianity. Because its impact was only temporary, it is tempting to play down the significance of the Vikings' reintroduction of paganism to parts of Britain and Ireland. Yet the arrival of pagan settlers in the ninth century called a halt to the apparently inexorable progress of the Christian religion. True, in the regions of the English Danelaw, the Vikings who settled in the late 860s and 870s appear to have accepted Christianity by *c.*900. This is suggested by the swift adoption of burial in churchyards, mostly, it seems, without the deposition of grave goods associated with pagan burial practices, as well as by the minting of coins bearing the names of saints—including, notably, St Edmund, the East Anglian king killed by Vikings in 869. In Scotland and the Isle of Man, however, adherence to paganism, including interments with grave goods, lasted longer. Likewise the Hiberno-Norse dynasty of Dublin, some of whose members also ruled York intermittently between 919 and 952, seems to have remained pagan until the 940s.

It is unclear why and how pagan Viking settlers adopted Christianity. Part of the answer is political coercion: Guthrum and his leading followers were baptized as one of the conditions of the peace agreed with King Alfred following their defeat in 878, Olaf (Amlaíb) Cuarán of Dublin and York was baptized in England in 943 with King Edmund as his sponsor, and Earl Sigurd of Orkney was forced to accept baptism by the newly converted Olaf Tryggvason of Norway in 995. Yet, important though such converted leaders may have been in ensuring that their followers in turn accepted the new faith, ministry to whole settler communities required the presence among them of priests—who alone could carry out baptisms—and therefore of churches. In other words, conversion would seem to imply an effective ecclesiastical organization. Paradoxically, however, conversion occurred more rapidly in the eastern Danelaw than in Hiberno-Norse enclaves such as Dublin, even though ecclesiastical organization almost certainly suffered far more disruption in the former region than in Ireland, including the immediate vicinity of Dublin. This may indicate that missionary work was undertaken in the Danelaw by priests in local churches that enjoyed greater continuity than bishoprics or minsters, or else by clergy sent from Wessex. By contrast, Irish clergy—and Irish kings, some of whom had no qualms in forming alliances with Vikings—perhaps lacked the inclination to try and convert pagan 'foreigners' whose settlements were in any case far fewer and smaller than those in Northumbria, eastern Mercia, and

East Anglia. In addition, contrasts in the chronology of conversion may indicate that different groups of Vikings responded differently to the competing claims of paganism and Christianity.

In the absence of written evidence for Viking converts' understanding of their new faith, much attention has been focused on the stone sculpture produced in areas of Scandinavian settlement in tenth-century Britain, namely northern and midland England, the Isle of Man, and to a lesser extent Scotland (the phenomenon is barely attested in the Scandinavian enclaves in Ireland). This sculpture witnesses to the enthusiasm of the settler elites for a distinctively Christian aspect of their host societies' material culture. In northern and midland England not only did stone carving—of which there was no tradition in Scandinavia—continue to be patronized on ecclesiastical sites that already had a tradition of producing it, but the number of sites containing sculpture tripled and the total quantity of sculpture produced increased fivefold by comparison with the pre-Viking period. This dramatic growth in sculptural production reflects an extension of patronage from monasteries, which used grave-slabs for burials of members of their communities and free-standing crosses to aid contemplation, to the numerous manorial churches established by lay landholders who sought to ensure the perpetuation of their memory through the erection of individual funerary monuments. This change in the function of sculpture, together of course with the proliferation of private churches, is graphic testimony to the Christianization of the Anglo-Scandinavian elite.

Admittedly a minority of monuments, notably in the Isle of Man, Cumbria, and Yorkshire, represent scenes from pagan Norse myth that raise the question of how far conversion had entailed the abandonment of pagan beliefs. What was in the minds of the tenth-century sculptors and patrons of, say, the Gosforth cross in Cumbria with its depiction of both the Crucifixion and scenes from Ragnarǫk, the myth of the fall of the pagan gods at the hands of monstrous evil that led to the emergence of a new world, or the Nunburnholme cross (Yorkshire), where the original depiction of a priest holding the chalice and host was recarved by a second sculptor in order to juxtapose the feast of Sigurð and Reginn, the equivalent of the eucharist in Norse legend? The precise nature of the accommodation between Scandinavian traditions and Christianity revealed by such images remains elusive. One interpretation of the evidence is that it reflects an intermediate stage between paganism and full Christianization, perhaps lasting for a generation or two, in which the Christian god was merely added to the pagan pantheon to create a hybrid or syncretist religion. Alternatively, however, contrasts and parallels may have been drawn between Norse mythology and Christian doctrine in order to make the latter more comprehensible and acceptable: thus the Gosforth cross could have been read as juxtaposing the world of the pagan gods with the world redeemed by Christ and the world which would end at Doomsday. In other words, paganism was pressed into the service of Christianity. More generally, the continuing fascination of Scandinavian converts with aspects of their pre-Christian culture probably made them no different from Anglo-Saxon Christians, whose religion had itself been grafted on to pagan beliefs and practices and remained embedded in a Germanic culture of patently pagan ancestry. In both cases, old gods were reimagined in the context of a new faith.

Belief and behaviour

With the possible exception of some pagan converts, adherence to Christianity was not a matter of individual choice but rather a collective obligation. Accordingly, the church had an impact on the lives of the laity that went far beyond the provision of pastoral ministry through rituals such as baptism, confirmation, or the saying of mass. For example, piety could be expressed by the freeing of slaves, often in a ceremony held at a church and sometimes recorded in a gospel book, as occurred at Llandeilo Fawr in the mid-ninth century and at Bodmin in the tenth and eleventh centuries. Such acts of manumission were intended above all to benefit the soul of the owner, and did not signal a fundamental objection to slavery on the part of the church, whose prelates were required to prevent the alienation of ecclesiastical property, slaves included. But manumission was only one of many ways that Christianity influenced social status and behaviour. In late Anglo-Saxon England kings sought to discipline their subjects by prescribing penance and other spiritual sanctions in addition to secular punishments for a variety of offences: for example, King Edmund (939–46) prohibited anyone guilty of blood-shed from entering his court until compensation had been paid to the victim's kindred and penance completed as instructed by the bishop. Oaths sworn on relics or gospel books played a central part in creating and maintaining obligations in early Irish and Welsh as well as Anglo-Saxon law, and perjury was thus regarded above all as a sin, even if it might also attract a secular penalty. Similarly, in England and Ireland, at least, uncertain cases were resolved by invoking God's judgment in the ordeal, a ritual presided over by clergy that subjected the accused to physical violence such as holding a red-hot iron; to survive the ordeal unscathed was accepted as proof of innocence. The clergy also intervened in disputes through the provision of ecclesiastical sanctuary. The laws of Alfred allowed a man fleeing from his enemies in a feud to remain protected in a church for seven days, without food: as elsewhere in Britain and Ireland, sanctuary helped to defuse violence by providing temporary protection and encouraging the termination of vendettas through compensation rather than revenge killings.

Marriage was a fundamental aspect of social life which had long been the subject of Christian teaching by 800. The strongest proponents of the ideal of monogamous marriage were ecclesiastical reformers such as Archbishop Wulfstan, whose influence on late tenth- and early eleventh-century English law codes is reflected in rules forbidding incest (marriage within the prohibited degrees of consanguinity), concubinage, and divorce. That it was considered necessary to issue these prohibitions suggests that in practice marriage customs fell far short of the standards to which reformers aspired. Nevertheless, the pressure in favour of distinctively Christian marriage is unmistakable and stands in contrast to the situation in Celtic Britain and Ireland, where there was probably greater ecclesiastical tolerance of secular marriage customs. Divorce was taken for granted in seventh- and eighth-century Irish law and seems to have continued to be permitted in the late eleventh century, much to the dismay of Archbishop Lanfranc, who had heard by c.1074 that in Munster 'a man abandons at his own discretion and without any grounds in canon law the wife who is lawfully married to him, not hesitating to form a criminal alliance—by the law of marriage or rather by the law of fornication—with any other woman he pleases, either a relative of his own or of his deserted wife or a woman whom someone else has abandoned in an equally disgraceful way.'[6] To judge by twelfth-century evidence, customs in Wales were little different, while a reforming council convened by Queen Margaret of Scotland (d. 1093) condemned marriage between a man and his stepmother or the widow of his deceased brother.

Attempts to control marriage reflect a wider attitude, especially prevalent among the more reform-minded clergy in England, which held that the laity needed constant policing if they were to lead truly Christian lives. Yet the laity's apparent reluctance to accept that marriage was the church's business points, not to a fundamental rejection of Christianity, but rather to a different understanding from that of reformers of the extent to which religion should penetrate society. Moreover, they contributed significantly to the process of Christianization on their own initiative, notably through endowing and founding churches. Although no doubt undertaken for a variety of motives, the foundation of English manorial churches in particular suggests that the clergy's pastoral services were valued by thegns. The same is shown by the five guilds whose statutes survive from tenth- and eleventh-century England. These were mutual benefit associations, consisting predominantly of laymen, which paid minster clergy to provide for the religious needs of their members, especially funeral rites and memorial masses: for example, at meetings of the early tenth-century guild at Exeter a mass-priest sang two masses, 'one for the living friends, one for the departed'; it was also stipulated that 'after a death each man (is to pay for) six masses or six psalters of psalms'.[7]

The laity's readiness to enlist the church's services at death is also reflected in the prevalence throughout Britain and Ireland in this period of burial in churchyards and at other ecclesiastical sites, as distinct from earlier ancestral cemeteries. Admittedly the shift to burial at Christian sites cannot be mapped precisely in either Ireland or Britain. Although Irish sources from the eighth century onwards both condemn burial among pagan ancestors and uphold the entitlement of local churches to bury those who died in their vicinity (on receipt of a fee), it remains uncertain how widely and rapidly these

---

[6] *The Letters of Lanfranc, Archbishop of Canterbury*, ed. and trans. H. Clover and M. Gibson (Oxford, 1979), 71.

[7] Whitelock et al. (eds.), *Councils and Synods*, i. 59.

prescriptions were followed in practice, as records of specific examples tend to be limited to burials of clerics, kings, and aristocrats in major churches like Armagh or Glendalough. Certainly it would be rash to assume that burial at churches or other ecclesiastical sites was universal among the Christian populations of Britain and Ireland. Several small groups of isolated burials, apparently of Christians rather than pagan Vikings, have been discovered in England from this period, and burials in fields and other unconsecrated ground are attested as late as the fifteenth century both there and in Ireland. Yet the laity's preference for overtly Christian burial cannot be denied. As we have seen, churchyard burial was rapidly adopted by most Scandinavian settlers in England, while the denial of burial in consecrated ground for certain offences in late Anglo-Saxon law codes implies that such burial was in demand. In addition, there is archaeological evidence from parts of northern and western Britain, including Wales, for Christian burials in cemeteries not associated with churches, although in some cases, such as Capel Maelog (Radnorshire), a church was subsequently built on the site.

One stimulus for the shift towards churchyard burial may have been a desire to be buried close to the bones of saints. The cult of saints was well established in Britain and Ireland by 800 and constituted the single most important focus of lay devotion throughout this period. Although formal canonization by the pope was not yet necessary for a person to be recognized as a saint, individual churches played an essential part in making saints and disseminating their cults, both through written texts—the *Martyrology of Óengus* commemorates at least one saint for every day of the year—and the promotion of shrines. It does not follow, however, that the laity who actively participated in saints' cults were merely gullible victims of ecclesiastical propaganda; rather, they turned to the saints because these were seen as uniquely accessible sources of supernatural power that belonged to two dimensions. On the one hand, they were advocates in heaven who helped to bridge the gulf between mere mortals and a remote God; on the other, they were still physically present in the world, principally through their corporeal relics, which consisted either of a whole body or fragments thereof, although secondary relics, objects associated with a saint such as enshrined gospel books, also attracted devotion (see Fig. 4.0).

The cult of saints and their relics explains the popularity of pilgrimage. Annalistic sources highlight the pilgrimages of the power-ful, such as those undertaken to Rome by Cyngen of Powys and Æthelwulf of Wessex in the ninth century, Hywel Dda of south-west Wales and Dwnwallon of Strathclyde in the tenth century, and Earl Thorfinn of Orkney, Echmarcach of Man, Macbeth, and Earl Tostig of Northumbria in the eleventh. Of course, rulers and lords no doubt calculated that such ostentatious acts of devotion would bring them prestige and power on earth as well as rewards in heaven: Athelstan, a renowned collector of relics, cultivated the support of the powerful community of St Cuthbert when he lavished gifts upon the saint's shrine at Chester-le-Street in 934, while Cnut's Roman pilgrimage of 1027 conveniently coincided with the imperial coronation of Conrad II. However, saints' Lives and miracle stories show that pilgrimage was restricted neither to the secular (and ecclesiastical) elite nor to distant places like Rome or Jerusalem; it also had a strong popular appeal, focused on numerous shrines in Britain and Ireland—in the early eleventh century a list was made naming over fifty resting places of saints in England. In Scotland, St Andrews seems to have become a major pilgrimage centre by the end of that century, for Queen Marga-ret provided pilgrims from Lothian with lodgings and free passage across the Forth. For many, pilgrimage to a saint offered the hope of relief from physical affliction. In the later tenth century St Swithun's shrine in the Old Minster, Winchester, drew huge crowds of people suffering from all sorts of deformities and illnesses so that, according to Ælfric, the monks had to rise up to four times a night to sing the *Te Deum* in thanksgiving for miraculous cures which resulted in the church's walls being covered with abandoned crutches and chairs.

The scenes at the Old Minster, whose community of monks had been established by the tenth-century Benedictine reform, illustrate how the experience of a faith with universal claims was mediated through particular contexts. While the church was clearly embedded more securely in the societies of Britain and Ireland by, say, 1050 than it had been in 800, its organization and influence varied across space and time. For example, even allowing for the dangers of distortion posed by the highly uneven character of the surviving sources, there can be little doubt that Viking disruption of ecclesiastical institutions was more severe and prolonged in the English Danelaw than in Ireland or Wales; that (as part of wider social, economic, and demographic changes) local churches proliferated in later Anglo-Saxon England to an extent unparalleled elsewhere in Britain or in Ireland; or that before the late eleventh century only England furnishes unambiguous evidence for a commitment to Benedictine monasticism and other reforming ideals heavily indebted to Carolingian example on the continent. Yet there were also important continuities in belief and piety which transcended such contrasts in infrastructure and ideology. Thus, in their devotion to St Swithun, both reformed monks and lay pilgrims shared common assumptions about the role of the sacred in society that played a fundamental part in the Christianization of Britain and Ireland throughout the period covered by this chapter. For the vast majority of Christians, both clergy and laity, religion was probably essentially a matter of tapping supernatural power through appropriate rituals rather than of internalizing the kinds of exemplary behaviour prescribed by ecclesiastical reformers.

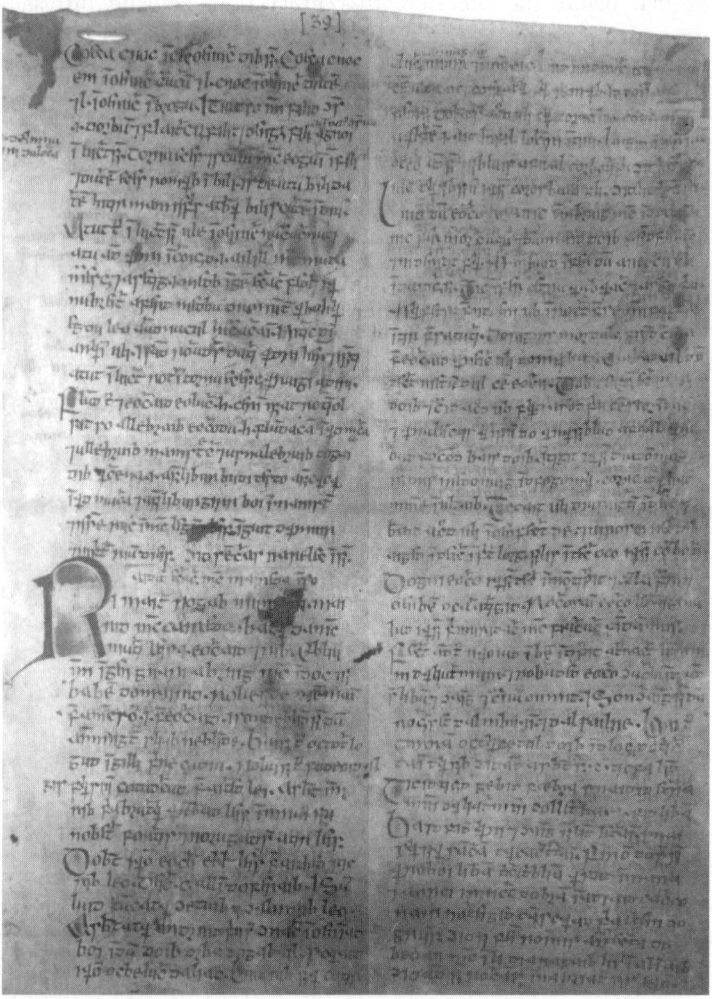

Figure 6.0 Dublin, Royal Irish Academy, MS 23E25 (1129) fo. 39ʳ. *Lebor na hUidre*. The oldest surviving manuscript written entirely in Irish (*c*.1100). The passage on fo. 39va, lines 15–21, contains the note about the book collections of two famous contemporary Irish scholars, Fland Mainistrech and Eochaid Ua Céirín. By permission of the Royal Irish Academy © RIA.

6

Writing

Dáibhí Ó Cróinín

In one of the most famous passages of medieval English literary history, the preface to the English translation of Pope Gregory the Great's *Regula Pastoralis* ('Pastoral care'), which Alfred the Great, king of Wessex 871–99, had commissioned, the king remarked how, at the time of his accession, 'learning had declined so thoroughly in England that there were very few men on this side of the Humber who could understand their divine services in English, or even translate a single letter from Latin into English; and I suppose that there were not many beyond the Humber either'. Modern discussion of literary culture in ninth- and tenth-century England has almost invariably centred on these words of Alfred's, with the pessimists inclined to accept them at face value as a true description of the sorry state of the country which had previously produced the Venerable Bede (d. 735), while the optimists have tended to see in them simply a rhetorical flourish, the better to flatter the king who had dragged England back from its 'Dark Ages' by emphasizing the seriousness of the decline to which learning and literature in England had fallen prey in the decades before he came to power. Alfred himself was quite adamant that the immediate cause of this disastrous decline was the Viking invasions of the mid-ninth century, but he also implies a general decline in learning throughout the eighth and ninth centuries, resulting in the desperate conditions that prevailed at the time of his accession. The Viking invasions he saw—like most of his contemporaries, in England and elsewhere—as a visitation of divine vengeance on a people that had fallen into decadent ways. The ransacking and burning of monasteries resulted in the wholesale destruction of books and libraries, with consequences that Alfred described as being nothing short of cataclysmic.

The Viking impact

It is, of course, the case that Viking attacks were experienced throughout Britain and Ireland in these years, not just in England, and their effects have been variously estimated by historians of England, Ireland, Scotland, and Wales. However, though Latin learning in Ireland, to take one example, has been judged to have suffered just as much as in England as a result of the Viking attacks, the evidence of the surviving manuscripts from this period tells a different story. We are alerted to the dangers of interpreting the situation in Ireland solely on the basis of books currently extant in Ireland because many important books have survived on the continent (some original and some as copies), and they reveal a familiarity with a wide range of Latin (and even some Greek) literature from late antiquity, as well as preserving an impressive variety of original compositions. If the surviving evidence in Ireland were to be our sole criterion, then we would be forced to see Irish learning in the second half of the ninth century and in the century following that in exactly the same terms as Alfred viewed his England. As it happens, we shall see that the English evidence in fact suggests that we need to beware of a too ready acceptance of the Alfredian picture in England itself; a more nuanced interpretation of the available materials might provide a more balanced picture.

That said, there is no gainsaying the fact that it would be difficult to argue for the existence of schools and scholarly activity in England during the ninth century. The continuity of the writing tradition which in previous centuries, in centres such as Monkwearmouth-Jarrow, had produced manuscripts written in the late Roman display scripts—namely uncial and half-uncial—appears to have been broken by the half-century of Viking disruption between 835 and 885. Those manuscript books that did survive appear to have been preserved because they were small and portable, but more particularly because they were valuable, many being lavishly decorated. Not one of them is written in the type of small, utilitarian script, called current minuscule, which was the common form of handwriting used in liturgical handbooks and schoolbooks in the seventh and eighth centuries. Even when we take into consideration the evidence of surviving English manuscripts on the continent, which do include the kinds of texts that one would expect to find in schoolbooks (Latin grammars, glossaries, computistical manuals like Bede's *De Temporum Ratione*, and a few standard authors like Isidore of Seville, Paulinus of Nola, and the native Aldhelm of Sherborne), the fact that they are for the most part in small format and written in current or cursive minuscule adds weight to the suggestion that the high-grade scripts appear never to have been used again in England after that time.

Continuity of learning and literature in Wales

If for England the evidence is slight and problematical, it is nonexistent in the case of Scotland, and almost so in Wales. It cannot seriously be doubted, however, that in Wales, at any rate, Latin learning can be traced back at least as far as the sixth-century writer Gildas—if not indeed further still, to sub-Roman times—and yet from Gildas (whose dates are uncertain) until the late eleventh century the surviving manuscript evidence is exceptionally meagre. Here, more perhaps than elsewhere in Europe, the Dark Ages are veritably dark. Of course, relations between Ireland and Wales were very close throughout our period, and can be traced back to the time of St Patrick and beyond. As the infant Irish church was heavily indebted to the activities of British missionaries and teachers, so, at a later period, when Latin learning had established a firm footing in Ireland, we have evidence of the presence of Irish ecclesiastics passing through Wales on their journeys to continental Europe, and some indeed who put down roots in Wales itself.

As we shall see below, these contacts between Ireland and Wales continued down to the later eleventh century, when Sulien, bishop of St Davids, spent some years studying in Ireland, before returning to his native land, where he and his family of sons presided over a renaissance in Latin learning. However, by stark contrast, the tenth-century manuscript evidence from Wales itself is desperately meagre. Principal witness is a manuscript that once belonged to Glastonbury Abbey, the so-called *Liber Commonei* ('Book of Commoneus', alias Cummeneus?), a single gathering of eighteen rough vellum leaves written by a number of apparently Welsh scribes in a bewildering variety of scripts in a composite volume now amongst the chief treasures in the Bodleian Library in Oxford (MS Auct. F.4.32 (SC

2176)). The manuscript is often referred to as 'St Dunstan's Class-book' from the fact that on fo. 1ᵛ there is a drawing of Christ with a monk at his feet, assigned by tradition to Dunstan, who was abbot of Glastonbury c.940–57 and who seems to have owned the codex at one time. Well known to Celtic scholars because of its glosses (i.e. annotations, both between the lines and in the margins) in Old Irish, Old Breton, and Old Welsh (the latter far more numerous), the collection is a fascinating assortment of bits and pieces, grammatical, computistical, liturgical, and biblical, in the latter case with two sets of Greek and Latin parallel texts (Fig. 6.1). The four separate sections of the codex are in turn of Breton (fos. 1–9), Anglo-Saxon (fos. 10–18), and Welsh origin (fos. 19–36, the *Liber Commonei*, and fos. 37–47, Ovid's *Ars Amatoria*); they are usually dated to the late ninth, tenth, and eleventh centuries. The Greek–Latin and Latin–Greek lessons and canticles are unique, while some of the other material (e.g. the computistical section on abortive moons) derives from earlier Irish sources, while the closing section, containing the Ovid, is the sole surviving copy of that work from Britain and Ireland in the early medieval period.

The presence in the *Liber* of what are usually taken as 'Irish symptoms' has led some to speculate that this section of the codex, at least, may have been copied in whole or in part in Ireland. Such a hypothesis is not impossible; but it is probably safer to view the collection as a witness to the eclectic nature of Welsh library holdings in the period c.900–c.1100. As such, it would indicate a striking degree of conservatism in Welsh ecclesiastical circles on the one hand (borne out, for example, by the use of older versions of the Latin Bible, and antiquated computistical texts), allied with a respectable interest in classical Latin literature, on the other. When, and in what circumstances, the codex came into Saxon hands is impossible to say for sure, but we may perhaps assume that it represents an example of the extensive importation of books from other parts of Britain and Ireland, and from the continent, that took place in the late Anglo-Saxon period, as a direct result of Alfred's support for the revival of learning and culture in England. It is perhaps no coincidence either that the Lichfield Gospels, now in Lichfield Cathedral Library, which contain numerous Welsh entries (including the oldest surviving piece of written syntactical Welsh), and Latin ones with Welsh names, came to Lichfield also during Dunstan's lifetime (d. 988). Even after the

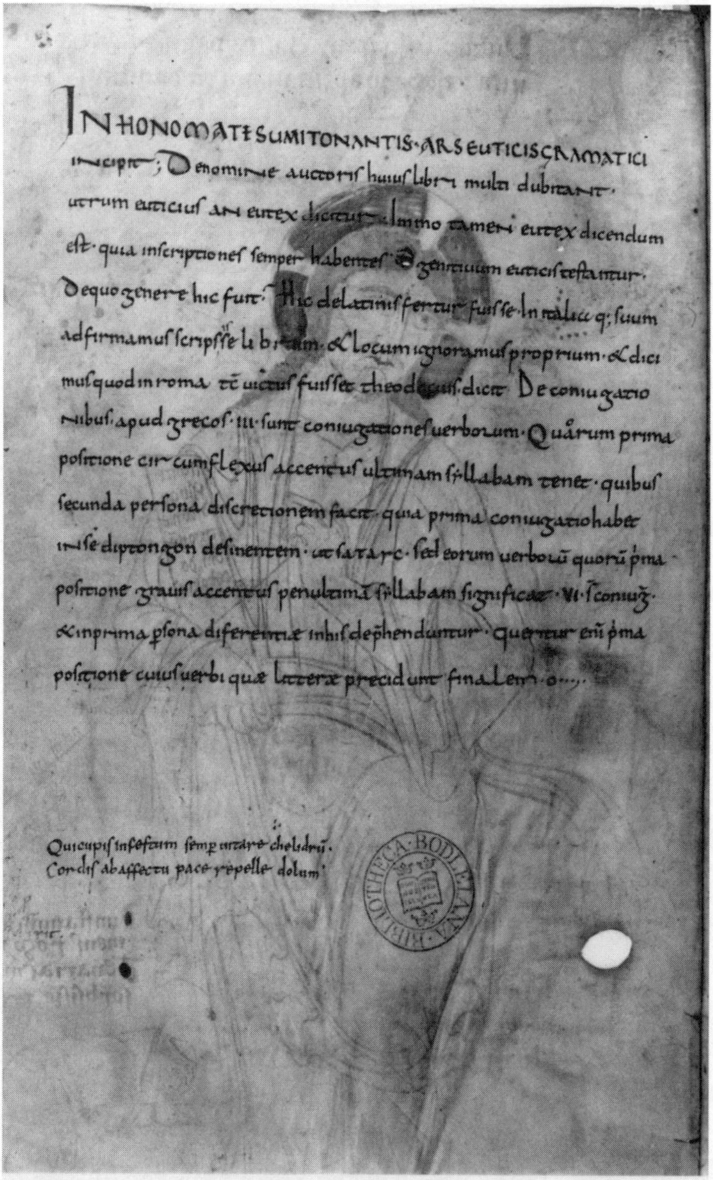

Figure 6.1 (a) Oxford, Bodleian Library, MS Auct. F.4.32, fo. l^v. The opening page of 'Saint Dunstan's Classbook', containing the Latin grammar of Eutyches in Caroline minuscule, with Old Breton glosses, ninth century. Reproduced by permission of the Bodleian Library, University of Oxford.

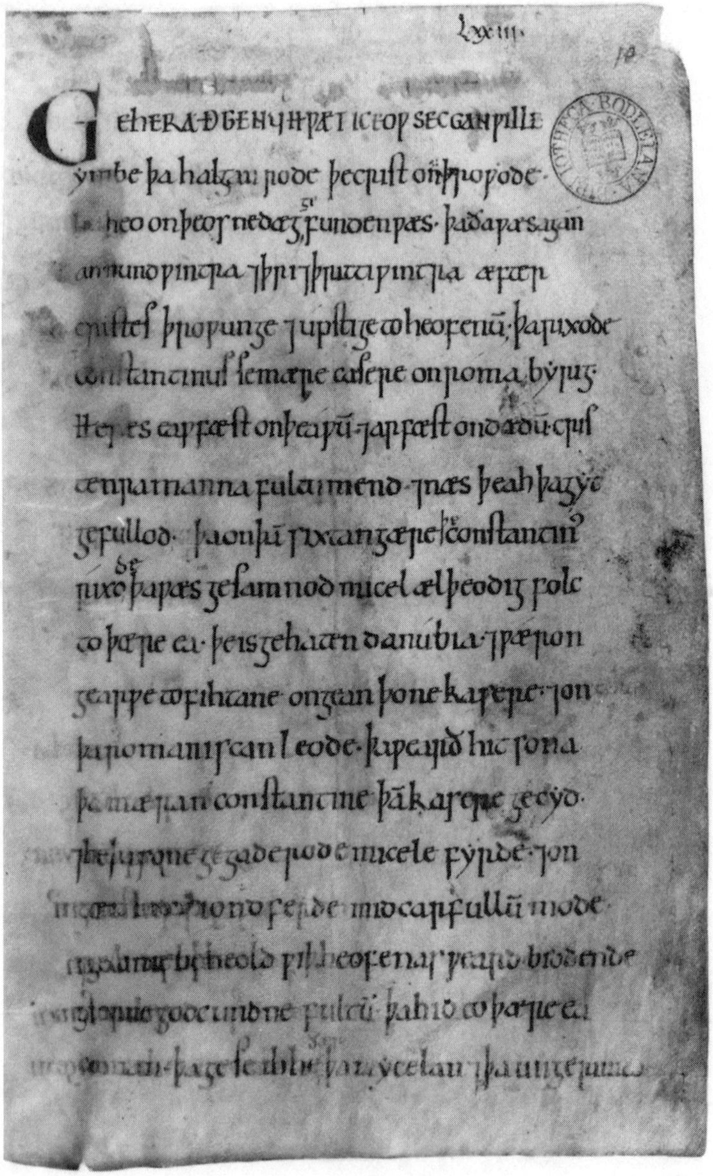

Figure 6.1 (b) Oxford, Bodleian Library, MS Auct. F.4.32, fo. 10ʳ. Homily in Old English on the 'Finding of the True Cross'. Script is late Anglo-Saxon mixed minuscule, second half of the eleventh century. Reproduced by permission of the Bodleian Library, University of Oxford.

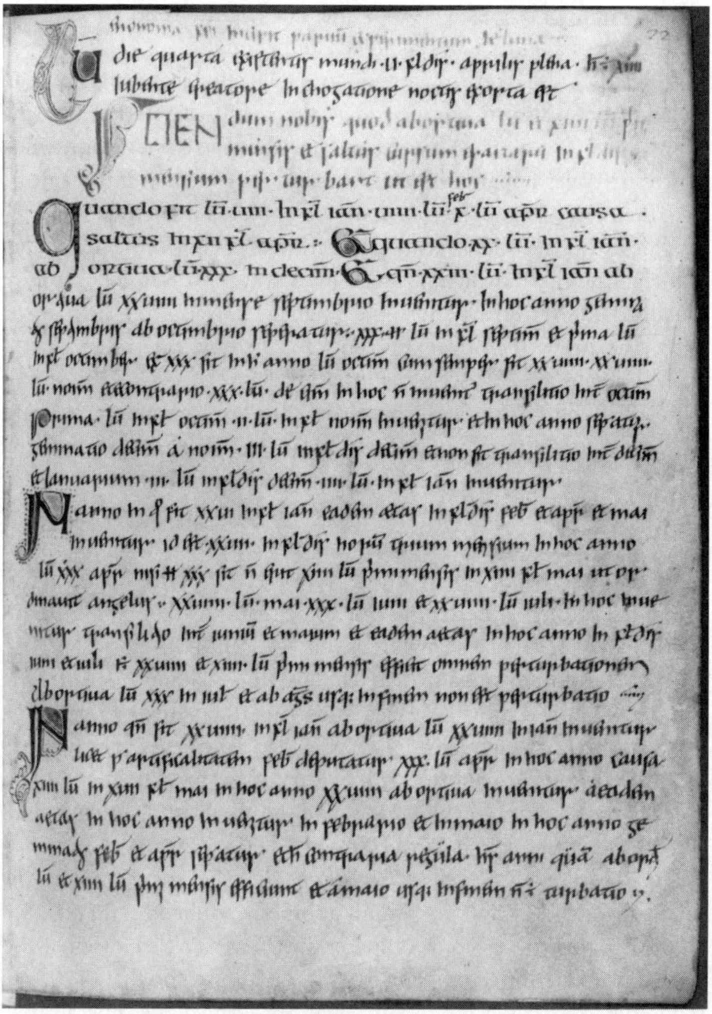

Figure 6.1 (c) Oxford, Bodleian Library, MS Auct. F.4.32, fo. 22ʳ. Opening page of the *Liber Commonei*, containing a miscellany of computistical tracts. Script is Welsh (?) minuscule, early ninth century. Reproduced by permission of the Bodleian Library, University of Oxford.

construction of Offa's Dyke in the late eighth century, contacts beween Mercia and Wales remained fluid enough.

A second well-known witness to intellectual contacts between Ireland and Wales in our period is the manuscript known as the 'Cambridge Juvencus' (CUL Ff.4.42) written at some unidentified centre in Wales apparently in the second half of the ninth century. Like the *Liber Commonei*, this book too contains numerous vernacular glosses (mostly Old Welsh). The scribe who copied the text added a note at the end in which he asked for a prayer for himself ('araut di Nuadu', 'a prayer for Nuadu'); the language is Welsh but the name is Irish, thus providing further evidence for the physical presence of an Irish scribe in a Welsh scriptorium at that time. The later (?) scribes who added the glosses clearly had access to a library well stocked with patristic texts (Jerome, Augustine, and so on) as well as post-patristic ones (such as Isidore's *Etymologies*), but strong affinities have also been noted with Hiberno-Latin biblical commentaries of an earlier age. On the other hand, Juvencus was never a popular author in the Irish schools (being much more frequently read in England, for example), so there is perhaps a case to be made also for Anglo-Saxon influence in the choice of materials that went into the glosses.

If, in addition to these two collections, one includes the surviving ninth- or tenth-century Welsh manuscript fragments of Boethius's translation of Porphyry's *Isagoge* in Leiden University Library (MS Voss. Q 2, fo. 60)—whose script is very close to that of the Ovid section in the *Liber Commonei*—and of the pseudo-Augustinian *Decem Categoriae* now in Bern (Burgerbibl. MS C 219 [4]), the manuscript of Martianus Capella's *De Nuptiis Philologiae et Mercurii* now in Cambridge (CCCC 153), and another Cambridge manuscript (CCCC 352), with a copy (apparently from a Welsh original) of Boethius's *De Arithmetica*, then one gets an impression that the Welsh schools had a strong interest in what are termed the 'liberal arts'. Unlike the early English manuscripts that survive on the continent from this period, which might have been penned in any one of the Anglo-Saxon foundations in Germany and elsewhere, or in England, there is little possibility that these Welsh books were written anywhere other than in Wales, since the Welsh—for whatever reason—seem never to have acquired the habit of *peregrinatio* which so characterized their Anglo-Saxon and Irish neighbours, so we are fairly safe in adding them to the weighing-scales when attempting to measure the level of achievement in the native Welsh schools. That this liberal arts tradition persisted into the early twelfth century is borne out also by the survival of a copy of Macrobius's *Commentary* on Cicero's *Somnium Scipionis* in a British Library manuscript apparently written at Llanbadarn Fawr in the time of Sulien's son Rhigyfarch (d. 1099).

One last collection of peculiarly Welsh interest is the set of Latin colloquies or conversational phrase-books in Oxford, Bodl. Lib., MS Bodley 572, written in caroline minuscule script (an imported continental script) of probably the second quarter of the tenth century (cf. Fig. 6.1a). The manuscript contains a number of glosses in Old Welsh and Old Cornish, but also has strong affinities with similar colloquies in two English manuscripts of the eleventh century (Oxford, St John's Coll., 154, and Oxford, Bodl. Lib., Bodley 865, SC 2737). It has been suggested that the underlying colloquy was composed in Wales and, moreover, that it was heavily indebted to the infamous *Hisperica Famina*, that 'culture fungus of decay', supposedly of seventh-century (?) Irish origin, in which the elementary Latin-language instruction of the early Insular schools was lampooned in grotesque and exaggerated language. The daily routine of monastic life is 'sent up' in a glorious pastiche of the simple phrases that beginners with Latin had to learn off by heart, though whether the original parody was composed in Ireland or in Wales is impossible to say. The English colloquies suggest that there was still traffic in such texts across the border down to the end of the millennium and beyond. The well-known colloquy attributed to Ælfric (author also of a grammar and glossary of Old English) is one of the earliest and most important educational documents from England in the later Anglo-Saxon period, and clearly follows in this long tradition.

Scotland

The Welsh evidence for the period 900–1100 is, as we have just seen, very thin. The evidence for Scotland, on the other hand, is non-existent. 'Where are the writings of early Scotland?' was the plaintive question once asked by Kathleen Hughes in a pioneering study; we are no nearer an answer today than she was when she posed it. In the case of Scotland the suggestion has been that all the early manuscript remains were deliberately destroyed, not by the Vikings—though they did raid and settle in Scotland—but by the religious reformers of the years 1559 and 1560, 'this promiscuous burning of religious houses, with the registers and libraries of churches', as Thomas Innes described it in 1729, a view which has been repeated down to our own day. Whether the hunt for 'popish stuff' really did put paid to Scotland's early history may be doubted. A pilot list of surviving books from medieval libraries of Great Britain includes volumes from Scotland of theology, philosophy, grammar and rhetoric, the church Fathers, sermons, liturgical books and bibles, jurisprudence, martyrologies, and church calendars, as well as chronicles, histories, and works of romance. But very few of these are from the eleventh century, some are from the twelfth and thirteenth centuries, while most are from the fifteenth and sixteenth centuries. So a lot of manuscripts did survive the Reformation in Scotland, but nothing of any note from our period.

There is frequent reference in Iona and Irish sources to the activities of Pictish kings and their subjects (and Bede too remarks that the Picts kept lists of their kings), but the sole surviving Pictish documentary text is just such a roll-call of kings, and that is preserved only in four Irish lists dating from the eleventh century and by the descendants of a twelfth-century Latin list in Anglo-Norman orthography. Not a single documentary or literary text in the Pictish language survives—if ever such a thing existed. And though there is evidence for the Pictish language on some of the so-called 'Pictish ogam' stones, no modern linguistic scholar has managed to produce a convincing interpretation of their inscriptions.

Apart, then, from a couple of artefacts dating from the eighth and ninth centuries, not a single scrap of continuous text, in Latin or in Pictish, has come down to us from Scotland. We can hardly suppose that whatever educational institutions were established in the Pictish kingdoms by Irish missionaries either failed to flourish or died out early. After all, when the Pictish King Nechtan (Naiton) wrote to Bede's abbot Ceolfrid at Monkwearmouth-Jarrow in 710 he must have done so in Latin. If Pictish clerics were able to handle the complexities of Easter tables (as both Ceolfrid and Bede imply that they were), then we cannot seriously doubt that they were thoroughly familiar also with the two other traditional branches of the early medieval school curriculum: biblical studies and Latin grammar, and doubtless all the other ancillary texts that were known and used by teachers and scholars in the Insular world. It is abundantly clear also from Adomnán of Iona's *Vita Columbae* (composed probably *c.*700) that there were numerous monks of Pictish origin in the Iona community from its foundation.

In trying to explain the disappearance of Pictish documents and manuscripts, therefore, it is not enough to say that they simply never existed. The failure must be one of written transmission, for which there ought to be a rational explanation. The Vikings, of course, have been blamed for this, as for every other deficiency in the Insular world, but they cannot have been the sole cause of the problem, at least in eastern Scotland. Even if the indigenous historical traditions of the Pictish peoples were, to whatever extent, subsumed into the more dominant Irish culture of the kingdom of Scotland, it is hard to understand why no trace whatever of those earlier traditions has survived (with the solitary exceptions of the so-called Pictish 'origin legend', which has survived both in later Irish sources and in Bede's *Ecclesiastical History*, and of fragmentary charter materials that presumably derive from Pictish contexts).

Anti-Irish kings in Scotland?

One scholar has pointed instead to the fact that the Scottish experience of Anglo-Norman expansion and domination in Britain and Ireland in the twelfth and thirteenth centuries, while, on the face of it, diametrically opposed to that of Ireland and Wales, wrought a strange and curious legacy. Because they remained largely unmolested until Edward I's famous onslaught, and, as a result, politically, Scotland was something of a success story, the kings of Scots enthusiastically embraced the new culture and language of the Anglo-Norman world, and turned their backs on the Gaelic traditions of their predecessors; the Irish and Welsh vernaculars by contrast retained their status as prestige languages under Irish and Welsh rulers. These 'anti-Celtic tendencies' (as they have been termed) among Scottish kings were to be found in both court and cloister, and by the time of Alexander I's death, in 1124, a significant shift in this direction had already taken place. We have no documents whatever written in the Irish (Gaelic) of Scotland before the twelfth century; the earliest extant example in its original manuscript—dated by its most recent editor to between *c.*1130 and *c.*1150—is preserved in the charters written into the ninth-century gospel book known as the Book of Deer. These *notitiae*, written in what must have been the vernacular of the upper classes of Buchan in the mid-twelfth century, are in almost every respect identical in their language with the contemporary written Irish of Ireland; they therefore represent the earliest linguistic evidence for a continuity of linguistic usage in Ireland and Scotland from the ninth century down to the twelfth, expressed by a Common Gaelic which was the lingua franca of the learned men of those two countries at that time. A liturgical office, of Irish type, entered, apparently towards the end of the eleventh century, on two pages of the manuscript originally left blank, is a ritual for the visitation and communion of the sick, closely related to those in earlier Irish manuscripts, and attests further to the continued contacts that must have existed between Ireland and Scotland down to that time.

The Gaelic notes in the Book of Deer were penned by a scribe whose native language was Irish. There was apparently a manuscript written *stilo scottico*, that is in the Irish style (whether in Irish script, or in the Irish language, we cannot be certain), in the monastery of Loch Leven before 1150, while the Cistercian abbey at Coupar Angus (founded in 1164) possessed and used a psalm book written in a twelfth-century Irish hand. An eleventh- or twelfth-century missal, later associated with the Scottish monastery at Drummond (now New York, Pierpont Morgan Library, MS 627), might have reached Scotland already in our period, though its provenance is thought to be Glendalough in Ireland. But the tide was clearly turning in Scotland in the twelfth century: the names in the Book of Deer *notitiae* are in Gaelic; in 1196 a royal grant made at Elgin is attested not by mormaers or abbots bearing Gaelic names but by clerics who have Anglo-Norman names, and by seventeen lords of whom only two have Gaelic names. We may deduce from all this that, if Irish was faced with a struggle for recognition in twelfth-century Scotland, then the possibilities of any Irish-language documents—not to talk of Pictish ones!—surviving must have been very small indeed.

Literacy and the laity

There are difficulties, then, when it comes to comparing the experiences of literacy and learning in England, Ireland, Scotland, and Wales. In the first instance, the evidence from the different countries is so random and haphazard that no truly valid comparison can be made. In the second place, we need to bear in mind that Ireland, for centuries before the period under discussion here, had a separate and distinct caste of learned men (*áes dána*), initially secular, whose professional training had equipped them in the linguistic and technical branches of a learning that was based entirely on the vernacular. The degree to which literacy was the exclusive preserve of the clergy—if it ever was—is a question that modern scholars find difficult to grapple with. When all due allowance is made for the pious belief that 'philosopher-kings' such as Alfred the Great were capable of reading and writing, the overwhelming evidence suggests that laymen (in England, at any rate) hardly ever acquired the capacity to write their names, let alone express themselves with the written word. This is in spite of the fact that a distinct (runic) alphabet existed for the expression of Anglo-Saxon, and may in fact have been widely used—much more widely than was once believed possible—for ordinary everyday purposes. Thus the survival, for example, of some 550 rune-sticks, with mundane personal messages, from Bergen in Norway (though admittedly of a much later, fourteenth-century, date) suggests at least the possibility, however slight, that such forms of communication might have existed for lay people in the earlier period under discussion here. But the bulk of the evidence for lay involvement in the production of written documents is provided not by literary texts but by charters, 1,500 of which survive from England alone, along with an assortment of related documents, all concerned with the conveyancing of property and the establishment of title, matters of obvious importance to the non-clerical elements in society as well as to the church.

Charters, wills, leases, and manumissions

It is generally assumed (probably correctly) that charters (records of property transactions) were an established part of legal practice in

Anglo-Saxon England from the time of the earliest Italian missionaries dispatched by Pope Gregory I in 597. Of course, the survival rate for such documents was often unpredictable: thus, although there is literary evidence for their existence in Northumbria in the seventh century, this type of document subsequently disappeared completely from there (and from eastern England), mainly, it is thought, because of Viking depredations. The earliest of these diplomas, drafted by clerics for clerical beneficiaries, are exclusively concerned with ecclesiastical property. But lay beneficiaries are attested by the late eighth century, and by the late Anglo-Saxon period most beneficiaries, in fact, were laymen. Even in those charters that have survived, however, where the beneficiaries might be mostly or entirely lay people, there are no autograph signatures of such individuals in the manuscripts, a fact that most scholars have seen as proof of illiteracy amongst those classes in society.

On the other hand, there is a notable tendency from an early date (i.e. from the late ninth century on) for charters and wills, leases and miscellaneous legal agreements, and manumissions to appear in gospel books or other liturgical manuscripts, written partly in Latin but partly also in Old English. The redemption of captives and freeing of slaves was regarded as a Christian duty from an early date (St Patrick mentions it specifically in his *Confession*, for example) and many Anglo-Saxon wills (though there are none preserved in gospel books) contain instructions about the freeing of the testator's slaves. A written record of the act of manumission was not essential to its validity, but we may assume that many people took the precaution of having their act recorded in writing in order to ensure that the freed slave was not subsequently challenged (thus depriving the former owner of his eternal reward earned by his charity at death). The earliest extant Anglo-Saxon manumission is one performed by King Athelstan immediately on becoming king in 925. Probably earlier in date, however, are the manumission and other documents in Welsh entered into the Lichfield Gospels ('Book of St Chad'). The most extensive collection of such documents, however, is in the Bodmin-Padstow Gospels, written in the tenth century in a caroline minuscule script probably at the monastery of Bodmin in Cornwall, and into which were entered, between the tenth and the twelfth century, a total of fifty-one such texts.

The fact is, however, that such documents are extremely rare outside England: there are no manumissions whatever from Ireland or Scotland in our period, and the earliest charters there date from the eleventh and twelfth centuries. Though there is a fleeting glimpse of charter material in Ireland c. 800 (in the Book of Armagh texts relating to St Patrick) there is nothing after that until the late eleventh century, while in Scotland, the charter evidence begins to appear for the first time in the eleventh and twelfth centuries.

Royal and secular documents in England

In England by contrast, by the later Anglo-Saxon period, royal administration and the upper reaches of lay society were using writing (and especially the vernacular) on a routine basis, which suggests that if the laymen involved could not actually read or write these documents, they at least could understand the contents when read to them. Previously, of course, literacy had been the exclusive prerogative of the clergy. Parallel to this development was the gradual encroachment of Old English into liturgical manuscripts—a few words initially, here and there, either as rubrics or headings, or simple instructions, in a prayer book or whatever. The only exception perhaps is in the area of penitential discipline, where it was felt necessary for the non-Latinate (both laity and most of the clergy) to participate more fully by being given direct access to the ceremonial formulas of the liturgy in a language they could readily understand. The evidence of the later *libri paenitentiales* (books of penance) is that the vernacular element came to predominate in that genre, while never of course being able to drive out the core of Latin *ordines*. Around the middle of the eleventh century in England the vernacular was 'nibbling at the margins' of the liturgy and was poised to assume a more substantial role in liturgical books. By then the need for material in the language of the people was felt to be much more pressing, and this is reflected in the vastly increased number of books in the vernacular produced in that period. Whether, however, one can deduce from these phenomena that there was a correspondingly significant increase in the level of literacy amongst the laity (with perhaps a corresponding decline in the use of Latin for such purposes?) is difficult to say. In the case of the Durham Collectar (Durham, Cathedral Library, MS A.iv.19), written c.900 but which came to Durham in the later tenth century, its Latin texts received a thorough Old English interlinear translation at the hands of Aldred, provost of Chester-le-Street—the same man who supplied the interlinear Old English translation in the Lindisfarne Gospels. Aldred's familiarity with Latin biblical commentary material and his capacity as a translator may be exceptional; the extraordinary glossing activity might imply that the canons of Chester-le-Street were incapable of understanding their liturgical texts in the original Latin language. In the absence of comparative evidence for Scotland and Wales, we cannot say whether there was any similar trend in those two countries in the years leading up to 1000, but in Ireland, although there are only sporadic fragments of manuscripts surviving, there is no conclusive evidence to suggest that, in liturgical and related church matters, the vernacular had replaced Latin for practical purposes.

Learning and literacy after Alfred's reforms

The suggestion has sometimes been made that Alfred set out to achieve for England what Charlemagne had attempted—and in large part achieved—in his realm a century previously. But there the comparison ends. The state of learning in the early days of Charlemagne's reign owed nothing to the depredations of invading armies, but rather was the result of a neglect, more or less benign, that had characterized the previous years of the Merovingian kings and Frankish bishops. The dire state of scholarship in England in Alfred's time—even if exaggerated by Alfred's supporters and admirers—was, in large part, due to the devastating effects of the Vikings on English monasteries and their schools and libraries. True, Bishop Waerferth of Worcester was sufficiently adept as a Latinist to be able to translate Gregory the Great's *Cura Pastoralis* and *Dialogues* into English, but the very act of translation seems to suggest that such a thing was needed in the first place because most of the English clergy were Latin-less.

Alfred's stated wish was straightforward enough, when he said that 'it seems better to me if it seems so to you that we also turn some books which are most necessary for all men to know into the tongue which we can all understand; and we do it, as we very easily can with God's aid, if we have peace, so that all the youth of England's free men who have the means so that they may apply themselves to it, be set to learning as long as they cannot be set to any other employment until such time as they know how to read English well. Afterwards let those be instructed besides in the Latin language whom one wants to teach further and to bring to higher office.' As a statement of policy it was admirable, but it hardly ranks with Charlemagne's *Epistola de Litteris Colendis* ('Letter on the cultivation of letters'). The level of Latin learning to be found at Alfred's court in his lifetime suggests that it was little more than a pious hope, while the achievements of Grimbald of St Bertin and of John the Old Saxon have left almost no visible trace. When English scholars came to read their *Carmen Paschale* of Caelius Sedulius and the like in later years, they did so on the basis of imported continental manuscripts and with the borrowed aid of Remigius of Auxerre's (d. 908) commentary on that text, not on a platform of native English scholarship. One aspect of Alfred's policy of renewal for the English church was a programme of book imports from Brittany, drawing on the current strength of Breton scriptoria in order to supply English churchmen with basic Latin texts. The great English liturgist Edmund Bishop even spoke of 'a veritable devotional *furore* in Bretonism' in the later tenth century, following an influx of Breton refugees during the early years of Athelstan's reign (913–19), when a Viking invasion succeeded in conquering Brittany and provoked a large-scale flight of members of the political and clerical classes.

What is clear, however, is that in the early years of the tenth century, a number of scriptoria were engaged in mass production of the English translations that Alfred had commissioned, and for that purpose a new form of script was created, to which the name Anglo-Saxon 'square minuscule' has been given.

It is quite striking that Alfred did not actively recruit Irish masters, as Charlemagne had done, considering the far superior state of Latin learning in Ireland in the mid-ninth century and after. A famous entry in the *Anglo-Saxon Chronicle* for 891 records how 'in this year the Viking army went eastwards, and King Arnulf with the East Franks and the Saxons and Bavarians fought against the mounted force before the ships arrived, and put it to flight', followed by this further entry:

And three Irishmen (*Scotti*) came to King Alfred in a boat without any oars from Ireland, whence they had stolen away because they wished to go on pilgrimage for love of God, they cared not where. The boat in which they travelled was made from two and a half hides; and they took with them only enough food for seven days. And after seven days they came to land in Cornwall, and then went immediately to King Alfred. Their names were Dubsláine, Mac Bethath, and Máel Inmuin. And Suibne, the greatest teacher among the Irish, died.

This anecdote might, at first sight, have the appearance of being apocryphal, but the names alone suffice to prove that it could not have been pure invention, for they are clearly authentic; Mac Bethath, in fact, is the form that recurs in the name of the famous Scottish king Macbeth (1040–57). Unfortunately, no manuscript trace of these three Irish scholars seems to have survived, but whatever they brought with them in the way of books, we can be pretty sure that most—if not all—of them were in Latin.

Vernacular writing in Ireland

There is no parallel in Ireland for the practice of translation into the vernacular from Latin, such as was the hallmark of Alfred's reform in England. The practice of glossing Latin texts in Old Irish (or a mixture of Latin and Old Irish) was, of course, commonplace in the Irish schools from c.700 at least, but, with only one or two exceptions, it never led to the wholesale production of full-length vernacular texts for the liturgy. What little evidence there is for the use of the vernacular in liturgical services derives from one solitary mass book (the 'Stowe Missal', Dublin, RIA, MS Stowe D.ii.3, ninth century) in which the rubrics throughout are in Old Irish, as is a vernacular exposition on the mass which was added at the end of the manuscript, probably in the later ninth century (see above, p. 180). It has often been asserted—though with no justification whatever—that the *Céli Dé* ('culdee') reform movement that emerged in the Irish church in the late eighth and early ninth centuries had as one of its effects (if not, indeed, aims) the replacement of Latin by Old Irish, and the encouragement of spiritual expression in the vernacular (particularly the so-called 'nature poetry' of the period). While it is true that the main house of the reform movement (Tallaght, Co. Dublin) did produce two remarkable Old Irish martyrologies, the one in verse and the other prose (see above, pp. 139), this is no evidence that Latin had gone into a terminal decline, either in the *Céli Dé* centres or in the Irish schools generally. That said, there is indeed a steady rise in the production of works of native literature in Old Irish (and its later form, Middle Irish), alongside the continuing practice of glossing Latin texts in both Latin and Irish, right down to the end of our period and well into the twelfth century.

This is manifested in a particularly striking way by the fact that, in Ireland, throughout the early medieval period, the native Irish script remained in use both for texts in the vernacular and for texts written in Latin. In England, by contrast, the Insular style of script came to be reserved for texts in Old English, with works in Latin being increasingly written in the imported continental script (caroline minuscule). Even more striking is the fact that in Wales, the caroline script came to be used for Latin and vernacular texts alike. It is still a matter for debate amongst Anglo-Saxonists whether retention of the native script could be interpreted as a statement of loyalty to the older traditions of pre-reform monasticism in England, or whether it merely reflects a change in attitude to the vernacular itself, writings in Old English now being viewed as lower in status. In Ireland, there does not appear to have been any such cleavage, but then in Ireland the *Céli Dé* movement, which seems to have concentrated its efforts on spiritual reform, was nothing like as significant in terms of educational initiatives as the Benedictine reform was in England, and does not appear to have exercised any influence whatever on the choice of scripts used for writing (nor, for that matter, on the choice of language, despite what some scholars have said to the contrary).

Continental influences in England after Alfred

The position in England in the decades following the Alfredian revival of learning owed more to continental input than it did to native scholarship, a fact which is reflected even in the language of the Latin writers of the period in England. Alfred's own description of the dire state of knowledge, in Latin and English, south of the Humber is borne out in striking fashion by the evidence of a series of original charters issued at Canterbury in the 860s, which reveal that the principal scribe, infirm and almost blind, could scarcely see to correct the appalling grammatical errors that he perpetrated. Alfred took measures to remedy that situation by importing books and scholars from the continent, thus gradually restocking the native libraries that had suffered during the ninth century. This educational revival was continued by his son Edward the Elder (899–924) and his grandson Athelstan (924–39). The emphasis among these men was on the twofold aim of restoring a literate clergy and providing monasteries which could train up such individuals. There is direct evidence for the continuation of the policy of importing continental know-how in some Latin poems composed by the man known as John the Old Saxon, one of the scholars whom Alfred had attracted to England, 'a man of most acute intelligence, immensely learned in all fields of literary endeavour, and extremely ingenious in many other forms of expression' (to quote Asser's encomium in his *Life of Alfred* of 893). In Oxford, Bodl. Libr., MS C. 697 (SC 12541), a late ninth-century miscellany written in north-eastern France but imported into England probably around the mid-tenth century, there is added at the end, on the last page (after the manuscript had come to England), an acrostic and telestich poem in eight lines written in Anglo-Saxon square minuscule, the first and last letters of each line spelling out the legends ADALSTAN and IOHANNES (Athelstan and John). John the Saxon outlived his patron Alfred (d. 899) and was active still during the reign of Edward the Elder, perhaps even longer, since two further acrostic poems of his may have survived in a manuscript now preserved in Bern (Burgerbibl. MS 671, fo. 74ᵛ; there are symptoms in the script that suggest a Cornish rather than a Welsh origin for it), again added in a blank space at the end of the main text, and again in Anglo-Saxon square minuscule of Winchester type. The codex passed subsequently to Great Bedwyn, Wiltshire, one of Alfred's estates, where four documents in Old English were added to it.

Another such continental scholar in England may have been Israel the Grammarian, who is described by continental chroniclers as Israel *Britto* or *Brittigena*, 'British—or Breton—born' (but in some manuscripts also *Scottigena*, suggesting a possible Irish origin). Israel had studied at Rome, was an expert Latin grammarian and knew Greek, and could turn his hand as well to philosophy. He was the teacher of Bruno (d. 965), brother of the German Emperor Otto the Great (912–73), who became bishop of Cologne in 953. At some stage in his career he seems to have entered the circle of Athelstan, for there is a note in the so-called 'Corpus Gospels' (Oxford, Corpus Christi

College, MS 122), an Irish gospel book written probably some time after 1140, in which is preserved a coloured drawing of a board-game called *alea evangelii* ('gospel dice'), accompanied by instructions on how to play it. The note says that the game had been brought back to Ireland by Dubinsi, bishop of Bangor, Co. Down (d. 953), who had learned how to play it at Athelstan's court 'from a drawing by a certain Frank and a learned Roman, i.e. Israel' (if indeed that is the correct interpretation of the Latin).

Hermeneutic style

The influence of these continental scholars is most readily to be seen in the style of their Latin, which has a baroque exuberance about it for which modern scholars have coined the term 'hermeneutic', i.e. bristling with archaisms, Graecisms, and sense neologisms in such profusion that many lines cannot be understood. Both in the literary productions of this period and in the charters that begin to reappear from 925 on, almost the entire text is composed in an artificial and inflated style, liberally sprinkled with rare and esoteric words and other exoticisms. The style appears to have been first practised by Frankish scholars such as Frithegod, who composed a *Breviloquium Vitae Wilfridi* at Canterbury during the decade after 940, which is by any reckoning one of the most difficult of all medieval Latin poems. (Some have proposed to see the origin of this style in one of the Celtic regions, in Brittany, or even in Wales, on the basis that these regions are the ones where the *Hisperica Famina* of an earlier age are supposed to have come into existence. Comparison has also been made with the seventh-century Anglo-Latin writer Aldhelm, whose puerile pomposity has been remarked upon. Alfred the Great is supposed to have expressed a liking for it, but we may doubt that he ever understood a word of it.) In a vein similar to Frithegod's, but later in the tenth century (the 980s), a version of the *Anglo-Saxon Chronicle* appeared in a Latin which is impressively impenetrable. Its significance lies in the fact that it was allegedly composed by a layman (an ealdorman) named Æthelweard. We may doubt whether that was the case; if it is true, then literacy among the Anglo-Saxon laity had reached unprecedented (and bizarre) levels. The two works by Frithegod and Æthelweard set the standard for Latin style in England for the late Anglo-Saxon period. They attest clearly to the revival of learning in the tenth century, but illustrate that, in its extreme form, learning could become pretentious and arcane.

Benedictine reform

Between the dates of these two works the English church and English education had been given a new direction and a new vigour by a Benedictine reform movement introduced in conscious imitation of the changes that had been carried out on the continent a century previously (see above, pp. 144). But the English reform was also inspired by more recent contact with the continent, personified by the three chief proponents of the movement in England, Dunstan, Æthelwold, and Oswald, who had links with Ghent and Fleury. Oswald, bishop of Worcester and archbishop of York (d. 992), received his earliest education at Canterbury under the tutelage of Frithegod, and perfected his knowledge at Fleury. His request to that house some years later for the assistance of someone who might teach the monks of his new foundation at Ramsey led to the dispatch, probably in 985, of Abbo, who presided for two years over the school there. Abbo was one of the greatest scholars in Europe at that time. At an earlier stage in his career he had studied with no less a teacher than Gerbert of Aurillac (later Pope Sylvester II), to some 'the most learned man of the tenth century', to others an *optimus negrimanticus* ('greatest sorcerer'), who by diabolical arts attained the archbishoprics of Rheims and Ravenna, and at last the papal see itself (in fact, he had pioneered the use of the abacus and paved the way for the introduction of Arabic science into the West). Gerbert was the leading scholar of mathematics in Europe and Abbo's own writings reflect these scientific interests, especially his knowledge of arithmetic and computus. But he also composed works on the more traditional subjects of the classical trivium and quadrivium: grammar, rhetoric, and dialectic, including one of the earliest known medieval treatises on logic. Abbo must have brought numerous books with him to Ramsey, amongst which were certainly his own computus and a copy of Macrobius's *Commentary* on Cicero's *Somnium Scipionis*, a text which formed the cornerstone of scientific instruction in the Carolingian schools.

There can be no doubting that the arrival of Abbo in the small fenland abbey of Ramsey wrought a revolution in educational practices there; certainly Abbo's foremost pupil Byrhtferth produced an impressive array of works on a wide variety of topics computistical, hagiographical, and historical, and was author of the most important scientific treatise that had appeared in England since the age of Bede. But the monastery itself almost succumbed to the consequences of the momentous political upheavals that took place in England during the later years of the reign of King Æthelred (978–1016), culminating in the battle of Assandun on 18 October 1016, when a Danish army led by King Cnut met the English army under Edmund 'Ironside' (Æthelred having died on 23 April of that year), as a result of which, the *Anglo-Saxon Chronicle* reported, 'all the nobility of England was there destroyed'.

Byrhtferth, however, was perhaps exceptional as a native product of Anglo-Saxon schooling (albeit trained by a continental master), though his near contemporary Ælfric (who ended his life as abbot of Eynsham) is generally regarded as superior in stature, whether as a teacher or as an exponent of the vernacular. Born probably in the 950s, he entered the monastery of Winchester while still in his teens, but by *c*.990 he had prepared and published the first in an impressive series of writings in Old English which were to establish for him an enduring reputation, a set of homilies. These were followed shortly thereafter by a second set; numbering eighty in all. Both had been commissioned by lay patrons and both collections were intended to be preached by ordinary parish priests to their congregations. There followed a handbook for priests, *De Temporibus Anni* ('On the times of the year'), and his most famous works, the Old English *Grammar*, with its accompanying *Glossary*, and his *Colloquium*, a Latin text with interlinear Old English gloss (which some scholars believe to have been the work of a pupil, rather than of Ælfric himself). In the *Grammar* Ælfric did what no previous Anglo-Saxon writer had done before him: he produced a standard grammar of contemporary English, and coined an appropriate technical terminology in which to express the rules of that language. While it might not be quite accurate to describe it as the first grammar in any vernacular, it was nevertheless a remarkable and original achievement.

It is doubtless no coincidence that the four major manuscript miscellanies that preserve the bulk of Old English poetry (the Exeter, Vercelli, and Junius manuscripts, with the *Beowulf* collection) are all products of the generation 970–1000. And yet it has been pointed out that, in England, the fine books of the eleventh century are nearly all Latin. The reason offered by scholars is that in the leading churches, with a necessary exception for sermons, there seems to have been a hardening against English as a literary medium. The comparison with contemporary Ireland could hardly be more striking.

Irish writing and learning

Renewed contacts between England and Ireland

We saw above how the tradition of *colloquia* pre-dated Ælfric, and how his own composition may have been directly influenced by earlier Latin colloquies of Celtic origin (i.e. from Wales or perhaps Ireland). Ælfric, on the other hand, in his homiletic writings seems to have deliberately avoided Irish works, and his homilies are virtually free of Irish influence. With him (and with Wulfstan, his younger contemporary) there is a conscious and deliberate turning back to patristic writers and continental sources, away from the earlier tradition of Hiberno-Latin biblical commentary. Theirs was not, however, an altogether typical reaction. The connections between Ireland and England in the tenth and eleventh centuries were strong: the world of these Irish monks was emphatically the world of the English monks of the tenth-century reform, and therefore of the post-Conquest communities of Evesham, Worcester, Glastonbury, Winchester, and Canterbury. One can point to Dunstan's Irish teacher, and the demonstrably Irish elements in his 'Classbook'; the Patrick, Brigit, and Indract legends at Glastonbury; how St Cadroe of Waulsort and Metz passed through England on a grand tour from north to south while on his way to the continent from Ireland sometime between 941 and 946, a journey which included a courtesy call on Archbishop Oda of Canterbury at Winchester. At Worcester the names of visiting Irish monks were entered in the Durham *Liber Vitae*; Bishop Patrick of Dublin (1074–84) was a monk at Worcester before his elevation, while letters addressed to Wulfstan by various Irish kings are reported in his Life. Worcester was also to be the centre for the English dissemination of Marianus Scottus's *Chronicle* (for which see below). And there is the survival in a Worcester manuscript of the letter from Pope Gregory

VII to the Irish king Toirdelbach Ua Briain, as well as other bits and pieces, all bearing witness to continued and (usually) friendly relations between the two clerical communities. The solitary exception is the Ramsey chronicle, which records how a penniless wandering Irishman murdered his benefactor, the abbot of the monastery. Everything leads us to think that there were many such callers, traders, pilgrims, teachers, and intellectual pedlars, and their lasting influence was demonstrated by the ubiquitous presence of Irish devotions in English prayer books of the late ninth and tenth centuries. The same monks would also have met on the continent, at places like Saint-Bertin in France or Ghent in Holland (where Dunstan had spent some years), or St Gallen, long a favourite place of pilgrimage for Irishmen, but where also (according to the Confraternity Book of that monastery) Bishop Cenwald of Worcester, in 929, passed through in the course of a journey undertaken on behalf of King Athelstan to all the monasteries throughout Germany. Amongst men like these there was a shared piety and learning, redolent of the past when Ireland and England enjoyed good relations. True, a too literal reading of Bede's *Ecclesiastical History* could give the impression to tenth-century readers that Canterbury had enjoyed a primacy over Ireland as far back as the sixth century, and that English kings had exercised dominion over it as well. It was not for nothing that the great James Ussher, Protestant archbishop of Dublin and primate of Armagh (d. 1656), published the famous *Altitonantis* charter for Worcester which claimed for Edgar that 'To me God has conceded together with the empire of the English all the islands of the ocean with their most fierce kings as far as Norway, and subjugated the greater part of Ireland with its most notable city of Dublin to the kingdom of the English'. Much more striking, however, is the inscription on the so-called Mac Durnan Gospels (London, Lambeth Palace Library, MS 1370) presented by Máel Brigte mac Tornáin to Athelstan, which Athelstan in turn presented to Canterbury:

> Maielbrithus MacDurnani
> Istum Textum per triquadrum
> Deo digne Dogmatizat:
> Ast Aethelstanus AngloSaexna
> Rex et Rector Dorvernensi
> Metropoli Dat per Aevum

i.e. 'Máel Brigte son of Tornán [abbot of Armagh 888–927] taught this gospel worthily for God's sake through the *triquadrum*; the Anglo-Saxon king and ruler Athelstan gives it for ever to the metropolitan church of Canterbury.' Athelstan was a well-known collector of precious books, and distributed them generously to various English churches (though in this regard he is not quite so impressive as King Cnut (1016–35), who is believed to have commissioned no fewer than fifteen lavishly illustrated gospel books). According to the Irish annals, Máel Brigte mac Tornáin died in happy old age (*felici senectute*), 'head of the piety of all Ireland and of the greater part of Europe'. Another Irish book, the Rushworth Gospels (Oxford, Bodl. Lib., MS Auct. D. ii. 19), also made its way to England in the tenth century, where it received a complete interlinear Old English translation that makes it one of the most valuable surviving Anglo-Saxon linguistic records. It was through such channels as these that Irish texts and Irish learning made their way to England, where their influence has been found particularly in Old English literary texts, both prose and poetry. To judge from the surviving manuscripts, these texts found a large audience in Anglo-Saxon England during the tenth and eleventh centuries.

Irish Latin learning

What Latin writings were in circulation in Ireland during the tenth and eleventh centuries we cannot say for certain; the material is too insecurely located, and manuscripts from the period are almost impossible to date with sufficient precision. In the British Library manuscript Egerton MS 3323, a miscellany of originally separate gatherings of various dates and provenances, there are two leaves from a schoolbook once belonging to Glendalough (Co. Wicklow), dating probably from the late eleventh century. It contains fragments of Clemens Scottus on grammar and, more intriguingly, *De Minutiis*, a treatise composed by a contemporary of Gerbert of Rheims. An English element in the transmission to Ireland is not demonstrable, but should not be discounted. That the traditional subjects of the curriculum (Latin grammar, biblical studies, and the calendar) were still being taught in Irish schools at this time is suggested by another surviving fragment, probably of the same rough date (TCD, MS C.i.8 (229)), which contains Priscian's *Institutiones Grammaticae*. Priscian was still the staple fare of Irish schools in the twelfth century, along with such texts as Lupus of Ferrière's *De Ratione Metrorum*, so it seems reasonable to assume a continuity of such teaching throughout the eleventh and twelfth centuries in Ireland.

Translations and vernacular writings

The eleventh century is marked in particular by a rash of translations, of the *Historia Brittonum*, for example (a Welsh composition of the early ninth century), the Irish *Sex Aetates Mundi*, a compendium of biblical history which preserves some remarkable apocryphal material, and a string of 'Roman' histories such as Lucan's *Pharsalia* (*In Cath Catharda*) and *Togail Troí* ('The Siege of Troy'). The real flowering in Ireland, however, was in the field of creative writing in the vernacular, both in prose and in verse, in a wide variety of genres, including history, pseudo-history, place-name lore (*dindshenchas*), women's history (*banshenchas*), and what would nowadays perhaps be called romance. Mindful perhaps of the rebuke that an earlier scholar, Cormac mac Cuilennáin (d. 908), had uttered, when he chided the 'careless Irish nation' (*imprudens Scottorum gens*) for having wilfully neglected their own history, Irish writers of this period developed a distinctive 'synthetic' view of earlier Irish history which was so effective and all-pervasive that it imposed on Irish people down to our own day. Men such as Cináed Ua hArtacáin and Eochaid Ua Céirín, Cúán Ua Lothcháin and Fland mac Lonáin (d. 1012), represented that distinct caste of historians who combined factual history (in so far as they could be said to have viewed things in that light) with a pseudo-history (or *senchas*, as they would have termed it) that filled the gap, as it were, in the history of Ireland in the centuries before the conversion to Christianity. But the bulk of the literary creativity, without a doubt, was original and in the Irish language. When, some time before 1100, the most famous Irish manuscript of the age came to be assembled, *Lebor na hUidre* ('Book of the Dun Cow', so-called because it was supposedly written on the hide of St Ciarán of Clonmacnoise's pet cow), its compiler was able to state that it had been put together by Ua Céirín and a contemporary, Fland of Monasterboice (Co. Louth, d. 1056), 'from the books of Eochaid Ua Flannacáin in Armagh and the books of Monasterboice, and from the other choice books, namely the Yellow Book which is missing from the safe in Armagh, and the Short Book that was in Monasterboice, but which the student stole and made off with across the sea, and which has never been seen since' (see Fig. 6.0). The proliferation of such collections is itself a good indication of the degree of 'mass production' that seems to have taken place in the eleventh century, no doubt consolidating and building on the work of a previous generation of such scholars. In fact, the list of names of Irish poets stretches unbroken from the ninth century down into the eleventh and beyond, and their compositions ranged over a wide number of topics, both didactic and literary. The scribal work was not entirely antiquarian, either; the text of what is probably the most famous prose saga in all of Irish literature, *Táin Bó Cuailnge*, has been carefully worked over in *Lebor na hUidre*, substantial passages being either rewritten or erased entirely, with specific reference to other extant copies. The two greatest compendia of the twelfth century, Oxford, Bodl. Lib., MS Rawlinson B 502 (*c*.1127, recently attributed to the monastery of Glendalough) and *Lebor na Nuachongbála* alias 'The Book of Leinster' (*c*.1167 and after), help to round out the picture of what was being composed in the 200 or so years before 1100. The most strikingly original composition of the period, the metrical biblical history known as *Saltair na Rann* ('Psalter of the verses', *c*.980?) is remarkable for its wealth of Old Testament apocryphal sources, though it is not unique among Irish texts of the period in this regard. It has been suggested by one Anglo-Saxon scholar that Ælfric deliberately eschewed the use of Hiberno-Latin biblical commentaries (though nowhere specifically identified by him in such terms) in his homilies precisely because they were replete with borrowings from biblical apocrypha long since anathematized elewhere, and therefore not to be trusted. His scathing reference to 'micel gedwyld' ('great foolishness'), which he had encountered in vernacular Old English writings, has been seen as a reaction against that Irish influence, which is well attested in Old English writings before 1000.

These Irish compositions in the vernacular were not viewed as a reaction to the emphasis on Hiberno-Latin literature of the previous centuries; rather, they were seen as complementary to that earlier tradition. Whereas the use of Irish certainly increases amongst Irish men of learning from the tenth century on, and there is a flowering of native literature, both prose and poetry, in the language, this does not appear to have been at the expense of Latin. Irish schools in the twelfth century give every appearance of having been thoroughly at home still in the traditional language of the church, and to have enjoyed a continuity of teaching in that language right through from the earlier centuries. In other words, there is a conservatism in the writings of Irish scholars in the eleventh century alongside a striking originality. The Fland Mainistrech of Monasterboice referred to above, for instance, composed a series of poems in Irish on Ulster kings and another on 'world kingship', the former set based naturally on native Irish materials, the latter on ecclesiastical sources such as Jerome's *Chronicle* and the *Historia contra Paganos* of Orosius. However, the best example of such a scholar is Marianus Scottus (Móelbrigte). Born in 1028, from 1052 he was a monk of Moville (Co. Down), but as a result of a minor breach of discipline he was banished in 1056 from Ireland, and he eventually found himself in Mainz in Germany, where he died in 1082. Marianus's interests were not so much in native Irish literature as in biblical studies, and particularly technical chronology or computus, of which he was a master. We are fortunate to have a partly autograph manuscript of his (Vatican, Cod. Pal.-Lat. 830) containing a collection of computistical tracts that are the same as those that were being read in Irish schools in the sixth and seventh centuries. More importantly, however, this Vatican manuscript preserves the original text of Marianus's *Chronicle*, consisting of a prologue and three books of 'world history', from Creation down to his own time, the work for which he is most famous, and which served as a model for such eminent English and continental chroniclers as Florence of Worcester and Sigibert of Gembloux, amongst others. Scattered throughout the manuscript, however, are marginal additions in the vernacular, some relating to Irish political history (a king-list, for example, the oldest we have), some to biblical apocrypha, some prayers in Irish, and other miscellaneous matter. Amongst the marginalia entered in Marianus' manuscript are records of the deaths of two Scottish kings, Mac Bethad mac Finlaeg in 1057 (i.e. Shakespeare's Macbeth), and Lulach in 1058, as well as the succession of a third, Móel Coluim, in that same year. The Scottish interest doubtless was due to the fact that one of Marianus's helpers had himself come in 1072 to Germany from Scotland *in peregrinitate* ('in exile'). He had written the manuscript, he said, 'out of friendship for you [= Marianus] and for all the *Scotti*, that is Irishmen, for I am myself an Irishman' (*quia sum ipse Hibernensis*). It is by such channels that Irish manuscripts made their way to Scotland in the eleventh and twelfth centuries, and doubtless by the same route Pictish king-lists made their way to Ireland.

Wales and Ireland

In England, at every point, it is clear that the course of the ecclesiastical revival hung on the king's nod, and its progress was entirely dependent on influence at court. The same could doubtless be said of Ireland too, where ecclesiastical matters are concerned, but since reform is conspicuously absent in the ninth and tenth centuries—the *Céli Dé* hardly count as anything more than a group of fervent ascetics, who left no programmatic statement of their reformist aims (if they had any)—then the obvious upsurge in writing (particularly historical writing) in Ireland can hardly be ascribed to the enthusiasm of pious kings. Ecclesiastical reform, when it did come in the twelfth century, seems to have produced no related literature of note. In Wales, on the other hand, the revival of law in particular is ascribed explicitly to the work of one man, Hywel ap Cadell, known as Hywel Dda ('Hywel the Good'), king first of Dyfed then of more extensive parts of Wales, until his death in 949 or 950. A conscious imitation of Alfred the Great's example has not been ruled out; as Englishmen like to see in Alfred the perfect paragon of a philospher king, so Welshmen too like to believe that Hywel really did initiate the revision and codification of Welsh law that bears his name. Whatever his contribution may have been, unfortunately, is buried in the later codebooks of Welsh law. In fact, apart from the memoranda in the Lichfield Gospels (mentioned above), and some mixed material in the Book of Llandaff, there is no contemporary written legal material that can be safely ascribed to the period before 1100.

The same applies, by the same token, to literary compositions. It is rare for texts in any medieval vernacular language to come down with their author's name intact (and Welsh is no exception), but a case has been made for attributing the Welsh tale 'Branwen daughter of Llyr'—and the Four Branches of the *Mabinogi* as a whole—to Rhigyfarch of Llanbadarn Fawr, or to his father Sulien, or to the two in collaboration. An alternative proposal, that the Four Branches were in fact the composition of a woman, Gwenllian, daughter of the prince of Gwynedd and wife of the prince of Dyfed who died in 1136, has found little favour (the most recent discussion has suggested dates ranging c.1050 × 1120, with one estimate putting it as late as c.1190).

That said, the importance of Sulien (1011–91), bishop of St Davids in the late eleventh century, and his family of sons for the cultural history of Wales at the close of our period is firmly based on solid knowledge. The contemporary Welsh chronicle *Brut y Tywysogion* ('Chronicle of the princes') described him on his death as 'the most learned and most pious of the bishops of the Britons, and the most praiseworthy for the instruction of his disciples and his parishes'. Two of his four sons, Ieuan (d. 1137) and Rhigyfarch (d. 1099)—for whose education Sulien was personally responsible—produced very creditable Latin compositions, but unfortunately, none of Sulien's own writings has come down to us. The school of Llanbadarn Fawr, where Sulien taught before being raised to the bishopric of St Davids, seems to have boasted a considerable library of Latin classical and post-classical authors. It was not the only one, however: the monastery of Llan-gors has been suggested as the likely place of origin for the Llywarch Hen cycle of poetry. The Llywarch Hen poems and much of the Welsh *englynion* material would fit neatly into this period of our discussion. The question then naturally arises: where did Sulien and his sons acquire their familiarity with these works? It is known from the poem by Ieuan on the life and family of his father (*Carmen de Uita et Familia Sulgeni*) that Sulien had, in fact, spent ten years in Ireland receiving instruction (and before that five years in Scotland—*Albania*—where, presumably, the instruction was along Irish lines). Besides their literary compositions, two decorated manuscripts intimately associated with the same two brothers have survived: the Psalter and Martyrology of Rhigyfarch (Dublin, TCD, MS. 50) (see Fig. 5.1) and a manuscript of Augustine's *De Trinitate* (Cambridge, CCCC 199), written and illuminated by Ieuan. These are the only two extensively illuminated early medieval manuscripts of known Welsh origin; the fact that they can be so closely dated, therefore, and their owners identified, makes them especially valuable witnesses to the level of learning and letters in late eleventh-century Wales. It is significant, therefore, that the decoration in both manuscripts is characteristically Irish in execution, so much so, in fact, that the style has been seen as directly redolent of Sulien's period in Ireland (c.1040–55), though more recent study has suggested that the decoration may owe more than was previously thought to earlier

Welsh traditions of manuscript illumination, as well as showing features of decoration which could have been shared by Ireland, Scotland, and Wales, and even traces of Anglo-Saxon influence as well. The Irish Sea province in the eleventh century was still a vibrant region of cultural contact and exchange between all the indigenous population groups of these islands. Sadly, one of Rhigyfarch's poems, the *Planctus* ('Lament'), on the ravages wrought by the Norman invasion of Wales, composed probably in 1094–5, not long before his death in 1099 at the relatively early age of 42 or 43 (his father Sulien died in his eightieth year in 1091), signals a change in the political climate in Wales which was in large measure to act as harbinger for developments everywhere in Britain and Ireland. The Norman conquest of Wales, as of England, marked a decisive turning point in the progress of insular culture, since after that time indigenous traditions of learning were replaced by continental tradition, and the poetry of (say) Gerald of Wales could scarcely be taken to represent indigenous Welsh-Latin learning. The same goes for England, Ireland, and Scotland, and after 1100 the writings of all four countries in these islands could be said to have shifted decisively from the paths that they had followed more or less in tandem for the previous 500 years.

Figure 7.0 William the Conqueror's great tower at Colchester Castle, now shorn of its top storey, but in area (110 by 151 ft) one third as large again as London's White Tower. A monument to Norman triumphalism, built on a site associated with the legendary British King Cole, and enclosing the podium of the Roman Temple of Claudius. Courtesy Anthony Kersting.

Britain, Ireland, and the South

John Gillingham

During the ninth, tenth, and early eleventh centuries, Britain and Ireland, two islands on the north-western edge of the known world, had not been much affected by contacts with continental European powers and cultures—much less so than in the seventh and eighth centuries. Merchants and pilgrims had always ensured that the populations of Britain and Ireland had not remained entirely impervious to the ideas and tastes of peoples living in mainland Europe and the Mediterranean region; such ideas had, for example, contributed to the attempts at monastic reform in mid-tenth-century England. Except, however, in Kent and London where commercial and cultural links with Flanders were close, influences from the south were slight when compared with the impact made by traders, settlers, and rulers coming from Scandinavia. From the 1040s onwards this was to change. A rapid intensification of relations—political, commercial, intellectual, and artistic—with the continent had transformed political and ecclesiastical culture in England by 1100 (Fig. 7.1). This 'process of Europeanization' had, however, barely begun to impinge on the Celtic societies of Britain and Ireland.

After 1066 French-style castles and Romanesque churches were erected on such a prodigious scale that the mark on the English landscape can still be seen today. Indeed England in 1100 has been described by Eric Fernie as 'a vast building site'. Significant developments had preceded the Norman Conquest. Edward the Confessor's Norman-style Westminster Abbey was, with the exception of the cathedral of the Salian emperors at Speyer, the largest church built

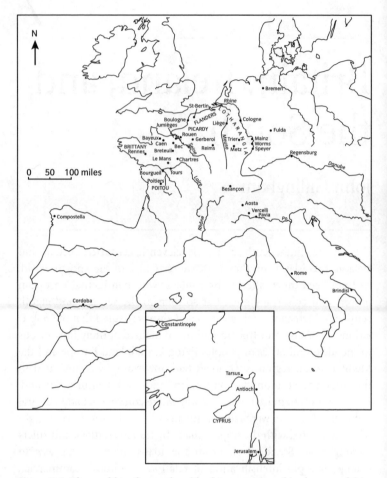

Figure 7.1 The world to the south, with places mentioned in the text of this chapter.

north of the Alps since the fourth century. Edward's French tastes are a well-known and obvious consequence of his prolonged exile in Normandy, but connections with and influences from other parts of continental Europe also mattered. Edward's is the first English royal seal to survive; the image of the king in majesty, enthroned with orb and sceptre, was borrowed from German models. A number of Flemish authors such as the hagiographer Goscelin of Saint-Bertin and the anonymous authors of the *Encomium Emmae* and the *Vita Ædwardi* spearheaded a revival of Latin letters. Robert of Lotharingia, bishop of Hereford (1079–95), brought to England a world chronicle written at Mainz by an Irish monk, Marianus Scottus, and John of Worcester then composed a continuation. This new writing marks an early stage of the Europe-wide cultural movement for which the term 'Twelfth-Century Renaissance' is a convenient shorthand.

There were three other momentous developments which once again brought these islands back into the Mediterranean and continental orbit which had been so dominant in the early centuries of Roman Christianity. In chronological order they were: the Gregorian Reform Movement, the Norman Conquest of England, and the First Crusade. These three developments affected the different parts of Britain and Ireland in different ways and at different speeds. It has been argued (by Robin Frame) that 'wealthy regions close to centres of learning and ruled by a strong unitary kingship were more likely to be receptive . . . than upland areas ruled by a collection of competing minor dynasties'. Certainly by 1100 only the kingdom of England had been transformed, though the importance and power of these currents from the south is plain from the fact that by 1200 Scotland, Ireland, and Wales had also been deeply affected by them.

Reform

England

1049 In this year was the great synod at Rheims; there was there: the pope Leo, and the archbishop of Burgundy, and the archbishop of Besançon, and the archbishop of Trier, and the archbishop of Rheims, and many more men, both ordained and lay. And King Edward sent there Bishop Duduc and Wulfric abbot of St Augustine's and Abbot Ælfwine, that they should report to the king what was decided for Christendom.

With these words the *Anglo-Saxon Chronicle* reports the council at which Leo IX launched a spectacular attack on ecclesiastical abuses— all the more theatrical for the fact that it was 300 years since a pope had last been seen north of the Alps. In 1050 Bishops Herman of Ramsbury and Ealdred of Worcester attended Leo's council at Rome, and Bishop Ulf of Dorchester attended another at Vercelli. A group of radical reformers, many of them—like Leo himself—coming from Lotharingia, had established itself at the papal court. They argued that priests should be sexually 'pure' and that prelates should not, as in the past, be appointed by laymen but instead should be 'freely' chosen by other churchmen. Like nearly everyone else at the time, the bishops from England no doubt regarded these assaults on long-held assumptions about sex, power, and property as unrealistic; on the other hand there were aspects of the Roman model which seemed eminently practical, the expectation, for example, that a bishop's cathedral would be sited in a town. In 1050 Bishop Leofric moved his see from Crediton to Exeter. Then Herman moved his cathedral from Ramsbury to Sherborne. There followed a series of moves which, together with the creation of two new sees at Ely (1109) and Carlisle (1133), resulted in a diocesan structure that lasted until the Reformation.

The greater English receptiveness may in part reflect a deep tradition, Bede's view of the English church as the special child of the papacy, but if so it was a tradition which had lain dormant since the eighth century. Its reactivation now may well have been due to the fact that in England—unlike Ireland, Scotland, and Wales—there were high-ranking clergy who had been educated on the continent. Cnut's pilgrimage to Rome in 1025 signalled a renewal of those continental cultural contacts. Duduc, the bishop of Wells who was sent to the 1049 council of Rheims, was a learned Saxon appointed by Cnut in 1033. Ulf was one of the Normans who came to England with Edward the Confessor. Herman of Ramsbury/Sherborne was a Lotharingian. The highly cultivated Cornishman Leofric of Crediton/Exeter had been brought up in Lotharingia; as bishop he reorganized his chapter according to the Rule of St Chrodegang of Metz. King Edward's promotions to the episcopal bench included two more Lotharingians and another Norman. Harold Godwinesson chose a Lotharingian, Adelard of Liège, as the head of his foundation at Waltham Abbey. As well as attending the Rome synod in 1050, the Englishman Ealdred of Worcester went on an embassy to Germany in 1054, spending nearly a year in Cologne; in 1058 he went to Jerusalem where, according to the *Anglo-Saxon Chronicle*, 'he offered a worthy gift for our Lord's tomb, a golden chalice of wonderful workmanship worth five marks'. In 1061 he travelled to Rome again in order to obtain his pallium as archbishop of York. Pope Nicholas II, taking his stand on canonical injunctions against pluralism, refused to give it to him until he had resigned Worcester, and when Ealdred returned to England in 1062 he was accompanied by two legates who oversaw the choice of Wulfstan as his successor at Worcester—papal intervention in English church appointments unparalleled since the eighth century.

In England then the papal reform movement had made itself heard well before 1066; none the less the pace of change was forced as a consequence of the Norman Conquest. William had obtained papal approval for his claim to the English throne. He knew how to use the papacy for his own ends, and was prepared to pay a price—though never to the extent of allowing any of his clergy to attend papal councils. In 1070 papal legates removed from office those English prelates whose loyalty William distrusted, at their head the all too influential Stigand who, by holding simultaneously the two richest sees, Canterbury and Winchester, had made unacceptable in reformers' eyes both his own position and the image of the English church in general. The legates held a council at Winchester before returning to Normandy where they helped persuade Lanfranc, abbot of St Stephen's, Caen, to become archbishop of Canterbury (1070–89). A monk of Bec and a scholar with a Europe-wide reputation, in the forefront of theological and philosophical debate in the Christian West, Lanfranc of Pavia was the most distinguished man to hold Canterbury since Theodore of Tarsus. In the opinion of Gilbert Crispin, Norman abbot of Westminster, Lanfranc revived *Latinitas*.

Lanfranc's aim was the monastic one of holding the entanglements of the world at bay, prohibiting simony and banning the clergy from participation in such activities as hunting, carrying arms, gaming, and—for the upper clergy above all—sex and marriage. He also wanted to regulate sex in the secular world. In 1075 he prohibited marriage within seven degrees (as calculated by Cardinal Peter Damiani) of kinship; in 1076 he decreed that no marriage should take place without a priest's blessing. It was not that monkish ambitions of this sort were entirely new ones. The idealistic monk Archbishop Wulfstan of York had responded to the early eleventh-century crisis of English defeat by calling for similar restraint. But his voice, though powerful, had been an isolated one. New in the 1070s was the sense of an orchestrated campaign, conducted from Canterbury, playing selected works from a programme composed in Rome—a programme which was itself driven forward with greater intensity after the election of the Roman monk Hildebrand as Pope Gregory VII in

1073. In summoning general councils of the English church with unprecedented frequency, Lanfranc was following where both popes and archbishops of Rouen had led since the 1040s. In 1072, with the aim of promoting ecclesiastical discipline, he ordered bishops to appoint first archdeacons—again following Norman practice—and then rural deans. Neither William I nor Lanfranc, however, had any intention of accepting the whole Gregorian programme. William, while agreeing to pay arrears of Peter's Pence, rejected Gregory's demand for tribute. Despite this partial rebuff, Gregory was right to recognize in William a king who was remarkably supportive of the clerical purity campaign. Not since the seventh century had there been so close a relationship between the papal curia and the English church.

Another of Lanfranc's achievements was to compile a new canon law collection. Although the *Penitential* composed by Wulfstan of York had begun with the words 'These are the customs which are observed across the sea', neither his outlook nor Cnut's German connections had resulted in the modern *Decretum* of Burchard of Worms being imported. Existing English canonical collections were of Carolingian provenance, regarded by eleventh-century continental scholars as thoroughly old-fashioned. Yet such was the accelerating interchange of ideas and scholars in the late eleventh century that Lanfranc's new collection was itself soon superseded by another, the *Panormia* (1095) of Ivo of Chartres. The new canon law elaborated conceptions of ecclesiastical jurisdiction and hierarchy, giving greater weight to the papacy's juridical supremacy within the church and, at the next rung, to the authority of metropolitans over bishops in their province. The latter certainly appealed to Lanfranc. He was the first archbishop to insist on receiving written professions of obedience from the bishops whom he consecrated. He developed the notion of Canterbury as the primate of all Britain, inevitably provoking a quarrel with York, and also, in his own eyes at least, reinforcing Canterbury's claim to be the conduit through which reform ideas were transmitted to the Celtic churches.

William II's misguided choice of Anselm of Aosta, abbot of Bec, as Lanfranc's successor in 1093 set a pattern for monk-archbishops of Canterbury that was not to be broken until the appointment of Thomas Becket in 1162. A greater theologian and philosopher even than Lanfranc, it is a measure of his standing in the wider world that at the papal curia he was asked to expound the doctrine of the Latin church at a meeting with representatives of the Greek church. Anselm took the idea of papal supremacy very seriously indeed. After some disagreements with Rufus—for to monks who equated long hair with effeminacy, the fashions, manners, and morals of the royal court were anathema—the king summoned him to a council at Rockingham in 1095 in the expectation of reaching a settlement. Instead Anselm announced that only the pope could settle the matter, for it was to the pope as the successor to St Peter, and not to any king or emperor, that Christ had given the keys of heaven. Anselm's stance came as a shock. When he had accepted Canterbury from Rufus, he had done homage, just like all bishops and abbots who held their estates from the king. Not surprisingly the other bishops of England told Anselm he was on his own. In 1097 he chose exile. At Easter 1099 he heard Pope Urban II issue decrees excommunicating all clergy who did homage to laymen and all who participated in lay investiture. When he returned to England in 1100, invited back by Henry I anxious to give a semblance of legitimacy to his sudden succession to the throne, Anselm brought with him this papal agenda, and challenged royal control of the church in England in ways that no king could—or indeed did— tolerate. Nonetheless the link between England and the papacy which had been forged by Lanfranc and Anselm grew stronger over the next two centuries. English representatives attended most twelfth- and thirteenth-century papal councils to which they were summoned. Moreover Anselm was allowed to summon a general council of the English church to London in 1102. He decreed that men should keep their hair short and ordered priests, deacons, and canons to put away their wives; he prohibited sons from inheriting their fathers' churches. Two Italian-born monk-archbishops of Canterbury had begun the radical attempt to overthrow the habits of centuries by abolishing both the family life of the clergy and lay control of the church. The campaign for clerical celibacy would have to be waged for many generations before it achieved even a measure of success; government control of appointments to the church would never be seriously weakened.

Wales, Scotland, and Ireland

None of the extant Irish or Welsh sources so much as mentions Leo IX at Rheims. This is not to say that there was no contact with the papal church. On the contrary the desire felt by some to pray at the tombs of saints and martyrs remained strong. Several Irish kings went on pilgrimage to Rome in the early to mid-eleventh century. So too did Macbeth, king of Scots (though this was reported only by Marianus Scottus), and Thorfinn the Mighty, earl of Orkney. Earl Thorfinn's pilgrimage probably lay behind the papal order, reported by the German historian Adam of Bremen, that Archbishop Adalbert of Hamburg-Bremen should send a bishop to the Orkneys—an order which fitted beautifully with that archbishop's own wide-ranging ambitions. But only in the case of Ireland—and only right at the end of the century—is there any indication that the reform movement was beginning to have any impact at all on the internal affairs of the Celtic or Scandinavian churches.

No sooner, it seems, had Gregory VII been consecrated pope in 1073 than he wrote to Toirdelbach Ua Briain and the Irish prelates offering them papal help should they be facing any difficulties. The kind of difficulty he had in mind is presumably indicated by a letter he wrote to Lanfranc at about the same time, urging him to reform, particularly in matters of marriage, not only those sinners living 'in the island of the English', but also the Irish. Given Lanfranc's contacts with Rome, it is not surprising that Gregory VII should think of Canterbury and the English church as a channel through which ideas of reform might reach Ireland, Scotland, or Wales. Indeed Gregory's letter to the Irish survives only in a Worcester manuscript. Moreover the earliest members of the Irish clergy known to wish to conform to the norms of the new eleventh-century canon law were Irish monks in English Benedictine houses. For such people one difficulty was the absence of a canonically consecrated metropolitan in Ireland. When Gilla Pátraic, a monk at Worcester, was chosen as bishop of Dublin in 1074 he asked Lanfranc to consecrate him. The surviving correspondence suggests that Gofraidh, king of Dublin and the Isles, as well as his then overlord, Toirdelbach Ua Briain of Munster, were—to say the least—closely involved in the choice of Gilla Pátraic. Probably the Irish and Lanfranc had both responded to Pope Gregory's urging. Moreover the kings evidently had no objection to Gilla Pátraic's approaching Lanfranc. In 1085 Patrick's successor as Dublin's bishop, Donngus, an Irish monk of Christ Church Canterbury, was also consecrated by Lanfranc. In 1093 Anselm wrote to the bishops of Ireland, suggesting that on matters of canon law they should consult him 'rather than fall under God's judgment as transgressors of his commandments'. In 1096 he consecrated two more Irish bishops: Samuel, a former monk of St Albans, as bishop of Dublin, and Malchus, a monk of Winchester, as bishop of Waterford. The professions of obedience of all these bishops were recorded in a Canterbury list— but for how long Irish bishops would want, or be allowed, to remain subordinate to Canterbury was an open question. Certainly Anselm was soon to be troubled by reports that the bishop of Dublin was acting as though he were an archbishop.

Malchus of Waterford was to be a key figure in the reform and reorganization of the Irish church; in 1111 he became the first archbishop of Cashel and was subsequently a supporter of the Cistercian Malachy. Meanwhile he remained in touch with Anselm. When the latter was in exile at the papal court, Malchus asked him for copies of his latest works. Precisely when it was decided to appoint a papal legate to Ireland is not known, but by 1101, the first such legate, Maol Muire Ua Dunain, chief bishop of Munster, had been appointed. If Gregory VII had seen Canterbury as an avenue of approach to Ireland, Anselm's quarrel with William II no doubt helped the papacy to prefer direct contact. As legate, Maol Muire Ua Dunain, together with Muirchertach Ua Briain, presided over a reform council held at Cashel. Like such councils elsewhere it focused on simony, clerical celibacy, and clerical immunity from secular exactions. Moreover Muirchertach's grant, also in 1101, of the Rock of Cashel to the clergy in perpetuity was an impressive demonstration of an ambitious ruler's piety.

The absence of Scottish sources means we know very little about the eleventh-century Scottish church. A letter of Lanfranc's tells us that the learned Queen Margaret of Scotland had written to him asking to be looked upon as his spiritual daughter. In his reply he informed her that he was sending three monks to her and to King Malcolm 'to do what ought to be done in God's service and yours' and asked her 'resolutely to endeavour to complete what you have begun for God and for your souls'. The outcome of this initiative was probably the foundation of a Canterbury priory at Dunfermline, the first 'regular' Benedictine house in the Scottish kingdom. Margaret had been educated in the German-dominated Hungarian court, but she was of English royal descent and only English sources report what she tried to do. Her biographer Turgot, prior of Durham (and from 1109 bishop of St Andrews), emphasized her role in summoning councils and in persuading the Scottish clergy to adopt her views in matters of Sunday observance, customs at mass, especially at Easter, and in the method of calculating the date of Lent. Here, it was a question of uniformity of liturgical observance, of conformity to what Turgot called 'the universal custom of holy church' rather than of Gregorian reform in the sense of attacks on simony and clerical marriage. But in the kingdom of the Scots it may well have appeared that it was the custom of England that was being imposed. According to Turgot, at these councils she spoke in English and her words were translated into Scottish (i.e. Gaelic) by Malcolm who had himself learned English while in exile. There is an English attitude of superiority in the Anglo-Saxon Chronicler's comment that she helped her husband 'and his people to turn to a better way and lay aside the evil customs which that nation had earlier followed'. It is not surprising that after the deaths of the king and queen in 1093 there should be an anti-English and anti-French reaction in Scotland to which dislike of unfamiliar southern impositions may well have contributed.

The church in eleventh-century Wales has been judged to have been archaic, backward looking, and probably more isolated on the eve of the Norman onslaught than in earlier centuries—this despite the claim in an eleventh-century Welsh poem that the holy power of Cyrwen, the pastoral staff of St Padarn, reached 'the limits of three continents'. Apart from the appointment of archdeacons and a fashion for English names among the clergy of south Wales—there was, for example, a bishop of Llandaff with the English name of Herewald—there is little evidence of any desire on the part of the Welsh to abandon their traditional ways in favour of the ideas being touted by reformers from continental Europe. The Normans imposed a Breton, Hervé, as bishop at Bangor in 1092, and Anselm began his archiepiscopate in 1093 by announcing that he had suspended the bishops of St Davids and Llandaff. However Canterbury's authority over Welsh churches existed only in the minds of archbishops, so whether or not anything came of these initiatives would depend upon military and political power on the ground. A Welsh fight-back in both north and south beginning in late 1093 led to Hervé being driven out, and the bishops reinstated. Not until 1107 when Anselm consecrated Urban to Llandaff was an archbishop of Canterbury able to repeat in Wales what he had begun more than thirty years earlier in Ireland.

Several factors help to explain the Irish church's greater receptiveness to reform. It must be significant that Norman armies invaded Wales and Scotland but not Ireland. Both William I and William II were said to have contemplated invading Ireland, the latter allegedly toying with the idea of building a bridge of boats from Wales. Continental involvements meant that neither did anything of the sort. There is no evidence of the presence of Welsh or Scottish clergy in English churches, whereas Irish monks trained in England had clearly played an important intermediary role. It is also noticeable that the churches of Dublin and Waterford were in the forefront of this movement. Although as time went by the people of the two closely connected ports of Dublin and Waterford, the Ostmen, were no doubt becoming increasingly Irish, they were still referred to as 'foreigners' in Irish annals. There was a more outward-looking culture in these two towns, the most important ports of Ireland, than in the rest of the island. Particularly important were the commercial links between them and Bristol, the chief seaport for the diocese of Worcester, and a place where Wulfstan, the saintly bishop of Worcester, often preached against the slave trade with Ireland. In one of Bishop Patrick's poems he recalls 'the dear home of Bishop Wulfstan'. The 1074 conjunction of an Irish Worcester monk being chosen as bishop of a Hiberno-Scandinavian seaport ruled by a king, Gofraidh, who also ruled the Isle of the Man and the Isles points to a vigorous Irish Sea culture contributing to reform. The fact that these initiatives were supported by the Ua Briain overlords of Dublin suggests that the most ambitious Irish kings of the late eleventh century were aware of both the new currents in the wider church and the prestige which accrued to William the Conqueror from his support for Lanfranc. In eleventh-century Scotland and Wales only Whithorn remotely approached Dublin and Waterford in importance.

Norman Conquest

English contacts with Gaul had been maintained for centuries. Diplomatic relations with ducal Normandy had been close since Æthelred married Richard II's sister Emma in 1002. But it was only with the accession of the half-Norman, French-educated Edward the Confessor in 1042 that the Norman connection came to matter in internal English affairs. In 1051 the Norman group at Edward's court outmanoeuvred Earl Godwine and his sons and drove them into exile. Only a year later the exiles returned in force and most of the Normans fled, generally back to Normandy, though Osbern Pentecost and Hugh went to Macbeth in Scotland. According to the *Anglo-Saxon Chronicle* the political struggles of 1051–2 brought men to realize that 'there was little of value except English men on either side'—an insight which was sealed at a meeting of the council which 'outlawed all the French men who earlier promoted illegality and passed unjust judgments and counselled bad counsel'. A few of the French were allowed to stay or return, as in the case of Bishop William of London (1051–75), but political rivalry during the rest of Edward's reign was between the houses of Godwine and Leofric, not between English and Norman.

Hence, and in marked contrast to Cnut's conquest which had reinforced trends apparent since the ninth century, the effect of the Norman Conquest was an abrupt and massive intensification of a recent trend. Moreover although an immediate effect of both conquests was a vast dispersal of English wealth abroad, in other crucial respects the two conquests had very different outcomes. A high proportion of the English aristocracy managed to survive the slaughter of the Danish conquest and was able to come to terms with the new regime. In contrast, as Domesday Book makes plain, by 1086 there were very few English lords. By 1100 not a single bishopric or major abbey was ruled by an Englishman. In the north of England it was not only the elite who had suffered. Here prolonged resistance had provoked William to a systematic harrying which amounted to massacre by famine, and reports of murder and cannibalism reaching Marianus Scottus at Mainz. Not all the new lords and prelates were Normans, but all were men who came from the south, among them

Bretons, Flemings, Poitevins, and Lotharingians. The Domesday Book entry for Shrewsbury tells a story that must have been replayed in many towns: 'The English burgesses of Shrewsbury state that it is very hard that they pay as much tax as they paid before 1066'. They claimed that of the 252 properties on which tax had been paid TRE (in the time of Edward the Confessor), 193 no longer contributed. Among the non-contributing properties were 51 demolished to make room for the earl's castle and 43 held by French burgesses. From the point of view of the elite in town and country the Norman Conquest was the greatest disaster so far in the entire course of English history. An entirely new French political order had taken over the kingdom by force—despite the fact that, as William of Poitiers, an author attached to the new king's headquarters staff, noted, 'the dearest wish of the English was to have no ruler who was not a fellow countryman'.

The organized wealth of southern England was in the hands of the conquerors and they celebrated their triumph in stone. Architectural reminiscences of the Danish conquest and rule are non-existent. By contrast nowhere else in Latin Christendom was so much built in so short a time as in England in the decades after 1066. New royal and aristocratic castles were dominated by distinctively French design features such as great towers and mottes. The old cathedral and monastic churches were demolished and entirely new ones were built in a new style, influenced by models from the German Rhineland as well as France (Fig. 7.2). St Albans, Winchester, York, Ely, Bury, and Durham were all bigger than the Confessor's Westminster Abbey. Secular buildings too, such as the Tower of London and Colchester Castle (Fig. 7.0) or Rufus's Westminster Hall were built on an imperial scale. Colchester, Winchester Cathedral, and Westminster Hall were the largest buildings of their kind to be erected in northern Europe since the fall of Rome. South and east of a line from Newcastle to Chester almost every city, town, and village had been touched, and sometimes massively so, by this unprecedented building boom. In town after town whole quarters were demolished to make room for the royal castles which represented both the extent to which towns were already central to England's political structure and William's determination to control that structure (Fig. 7.3). Built by English labour, paid for by English taxes and dues, lived in by Frenchmen, these were the monuments of a deeply divided society. Although in the 1090s the English author of the *Anglo-Saxon Chronicle* felt able to

Figure 7.2 Cathedrals and major abbey chuches built, 1050–1100. During this period no churches on this scale were built anywhere west or north of the areas shown. Here the south and east of England, together with the Severn and Thames valleys, are prominent.

refer to Rufus as 'our king', the continuing exclusion of the English from the high office to which they felt their birth or talents qualified them still rankled.

But north and west it was a different story. Towns and villages were few and far between. What was newly built in the later eleventh century was built in entirely traditional ways; buildings remained small, indeed minuscule compared with some of the monsters in England. In 1120 Urban of Llandaff claimed that his cathedral church was no more than 40 feet long and 15 feet wide. The old settlement patterns remained in place, and so did the old rulers. A sharp faultline now ran diagonally across Britain. West and north of that line sub-

Figure 7.3 Important Norman castles built by 1100. The grip of royal castles is noticeably weaker in the west and north.

jects and rulers spoke the same languages. South and east, subjects spoke English and their rulers spoke French (which they called 'Roman').

The myth of feudalism

Long before 1066 English political society was focused on forms of lordship in which many of a lord's dependants were also his tenants, paying rent in many forms, including obligations to provide all sorts of service, including military service. After 1066 French lords from the king downwards wielded greater power over their French and English tenants than had their English and Anglo-Scandinavian predecessors. But this was not because the conquerors introduced

Norman or French customs previously unknown in 'pre-feudal' England. It was rather that the military circumstances of the Conquest and the opportunities for an entirely new landholding class generated by the elimination of the former elite resulted in a tightening of the bonds of lordship to a degree which was even more foreign to France (including Normandy) than it was to England. The gradual spread after 1066 of a tenurial vocabulary in which the word *feudum* was prominent marked a terminological shift, not significant social change. The notion that the Normans introduced a new framework of lordship, the 'feudal system' or 'feudalism', is a myth which emerged in the seventeenth century in association with the then highly politicized idea of 'the Norman yoke'.

In the generation after 1066 far more Frenchmen married English women than had ever been the case before. One curious consequence of this seems to be the widely held nineteenth- and twentieth-century notion of another 'Norman yoke' putting an end to an Anglo-Saxon 'Golden Age' for the property rights of women. In the scramble by the victors for property in a defeated country, it was worth trying any claim to gain an edge over rivals, and one was to claim that the property in question had been lawfully held by one's wife. Whether women had really possessed as much land TRE as the Domesday commissioners were told they had held is another matter.

Scotland, Wales, and the Normans

Concentration of English wealth into few hands not only allowed the new French lords to build on a gargantuan scale, it also allowed them to drive further into north and west Britain than any previous rulers of England. At this stage of economic development a conquest of Scotland or Wales in the manner of the Norman conquest of England was ruled out by the absence of towns there and the logistical problems involved in maintaining armies for long periods in relatively thinly populated regions. So far as the Norman kings were concerned it could only be a question of overlordship, of reprisals against Scottish and Welsh raids, and, perhaps, the exaction of tribute from subordinate kings. Malcolm posed a real threat to William. The survivors of the English royal dynasty, led by Edgar the Atheling, fled to Malcolm's court in 1068. Malcolm's marriage to Edgar's sister Margaret gave the many other noble northern English refugees in Scotland reason to hope for military assistance from a king who had already raided Northumbria in 1061 and 1070. In 1072 William reacted. While his fleet blockaded the eastern estuaries, William took an army over the Forth. At Abernethy Malcolm gave hostages, including his eldest son, presumably promising to launch no further raids.

Northumbria, like Wales, Ireland, and the Irish Sea, remained a zone where military and political power fluctuated wildly and where outside forces, Normans, Scots, and Scandinavians, often intervened with dramatic effect. Malcolm raided again in 1079 and 1091 provoking Norman counter-raids in 1080 (by Robert Curthose who on his return south built a new castle on the north bank of the Tyne) and in 1091. According to William of Malmesbury (c.1120), Malcolm carried off so many captives that there was still no Scottish household without its English slave woman. But his fifth great raid ended with his, and his son Edward's, death near Alnwick in 1093. This precipitated a three-cornered struggle for power in Scotland between his brother Donald Ban and two of his sons: Duncan (a hostage in England since 1072, and the Norman candidate) and Edmund, a son by Margaret. In this struggle one important factor was the resentment felt by some Scots towards both English and French. In 1097 Anglo-Norman power was decisive, defeating Donald Ban, and putting Edgar, another son of Malcolm and Margaret, on the throne as William II's client king. Client kings tended not to stay clients for long. But, as it happened, Edgar's accession was followed by a generation of peace on the Anglo-Scottish border as a result of the marriage of Henry I in 1100 to Edith/Matilda, sister of successive Scottish kings.

More significant for the future was an event in 1092. Rufus took Carlisle from the Scots, built a castle, and then, in the words of the *Anglo-Saxon Chronicle*, 'afterwards returned south here and sent very many farmers there with wives and livestock to live there and cultivate the land'. Demographic growth and economic development allowed the quest for overlordship and tribute to be replaced by a policy of conquest accompanied by settlement and further economic development. The twelfth-century Scottish kingdom was powerful enough to be able to contain the colonial expansion of English settlers, but not so Wales and Ireland.

In 1081 William went much further west than any previous king of England. According to the Welsh *Brut*, he went to St Davids to pray; according to the *Anglo-Saxon Chronicle* he 'freed many hundreds of men'. Presumably Rhys ap Tewdwr was brought to acknowledge William's overlordship. Coins in William's name were minted at St Davids and Domesday Book records that Rhys ap Tewdwr paid £40 a year for Deheubarth. According to the author of the *Brut* (who might have seen him pray at St Davids), by the time of his death William was 'prince of the Normans, king of the Saxons, Britons, and Scots'.

It was not the king but the marcher earls of Hereford, Shrewsbury, and Chester (William FitzOsbern, Roger of Montgomery, and Hugh of Avranches) who led the Norman onslaught on Wales. When Roger of Montgomery's son Arnulf captured Pembroke in 1093, he presumably came from the sea, but what, in military terms, struck the Welsh about the invaders was not their fleets but how well supplied they were with arms and armour, and how systematically they built and used castles. In the words of the twelfth-century Welsh *History of Gruffudd ap Cynan*, Earl Hugh 'built castles and strong places after the manner of the French, in Anglesey, at Caernarfon, Bangor, and Meirionydd. He placed in them horsemen and archers and they wrought such evil as had not been done since the beginning of the world.' The raids which Robert de Tilleul (or 'of Rhuddlan') launched across north Wales were so destructive of Welsh political structures that, according to Domesday Book, it was Robert who paid the annual render of £40 for the kingdom of Gwynedd. When Rhys ap Tewdwr was killed by the French in 1093, the *Brut*'s comment was: 'then fell the kingdom of the Britons ... the French came to Dyfed and Ceredigion and they fortified them with castles.' The most eloquent expression of what the *Brut* called 'French tyranny' came from the pen of Rhigyfarch:

> The people and the priest are despised
> By the word, heart, and deeds of the Frenchmen.
> They burden us with tribute and consume our possessions.
> One of them, however lowly, shakes a hundred natives
> With his command, and terrifies them with his look.

By 1100 a Welsh fight-back in the north had forced the Normans to withdraw to the line of the River Conwy. In part this retreat reflected the dramatic return to the Irish Sea of a force for long not seen here, the war-fleet of the king of Norway, overlord of the Orkneys and Western Isles (see above, p. 70–1). But in south Wales, despite some losses, the Normans still held Pembroke, Glamorgan, Brecknock, and

Gwynllŵg. After 1100 the Norman advance into south Wales was resumed. Behind the armies came the English settlers and the English inhabitants of new towns such as Monmouth, Chepstow, Cardiff, Abergavenny, Brecon, Builth, Carmarthen, Pembroke, and Swansea. By 1135 it seemed to one observer that the Normans had turned Wales into a 'second England'.

Crusade

In 1096 'at Easter there was a very great stir throughout all this nation and in many other nations through Urban who was called pope though he had nothing of the seat in Rome. And countless people, with women and children, set out because they wanted to war against heathen peoples' (*Anglo-Saxon Chronicle*). Although no extant Irish or Welsh source so much as mentions Urban II's call for an armed pilgrimage to Jerusalem, Britain, Scotland, and Ireland are among the countries listed by continental chroniclers trying to give an impression of the extraordinary scale of the response. Except for Lagmann, king of Man and the Western Isles, full of remorse for the sin of blinding and castrating his own brother, none of the rulers of Britain and Ireland were among those who took the cross. But Robert Curthose did, and among those who followed him were men with great estates in England such as William Percy and Eustace of Boulogne. Indeed English taxpayers contributed far more than they wanted to the 10,000 marks raised by William II so that Robert could go to Jerusalem and he could get his hands on Robert's duchy. In the crisis of the crusade from the siege of Antioch to the capture of Jerusalem, English ships and sailors brought vital supplies from Cyprus to the army. English ships were to operate in those waters again in 1102, 1107, and 1112. Edgar Atheling went there in 1101–2. One English pilgrim Saewulf wrote an account of his 1102 journey from Brindisi to the Holy Land and back to Constantinople. His narrative of storms, Saracens, and Greeks, his descriptions of sites linked with Helen and Paris as well as with Christ, vividly illustrate the wider world into which the English were now moving. The First Crusade came at a time when people in the West were becoming a little more familiar with the Mediterranean. In the early 1090s a Canterbury monk on his way back from Jerusalem was helped by some of the

English in the Byzantine emperor's service when he tried to buy relics of St Andrew from the imperial chapel in Constantinople. By 1100 pilgrims from England joined those heading for Compostella. The English word 'cordwainer' derives via Latin/romance from Cordoba, famous for its high-quality leather; by William I's time there was a guild of cordwainers at Rouen, and by 1130 at Oxford. But it was not only England that felt some of these ripples from the Mediterranean. In 1105 Muirchertach Ua Briain was given a camel by Edgar, king of Scots.

Lay lords and lay culture

As everywhere in Europe, the lay lords throughout Britain and Ireland were warrior elites. In the north and west where towns and markets were few, plunder and tribute remained central to the circulation of wealth. But by the eleventh century England south of the Humber (or perhaps the Tyne) had already gone through the process of urbanization and monetization which has been aptly described by Rees Davies as the transition from 'an economy of plunder' to 'an economy of profiteering' (see above, pp. 79–82, 92–104).

Norman knights and castles

South of the Channel small-scale wars were routine continuations of local politics by other means. Castles were both the main bones of contention and the focal points around which the wars revolved. England before 1066 was different. Here an unusually centralized government kept the peace; hence there were very few castles—just one or two on the Welsh border. Although English lords continued to think of themselves as warriors, only those who lived on the Welsh and Scottish borders had much experience of war. In this sense the English were different not only from Celtic and Scandinavian aristocracies, but also from those who lived in France. The French author of *The Song of the Battle of Hastings* described the English as 'a people ignorant of war' and the French as 'well versed in stratagems, skilled in warfare'. In his sycophantic account of William I's deeds, William of Poitiers chose to portray the young duke not just as a model ruler but also as an accomplished knight. William's cavalry was capable of carrying out manoeuvres as risky as the feigned retreat—as at Hastings. In its possession of the crossbow, William's army was equipped with up-to-date military technology, and since missile weapons were much the best way to disrupt infantry drawn up in defensive formation (like the English at Hastings), it is not surprising that the earliest technological explanation for the Norman victory (offered by Henry of Huntingdon) was the French superiority in archery. In William's camp there were men who believed that a land without castles was virtually indefensible. Naturally he and his followers set about making their conquest defensible. By 1087 as many as 500 castles had been built. The English landscape began to look like the land south of the Channel.

Inevitably this had an impact on the lifestyle and political values of the ruling elite. William's seal, in representing a warrior on horseback on one side, differed from that used by Edward the Confessor. The earliest surviving example of a secular noble's seal, Ilbert de Lacy's of *c*.1090, imitated this military royal model. By 1075, as again in 1088, 1095, and 1101–2, Norman nobles were prepared to provision and garrison their castles in England and Wales as centres of rebellion against the king. The Norman introduction of the judicial duel, sometimes known as trial by battle, a standard component of the Carolingian judicial system, may also reflect these warrior values.

French chivalry

Where the dominance of the castle led to protracted campaigns with sieges usually ending with a negotiated surrender, it made sense for a convention to develop whereby the wealthy (those with negotiable assets) would be taken prisoner rather than—as so often before—be killed or mutilated. For the elite such a convention offered both the prospect of financial gain (ransom) and an insurance policy against the day when they were on the losing side. This chivalrous convention had become an established part of political life in France and Germany long before 1066. But political values in Anglo-Scandinavian England were different. Cnut engineered the destruction of the old royal kindred in the bloodbath of 1016–17. In 1036 the Atheling Alfred was fatally mutilated and many of his companions killed. As late as 1064 a Northumbrian noble, Gospatric, was killed at court, allegedly on the orders of Queen Edith. Both Norman apologists for the conquest, William of Jumièges and William of Poitiers, justified it as fitting retribution for the murderous cruelty of the Danish kings and their English helpers such as Earl Godwine and Harold Godwinesson. Even after the Conquest native English nobles continued to kill each other in ways the Normans found offensive, just as they also disapproved of the custom of decapitating dead enemies that was practised by both English and Celtic peoples.

The Norman Conquest ushered in a period when politics in England became a less bloody business for the leaders. The hanging of William de Alderie by Rufus in 1095 was the last time for 200 years that an aristocrat would suffer death for rebellion in England. Although twelfth-century kings of England branded many aristocratic rebels as traitors, they put none of them to death. In Maitland's words, 'for two centuries after the Conquest, the frank, open rebellions of the great folk were treated with a clemency which when we look back to it through the intervening ages of blood, seems wonderful'. Clemency indeed, according to William of Poitiers, was one of the conqueror's outstanding qualities. And up to a point it was. Ready to massacre thousands by famine in the Harrying of the North, he none the less, with one exception, punished the leaders of the English resistance by imprisonment, exile, and confiscation of their property, not by executing or mutilating them. The one exception was the beheading of Earl Waltheof in 1076 and in this case, wrote Orderic, English rather than Norman law was explicitly invoked.

The generosity of William I's treatment of Edgar Atheling is both remarkable and highly significant. By 1069 Edgar was old enough to head the English resistance. Yet in 1075, after years of fomenting rebellion, he was received at court. In 1097 he was given command of the Norman army which put Edgar on the Scottish throne. The freedom and power accorded the Atheling is extraordinary, and must have something to do with the Norman kings' assessment of his character. But the mere fact that he was not mutilated or killed when at William's mercy stands in contrast not only with Cnut's and Harthacnut's treatment of rivals to the throne, but with all earlier English practice.

There is a contrast too between the new French political style and that practised in Celtic Britain and Ireland. Between 1072 and 1081 no less than five members of the ruling dynasty of Deheubarth were put to death by their own kindred. In Ireland the mortality rates of royals were high. The *Annals of Innisfallen* report the killings of royals either treacherously or in battle in twenty out of the twenty-five years between 1076 and 1100. In the 1093–7 struggle for the Scottish throne Duncan was killed—allegedly by the treachery of his uncle Donald Ban and his half-brother Edmund. There are conflicting accounts of Donald's own fate. According to William of Malmesbury, he was killed by the cunning of his nephew David; according to later Scottish accounts he was merely blinded and imprisoned. Either way his blood was shed. In the Anglo-Norman realm too there were violent struggles for dominance within the ruling dynasty. Robert rebelled against his father and fought against him at Gerberoi in 1079; after 1087 the three brothers often took up arms against each other. But none of them was killed. When Robert was captured by his brother Henry in 1106 he was imprisoned, not killed or mutilated. Not even Henry felt able to keep a child, Robert's son William Clito, in prison, despite the foreseeable problems which would—and did—arise when the boy grew up. When King Stephen was captured in battle in 1141 he too was imprisoned, and soon released. Only if we believe that Henry I was responsible for his brother's death in the New Forest—a conspiracy theory of murder that occurred to no one living at the time—is it possible to think that the Norman royal dynasty engaged in the kin-slaying common elsewhere in Britain and Ireland. (And if it had, the new political morality required that it be kept secret.)

In the warfare which took place on English soil after 1066 very few nobles were killed. This stands in marked contrast to the high rate of royal and aristocratic casualties not only at both Hastings and Stamford Bridge in 1066, but also in most if not all earlier battles in England. After 1066 there was more violence and civil war—and notoriously so in Stephen's reign—than there had been in the fifty years before the Norman Conquest, but it was now violence controlled so as not to spill blood of nobles. Although in 1100 Celtic Britain and Ireland showed no signs of being influenced by these French political values, both Wales and Scotland would gradually come to adopt them during the course of the twelfth and thirteenth centuries. In the fourteenth century, of course, and in both England and France, the 'ages of blood' returned.

Fashionable lifestyles

According to William of Poitiers, when aristocratic English hostages were taken to Normandy in 1067 and paraded as part of the spoils of conquest, 'these long-haired sons of the North with their almost feminine beauty' were regarded as objects of curiosity by the French nobles. The designer of the Bayeux Tapestry was clearly struck by the difference between Norman and English male hairstyles. Long hair was back in fashion at the court of William Rufus, but after 1066 there is no doubt that all who wished to make a name for themselves in England had to take account of French styles. According to Orderic Vitalis, 'You could see many villages or town markets filled with displays of French wares and merchandise, and observe the English, who had previously seemed contemptible to the French in their native dress, completely transformed by foreign fashions.'

Symeon, a French scribe who became a monk at Durham in the 1090s, claimed that under Margaret's influence Malcolm of Scotland laid aside his barbarous ways and became more civilized (*civilior*). Turgot, her biographer, emphasized clothes of more varied colours and greater elegance when he observed that she had merchants from various regions bring in precious goods hitherto unknown in Scotland. However the comment of the Picard Guibert de Nogent, that Scots looked ridiculous 'with their bare legs, shaggy cloaks and purses hanging from their shoulders', suggests that the more cosmopolitan style espoused by their English queen made little impression. As late as the 1120s William of Malmesbury believed that King David of Scotland was offering tax rebates 'to all of his subjects who could learn to live in a more cultivated style, dress with more elegance, and learn to eat with more refinement'. But within limits Margaret's influence is clear. She bore eight children who survived into adulthood. Their names: Edward, Edgar, Edmund, Æthelred, Alexander, David, Edith, and Mary. The names Alexander, David, and Mary probably refer to great kings and the queen of heaven. The other five were names used by the royal house of Wessex. Entirely absent were the names of Malcolm's ancestors and predecessors. Name-giving was evidently a sphere in which Margaret counted for much, no doubt because she represented the cultural pull of Scotland's richer southern neighbour.

In post-Conquest England French names—in most cases names

from fathers' families—became immediately fashionable. A Winchester survey of *c.*1110 referred back to an earlier one made TRE (probably *c.*1057). Estimates on the basis of the names in this and subsequent Winchester surveys suggest that *c.*1057 85 per cent of Winchester names were Old English, and 15 per cent foreign; by 1110 the proportions were 30 per cent Old English and 70 per cent foreign; by 1207 only 5 per cent of recorded names were Old English. In pre-Conquest Winchester the favourite names were Godwine and Alwin; by 1110 they were Robert and William.

Chess, a new game which came to western Europe via the Arab world, had in all probability reached England by 1100. At any rate by 1108 the word for a chessboard (*scaccarium*) was being used as a term for the abacus-cloth of what became the English exchequer. One advantage of chess was that as a fashionable game of skill played by girls as well as boys it provided quiet opportunities in which young men could, as the twelfth-century *Romance of Alexander* put it, 'speak courteously of love to ladies'. But if any courtly romances were composed in eleventh-century Britain and Ireland, none survive.

Clerical culture

Wales and Ireland

'In that year [1099] died Rhigyfarch the Wise, son of Bishop Sulien, the most learned of the learned men of the Britons, ... the man whose equal had not arisen in the ages before him and whose peer it is not easy to imagine will arise after him.' The author of this passage from the Welsh *Brut* claimed that Rhigyfarch had been highly praised 'by the neighbouring peoples, that is English and French and other peoples beyond the sea'. He nonetheless also made a point of saying that Rhigyfarch 'had received instruction from no one save his own father'. From whom then had Sulien received instruction? None of his own writings survive, but in a poem written by another of his sons, Ieuan ap Sulien, we are told that his father spent five years in Scotland and ten years in Ireland before returning to Wales to teach in Llanbadarn Fawr (see above, pp. 151, 199). Whereas Sulien's own career and teaching had been confined to the Irish Sea cultural province, the *Brut* author insisted that Rhigyfarch's learning was appreciated by the English and the French—precisely those peoples who were founding new religious houses on estates stolen from Welsh churches and who were, no doubt, disparaging that traditional Welsh clerical culture of which this author was defiantly proud. Similarly Ieuan ap Sulien boasted of his descent from those Britons who had withstood the might of the invading Romans, who had made even Julius Caesar retreat, and he did so in accomplished verse which, together with Rhigyfarch's prose *Life of St David*, proclaims a late eleventh-century Welsh renaissance in Latin learning put to use in defence of their British heritage.

Irish clerical culture continued to admire those who left their homeland, men such as Marianus of Donegal (d. 1088), who founded St Peter's at Regensburg, or Marianus Scottus at Cologne, Fulda, and finally Mainz, the chronicler and computist whose iconoclastic chronological calculations were admired even by William of Malmesbury (see above, p. 197). If few who went so far returned to Ireland, this was not the case with those who went to England. In his poem *Perge carina* ('Onward, my barque'), Bishop Patrick of Dublin sent his words to the 'fields of England' (*anglica rura*), to the 'dear home', i.e. Worcester, where 'kind Bishop Wulfstan' and his own friend Aldwin were to be found. But the classical Latin of Patrick's verse was far removed from the rhyming of Mael Isu Ua Brolchain whose poetry in both languages (i.e. Latin and Irish) received warm praise in the Ulster annal for 1086. On the whole Irish Latin remained insular and conservative. William of Malmesbury reflected mainstream twelfth-century opinion when he wrote of Irish scholars: 'though they promise great things today of their knowledge of language and grammar, they are less than safe guides to the formation of Latin words and the proper speaking of Latin.'

England

Nothing could have prepared English clerks for the shock of the Norman Conquest and its overwhelming destructiveness. Their finest manuscripts, high-status books, were treated as plunder and sent abroad. In the ears of the new French lords and their clerks, English had a barbarous sound, and there followed an onslaught on the old vernacular. Coleman's Old English *Life of Wulfstan* was composed at

Worcester where the revered Bishop Wulfstan had been able to stay in office until his death (1095), but otherwise Old English book production came to an end. To Goscelin of Saint-Bertin it was the Normans who were the barbarians.

However a church led by Lanfranc was bound to put a high value on Latin education. He arranged for a canon of St Gregory's, Canterbury, to be responsible for a city school in which boys could be taught the liberal arts. Thomas of Bayeux, archbishop of York (1070–1100), provided his cathedral with a schoolmaster. By 1100 the Norman bishops of Salisbury and London had done the same. This was to be standard practice in twelfth-century England. The ecclesiastical reformers' objections to a son succeeding his father in the priestly office meant they were acutely conscious of the need to provide alternatives to the home as places of education. In 1100 and for some time to come, however, those whose own family origins lay in France tended to think that the best schools were in France. John of Tours sent the English Adelard (born c.1080) to Tours to study the liberal arts. There Adelard 'of Bath' not only learned to play the cithara well enough to be called upon to perform before Henry I's queen, he also developed that passion for Arabic science that was to take him to Spain.

Since the earliest extant works in Anglo-Norman French date from the first or second decade of the twelfth century, the literary language which first clearly gained at the expense of English was Latin. Eadmer, an English monk born c.1060, educated in Lanfranc's Canterbury, became a considerable stylist. William of Malmesbury, born c.1090, reckoned that it was under Godfrey of Jumièges, abbot from c.1090 to 1106, that the monks of Malmesbury went from babbling in the old vernacular to speaking good Latin. Godfrey's library acquisitions policy, as described by William, can be paralleled in many other churches. Newly appointed French abbots and bishops found existing English libraries inadequate. Not just because they had been plundered but because the Conquest coincided with a European Renaissance which greatly valued the works of Latin antiquity, including the works of non-Christian authors. New manuscripts were imported from the continent, and especially from Lotharingia and the Low Countries. In this way, for example, the canons of Salisbury quickly acquired their copies of Cicero and Plautus. The classicizing works of eleventh-century French poets such as Marbod of Rennes,

Baudri of Bourgueil, and Hildebert of Le Mans were to dominate English anthologies of Latin poetry for centuries to come. At Canterbury a bilingual (Latin and English) version of the *Anglo-Saxon Chronicle* was composed *c.*1100, presumably to help those whose reading knowledge of English was now uncertain—a sign of a new Anglo-Latin cultural synthesis.

Towns and trade

Growing urbanization in the tenth and eleventh centuries strengthened contacts in all directions, including north and west to Iceland and Greenland and, perhaps, even as far as Markland across the Atlantic. But given the wealth and commercial sophistication of regions such as Flanders, the Low Countries, and the Rhineland, it is anything but surprising that the number and location of eleventh-century English ports should suggest that most important trade was with the south. In the *Encomium Emmae* Sandwich was described as 'the most famous of all the ports of the English'. By 1066 English towns had already achieved that combination of corporate solidarity and administrative separation from the country which would later be reflected in borough charters, but it was the towns with which they traded in the Rhine and Meuse valleys which were in the forefront of the movement for privileged status. It was in Flanders, Lotharingia, and France that the word 'burgess' was first employed to mean a full member of an urban community with laws and customs of its own. Not surprisingly, when Norman lords founded or promoted towns in England, it was their experience at home on which they relied. Thus William FitzOsbern as earl of Hereford transferred 'the law of Breteuil' to Hereford, and Robert de Tilleul gave to his borough of Rhuddlan 'the laws and customs of Hereford and Breteuil'.

Jews

According to the *Annals of Innisfallen* for 1076: 'Five Jews came over the sea with gifts to Toirdelbach, and they were sent back over the sea.' Why the Jews came to the court of the Ua Briain high-king—whether, for example, they hoped to inaugurate a settlement in an

Irish trading centre such as Waterford or Dublin—is entirely unknown. Whether or not they obtained what they came for, they were sent back. It seems clear that if any Jews visited England or any other part of Britain before 1066 they too were sent back. But after the Norman Conquest it would be different. There was a prosperous and flourishing Jewish community in Rouen. Christian monks who disliked Rufus were appalled by his relaxed dealings with Jews. Other clerics such as the royal chancellor Gerard (bishop of Hereford 1095–1100, archbishop of York 1100–8), who owned a Hebrew Psalter, were evidently more tolerant. It seems likely that by 1100 Jews from Rouen had settled at London. Certainly in the later twelfth century Jewish settlements could be found in towns as far north as Newcastle and as far west as Bristol.

The slave trade

The last known reference to the slave market in Rouen dates from the 1030s. In England by contrast there is a reference to a slave market at Lewes (Sussex) as late as 1086 and, according to William of Malmesbury, it took a strenuous campaign by Bishop Wulfstan of Worcester (1062–95) to put a stop to the export of slaves from Bristol to Ireland. As late as 1102 the Council of Westminster decreed: 'henceforth no one is to dare to carry on that shameful trade by which in England people used to be sold like animals.' This was not the first church council in England to ban the slave trade but it was, significantly, the last. By the time William of Malmesbury was writing (the 1120s), he clearly regarded the slave trade as a barbarous thing of the past. In his view the first Norman king of England deserved to be praised for taking Lanfranc's advice and banning the sale of slaves to Ireland— despite the fact that hitherto the king had enjoyed a share of the profits from the trade. It seems likely that demographic growth and the commercialization of labour were already tending to the decline of slavery in England before 1066. Moreover not all Normans were as ready as their kings to renounce a lucrative source of income. Orderic denounced Robert of Rhuddlan for a merciless onslaught on the Welsh: 'some he slaughtered on the spot like cattle . . . others he put in chains or forced into harsh and unlawful slavery.' (Presumably many were exported to Ireland from Chester.) Even so by 1066 people who lived in France were no longer accustomed to seeing slaves for

sale at home, and so the views of moralists such as the Italian Lanfranc and the English Wulfstan seemed only natural to the new
French lords of England. Once the slave trade had been abandoned,
so too was war as slave raid. By the 1130s English authors were describing Scottish and Welsh raids into England in language which reveals
just how appalled they were by the methods of that old-style warfare
which they themselves had only recently given up. For to capture
young women and sometimes young men too, and drag them off into
slavery, involved a kind of total war, the killing of anyone who got in
the way, not just husbands and fathers who put up a fight, but also
elderly parents and small children, those whom it was uneconomic to
put to work, but whose lamenting, clinging presence endangered the
whole operation. Slave raiding and trading very rapidly came, in the
eyes of the elite of England, to be identified as markers of the barbar-
ism of the Irish, Scots, and Welsh. By the early twelfth century the real
differences between England and the rest of Britain and Ireland, differences in economic development, in family law, and in the conduct
of war, were such that Christian intellectuals in England turned to
the Graeco-Roman concept of the barbarian and applied it to the
Christian Celts of their own day. The newly constructed contrast
between Celtic savages and the civilized in England was to become
deeply entrenched in English thought. In the history of Britain and
Ireland this was a decisive moment, the creation of an imperializing
English culture.

Conclusion

Wendy Davies

In a short book one cannot do everything. Some readers are bound to reach this point and feel that a favourite theme has been unjustifiably omitted. We are sorry to let them down but we have chosen to emphasize what we as individuals regard as interesting and significant, rather than cover all expected or standard topics. Given, then, the different backgrounds and locations of the contributors, it is particularly noteworthy that some consistent themes emerge.

Ethnicities and identities

Those of us who were brought up in Britain or Ireland tend to remember the dramas of political narrative from childhood histories: Vikings arriving with rape and pillage; Alfred burning the cakes; Rhodri saving Wales; Kenneth 'unifying' Scotland; Brian almost unifying Ireland, dying in glory on the field of Clontarf; Normans conquering everything. While obviously emphasizing the role of individual kings, these images also emphasize ethnicities, and with that enmities. Vikings and Normans arrived, with hostility, from outside the islands; the English stood opposed to the Welsh, to the Cornish (West Welsh), and to the Scots; Picts succumbed to Scots, as did the north British. Of course, the extent to which either residents or incomers identified themselves in such broad ethnic terms is arguable but contemporaries could be conscious of cultural difference on this scale and could express it pointedly: the massacre of Vikings on St Brice's Day is but an extreme case of this. More passively, the Welsh writer of the mid-tenth-century poem *Armes Prydein* envisaged a time when all the peoples of Britain, aided by the Irish and the 'foreigners' of Ireland (i.e. Norse), would unite to expel for ever the arch-enemy, the Saxons, from the island of Britain. In fact, though he saw the Cornish and the north Britons as fellow countrymen (*Cymry*), he nevertheless differentiated between them. So too the annalists of the *Annals of Ulster*, who most frequently called the Viking incomers 'foreigners' (*Gaill*), sometimes differentiated between 'dark' and 'fair' foreigners.

Despite the contemporary sense of difference (a sense sustained in Ireland until the late eleventh century), interaction between the groups is increasingly evident. Modern writers freely use labels like Hiberno-Norse, Gall-Gaedhil (literally foreigner-Irish), and Anglo-Scandinavian of this period, thereby emphasizing the mixed origins of warrior bands, or seafarers, or artistic styles. Anglo-Norman comes a little later for modern writers: while the incomers are called Norman in the eleventh century they are Anglo-Norman by the twelfth. Just as Cnut the Dane had run the English state, so did William the Norman, and both thereby became Anglicized to an extent. Gruffudd ap Cynan, who had a Welsh father and a Scandinavian mother, was brought up in Dublin, whither his father seems to have fled. Indeed, although we have so little evidence from Wales, we can see from Welsh library holdings that books, and ideas, came in from abroad; the 'Irish Sea province' was in this sense too a region of 'vigorous' and 'vibrant' cultural contact, not just an arena for traders and seafarers (see above, pp. 199, 227–8). Cross-cultural contact, and influence, was common, particularly in towns (see above, p. 91); people of different backgrounds negotiated with each other, borrowed styles and ideas, went raiding together, and adopted new names.

Although contemporary writers sometimes wrote in terms of very broad ethnic groups, smaller-scale identities were recognized too, from the relatively large groups of Ulaid or West Saxons to the much less extensive Irish Luigne or Galenga (see above, pp. 15–16). People were also frequently identified by reference to their place or region of origin: Munstermen (*Muminenses*) or men of Brega (*fir Bregh*), appear already in the early ninth century, people from Gwent (*Went-saete* and *gwyr Guenti*) in the tenth, and Flemings and Lotharingians in the late eleventh, just as people came from Dublin or London or the River Clyde. The 'foreigners of Dublin' appear consistently across a century (replacing the earlier, ninth-century, 'pagans (Gentiles) of

Dublin'). For Ieuan (for whom see above, pp. 152, 199, 227–8), the land of Ceredigion was the fatherland in the late eleventh century, although he classified himself as a Briton: he was as aware of the very broad group identity as he was of the much smaller homeland.

Cultural identity, then as now, was complex and people could easily acknowledge membership of more than one group. There is a sense too in which identity in its broadest sense was defined linguistically. The hated Saxons spoke English; the 'foreigners' spoke Norse; the Britons spoke several languages, all derived from British, that is—by the ninth and tenth centuries—Cornish, Welsh, and Cumbric; the Irish of Ireland and of Scotland spoke Irish; the Normans spoke French. So the Britons recognized their fellow countrymen, who are mentioned in approving terms, by the tongue they used. By contrast, Latin, the language of learned literacy, was shared thoughout the islands, in greater or lesser degrees of competence, and did not define distinctive ethnic identities. Similarly, the establishment of learned literacy in English and in Irish vernaculars had more to do with the culture of scholars than with ethnicities, though the development of these vernacular literacies remains one of the outstanding developments of our period (see above, pp. 185–7, 196). Scholars certainly acquired competence in several languages (see above, pp. 176, 191). But others, outside the scholarly world, learned to use more than one language too. In England and in Ireland, especially, words of Norse origin were adopted—just as French words were adopted at a slightly later date—bearing witness to linguistic interchange *beyond* the worlds of scholarship and thereby enriching the languages too. While there is not much direct evidence of the range of languages used, and of the skill of the users, towns like Dublin, London, and Chester, and others like Winchester, Whithorn, and maybe even an emergent Swansea, must have known several languages in daily use. And even outside the towns we know, for example, that King Malcolm of the Scots spoke English and Gaelic (see above, p. 212). While it is reasonable to suppose that many people continued to live in a monoglot world, there were multicultural societies in Britain and Ireland at this time too.

Wealth

The most striking of all the developments of the period covered by this book is the increase in the accessibility and conspicuous use of wealth. Wealth became easily portable and realizable; individuals and churches accumulated wealth on a scale not seen before in this part of the world; English kings, in particular, tapped the productive capacity of their subjects, establishing effective monetary and fiscal mechanisms for doing so (see above, pp. 36–7, 77, 81, 121–2). The portability of wealth was symbolized by its availability as silver: enormous sums were collected, in coin, and paid to Viking raiders of England in the late tenth and early eleventh centuries; a silver arm-ring 'currency' was developed by Vikings of the Irish Sea area (see Frontispiece, p. xviii); large silver brooches were worn in ever more elaborate display in Ireland. The quantities of silver were more evident in England than elsewhere, but even in Wales Maredudd collected silver to pay off the Vikings in 989. Availability—conversion—accumulation—and, above all, display. Churches were wealthy all over Britain and Ireland: the reliquaries of insular origin, or fragments of them, that turn up in silver hoards in Scandinavia make the point (see above, p. 158).

Silver was one very prominent aspect of wealth; land, of course, and produce, remained fundamental to wealth and it was the availability of surplus produce that could be *converted* to cash that made the difference. The wealth of churches was often manifest in the erection of stone monuments, especially fine sculptured crosses; they can be found in all parts, from the eloquently Christian slabs of late Pictish society to the great high crosses of Ireland and the increased quantities of sculpture in (Scandinavian) northern and midland England (see Figs. 8.1, 5.0). Churches also benefited from the piety of the laity, who expressed their patronage not only by modestly commissioning homilies but by flamboyantly giving arrestingly visible things—the crosses, books, even churches (see above, pp. 149, 153–4). Of the thousands of new local churches of this period in Ireland, and especially in England, many were provided by the laity. In England a flurry of building in stone, secular as well as ecclesiastical, marked the later tenth and eleventh centuries—by the second half of the eleventh century on a scale unseen before (see above, pp. 95, 133, 215).

Figure 8.1 The Pictish cross-slab in Glamis. © Royal Commission on the Ancient and Historical Monuments of Scotland.

If England was marked out from the rest of Britain and Ireland by the quantity of its stone building by 1100, it was also distinguished by its conspicuous consumption. Even after kings had taken tax and Vikings had taken geld, there was something left for self-indulgence, prestigious projects, and fun. People did more with their wealth in

England: they acquired fine clothes (embroidery using gold thread was an option), their robes grew longer, they ate good food, they developed a cuisine (see above, p. 127). London and York were towns where a great range of goods was made and sold—places with an array of practical, rich, and fine things available to the purchaser (see above, pp. 88, 99). Commercial cultures—genuinely commercial, with people buying and selling at a price—were developing (see above, pp. 102, 121–2).

Of course, urbanization itself was a distinctive characteristic of this period across western Europe. Although Ireland had its urban take-off in the eleventh century too, there were more towns per hectare, and bigger towns, in England, especially in the south and Midlands; and the further east you travelled, the larger the towns were (see above, p. 98). Wales and Scotland, on the other hand, still had strikingly low levels of urbanization in 1100, much lower than western European norms; and Welsh texts—unlike Irish or English—are strikingly devoid of references to merchants, markets, mints, and mechanisms for the control of the profits of exchange (see Fig. 3.5).

English expansion and Celtic reactions

This was the time when the foundations of the 'first English empire' were laid. England—state, monarchy, territory—was established by the early twelfth century. English (or Anglo-Norman) interest in Scotland had begun; that in Wales was quite far advanced; that in Ireland was largely still to be developed. The English king in 1100 also had substantial continental interests and territory, albeit by virtue of the fact that this was the home dominion of the Norman dukes who had settled in England.

England was different from the rest of Britain and from Ireland by virtue of its expansive tendencies. It was also different in its patterns of consumption, as we have seen—Robin Fleming's chapter is central to the differences between England, Scotland, Ireland, and Wales. But if England was different, it was certainly not set against a single undifferentiated other. There was no Celtic norm (cf. above, pp. 12–16). It is strictly anachronistic to talk of Ireland, Scotland, and

Wales in this period, although it is worth remembering that there are distinctive Irish, Welsh, and Scottish bodies of law, and that the latter two began to take shape in our period (the Irish had already done so by then). Ireland, Scotland, and Wales were as different from each other as they were from England, although there was plenty of interaction between Irish and Welsh on the one hand and Irish and Scottish on the other (see above, pp. 180, 200). An effective monarchy developed in Scotland, but political power in Wales was exceptionally fragmented and was to remain so until the Edwardian conquest, and to some extent thereafter; and in Ireland, despite the gradual erosion of the *tuath* and growth of provincial overkingships, kingship was still multiple in the middle of the twelfth century. The scale of effective units of political authority therefore varied widely, and this had a bearing both on the relationship between ruler and subject and on the rate of development of administrative machinery.

There were other kinds of difference too. Clientship seems to have been more important to the functioning of Irish agricultural society than it was to Welsh. More women seem to have had access to more property rights in Ireland than they did in Wales, and women there clearly seized the opportunities offered by the Christian church more enthusiastically than those in Wales. The veneration of female saints was already prominent in ninth-century Ireland; it was rare in Wales. There were probably more bishops in Ireland, but also, in the tenth and eleventh centuries, more abbots with administrative powers. The rate of economic change was certainly much faster in Ireland at that time than it was in Wales, and probably in Scotland—where the comparison, as ever, is limited by the paucity of available source material.

There are many ways in which Irish development was strikingly different from that of Wales, and apparently different from that of Scotland. There is of course no reason why these should have been similar but if we think about deep currents and long-term trends— the forces that made for change in European history irrespective of political fortune and the capacity of individuals—we have to ask why Irish development, though distinctive, was more like English development than was Welsh. One is inevitably drawn back to the fundamentals of demography, geography, and climate change. People and produce—how many and how much of each, for a start; add lordship—landlords, rulers, leaders of warrior bands or sea bands. The subtle relationship between numbers of people, quantities of surplus produced, control of surplus, and conversion of surplus made for faster or slower development—rather than proximity to any notional continental mainstream.

Those who have been brought up speaking English have on the whole been influenced by English nationalist historiographies: the English and Anglo-Norman military successes of the tenth and eleventh centuries were the necessary prelude to the making of Great Britain and its empire, and to the export of democracy to a waiting world. But Scotland has had a strong and independent identity since the central middle ages, a land of implacably independent chiefs, a land which ultimately gave its king to England; the symbols of historic Welsh identity have continued to be clearly associated with resistance, prolonging the theme set by *Armes Prydein*; and, although the perspectives of tenth-century Irish historians exerted a long influence (see above, p. 195), the twentieth century has seen the development of powerful Irish counter-histories, rooted in Gaelic experience, emphasizing an early medieval culture that brought learning to the western world. In the nineteenth and twentieth centuries there has also been powerful myth-making about a pan-Celtic past of spirituality and mysticism—a world of saints on islands, talking to the birds, and a hoped-for counter to English practicality, pragmatism, and control. Most of this is wishful thinking—a search for alternatives, a refusal to recognize difference, and a wilful disregard for chronology and historical context.

We can see, in the early years of the twenty-first century, how critical was the period 800–1100 for the various histories and polities of the people of these islands. This was the time when England and Scotland took political shape, when writing began to be used on a significant scale, when commercial exchange took off, when towns became established. But the political history of Britain and Ireland is now set to change, under the dual influences of devolution in Britain and the enlargement of the European Union. Both threads give opportunities to smaller states and smaller cultures that have not been seen for many a century. Scotland and Wales both now have their own political assemblies, and there are moves in the wind to bring Northern Ireland into a closer relationship with the Republic of Ireland. Such changes are bound to influence the writing of history, even of that of 1,000 years ago. What the next generation will make of that past is just as interesting as the past itself. We can look forward to building in those new perspectives in another twenty or thirty years.

Further reading

Introduction

In addition to the works detailed in the sections that follow, N. Edwards, *The Archaeology of Early Medieval Ireland* (London, 1990), is an exceptionally useful guide to Irish archaeology; there is a brief guide to recent Welsh archaeology of the period in W. Davies, 'Thinking about the Welsh Environment a Thousand Years Ago', in G. H. Jenkins (ed.), *Wales and the Welsh 2000* (Aberystwyth, 2001). For inscriptions on stone in Scotland, Ireland, Wales, and the Isle of Man, the easiest mode of reference is to use the online Celtic Inscribed Stones database at http://www.ucl.ac.uk/archaeology/cisp/database.

Chapter 1

On Ireland in this period see D. Ó Corráin, *Ireland before the Normans* (Dublin, 1972), F. J. Byrne, *Irish Kings and High-Kings* (London, 1973), and D. Ó Cróinín, *Early Medieval Ireland, 400–1200* (London, 1995). T. M. Charles-Edwards, *Early Christian Ireland* (Cambridge, 2000) covers a slightly earlier period but is full of insight into the working of early Irish, and early medieval, society and rule. D. Ó Corráin's 'Nationality and Kingship in Pre-Norman Ireland', in T. W. Moody (ed.), *Nationality and the Pursuit of National Independence* (Belfast, 1978) is an important corrective to views which see Ireland as fundamentally different from the rest of Europe, as is P. Wormald, 'Celtic and Anglo-Saxon Kingship: Some Further Thoughts', in P. Szarmach (ed.), *Sources of Anglo-Saxon Culture* (Kalamazoo, Mich., 1986). On Wales, W. Davies, *Wales in the Early Middle Ages* (Leicester, 1982) and her *Patterns of Power in Early Wales* (Oxford, 1990) are essential. R. R. Davies, *Conquest, Coexistence and Change: Wales 1063–1415* (Oxford, 1987; reissued 1991 as *The Age of Conquest: Wales 1063–1415*) is important for the eleventh century. His introduction and chapter 'In Praise of British History' in *The British Isles 1100–1500: Comparisons, Contrasts and Connections* (Edinburgh, 1988), and his Royal Historical Society presidential lectures 'The Peoples of Britain and Ireland 1100–1400', *Transactions of the Royal Historical Society*, 6th ser. 4–7 (1994–7), are largely concerned with a later period, but have much to say relevant to this one and are inspirational. On Scotland A. A. M. Duncan, *Scotland, the Making of the Kingdom* (Edinburgh, 1975) is essential, full of information and judicious insight though not easy to use. For the period after AD 1000, G. W. S. Barrow, *Kingship and Unity, Scotland 1000–1306* (London, 1981) is excellent. Important new work is rethinking early Scottish history: see, for example, D. Broun, 'The Origin of Scottish Identity', in C. Bjørn, A. Grant, and K. J. Stringer (eds.), *Nations, Nationalism and Patriotism in the European Past* (Copenhagen, 1994), 35–55; contributions by him and Cowan to E. J. Cowan and R. A. McDonald (eds.), *Alba, Celtic Scotland in the Middle Ages* (East Linton, 2000); and A. Woolf, 'The "Moray Question" and the Kingship of Alba in the Tenth and Eleventh Centuries', *Scottish Historical Review*, 79 (2000), 145–64. Woolf's 'Pictish Matriliny Reconsidered', *Innes Review*, 49/2 (1998), 147–67 is the most recent and important thought on this vexed topic. On England see P. Stafford, *Unification and Conquest: A Political and Social History of England in the Tenth and Eleventh Centuries* (London, 1989); S. Keynes, 'King Alfred and the Mercians', in M. A. S. Blackburn and D. N. Dumville (eds.), *Kings, Currency and Alliances* (Woodbridge, 1998), 1–45; and P. Wormald, 'Engla-lond: The Making of an Allegiance', *Journal of Historical Sociology*, 7 (1994), 1–24.

On early law, F. Kelly, *A Guide to Early Irish Law* (Dublin, 1988) is an indispensable text and invaluable; T. M. Charles-Edwards, *The Welsh Laws* (Cardiff, 1989) is an excellent introduction, and not only to Welsh law; P. Wormald's work has transformed our understanding of early English law. Wormald's *The Making of English Law: King Alfred to the Twelfth Century*, i: *Legislation and its Limits* (Oxford, 1999) is concerned particularly with the texts but has much on kings and law. His collected essays, *Legal Culture in the Early Medieval West: Law as Text, Image and Experience* (London, 1999), collects much of his important work not only on English law but on early law more generally, including his seminal essay '*Lex Scripta* and *Verbum Regis*: Legislation and Germanic Kingship from Euric to Cnut'.

Chapter 2

The standard—and only—textbook on the Vikings in the whole of Britain is H. Loyn's *The Vikings in Britain* (Oxford, 1977, 1994), although *The Oxford Illustrated History of the Vikings* (ed. P. Sawyer, Oxford, 1997) has one chapter on 'The Vikings in England *c*.790–1016' by S. Keynes, and one chapter on 'Ireland, Wales, Man, and the Hebrides' by D. Ó Corráin. The book of the BBC TV series 'Blood of the Vikings' by J. Richards (London, 2001) covers all the British Isles, with the heaviest concentration on England.

For England J. D. Richards's *English Heritage Book of Viking Age England* (London, 1991, 2000) primarily focuses on the archaeological evidence. *Alfred the Great: Asser's Life of King Alfred and Other Contemporary Sources*, translated with an introduction and notes by S. Keynes and M. Lapidge (Harmondsworth, 1983, and many reprints) still provides the essential textbook of the written sources for King Alfred's struggle with the Vikings, while P. Cavill's study *The Vikings: Fear and Faith* (London, 2001) is a new and very interesting assessment of the historical and literary sources for the period. A recent collection of multidisciplinary papers in the Proceedings of the Thirteenth Viking Congress, *Vikings and the Danelaw*, ed. J. Graham-Campbell, R. Hall, J. Jesch, and D. N. Parsons (Oxford, 2001), provides up-to-date contributions by scholars on many different aspects. In general, the focus has been on reassessing Sir Frank Stenton's theories about the Danelaw and its Danish character (as in *The Oxford History of Anglo-Saxon England*, Oxford, 1971, with many reprints and still valuable), particularly by D. Hadley in *The Northern Danelaw: Its Social Structure* (London, 2000) and in the papers edited by D. Hadley and J. D. Richards, *Cultures in Contact; Scandinavian Settlement in England in the Ninth and Tenth Centuries* (Turnhout, 2000). This reassessment builds on the earlier controversies over the size of the great army and the extent of Danish settlement in eastern England: see K. Cameron's papers collected in *Place-Name Evidence for the Anglo-Saxon Invasions and Scandinavian Settlements* (Nottingham, 1975) and his *English Place-Names*, 3rd edn. (London, 1996). For detailed local studies of the toponymy see G. Fellows-Jensen's *Scandinavian Settlement Names in Yorkshire* (*Navnestudier*, 11, 1972), *Scandinavian Settlement Names in the East Midlands* (*Navnestudier*, 15, 1978), and *Scandinavian Settlement Names in the North-West* (*Navnestudier*, 25, 1985). More recently, *Wirral and its Viking Heritage* by P. Cavill, S. Harding, and J. Jesch (Nottingham, 2000) puts the Scandinavian place-names admirably into the context of the Viking impact on a localized area.

Moving north, a collection of interdisciplinary papers in *The Viking Age in Caithness, Orkney and the North Atlantic*, ed. C. Batey, J. Jesch, and C. D. Morris (Edinburgh, 1993) resulted from the Eleventh Viking Congress in Orkney, with a similar collection for Ireland in *Ireland and Scandinavia in the Early Viking Age*, ed. H. B. Clarke, M. Ní Mhaonaigh, and R. Ó Floinn (Dublin, 1998). D. Ó Corráin's article 'The Vikings in Scotland and Ireland in the Ninth Century' in *Peritia*, 12 (1998) takes a new broader look at Viking activity in north Britain and Ireland. Otherwise the general histories of Scotland and Ireland discuss the impact of the Vikings on the two countries as being more or less important. Those which do take the Vikings seriously are D. Ó Cróinín's *Early Medieval Ireland 400–1200* (London, 1995), A. P. Smyth's *Warlords and Holy Men: Scotland AD 80–1000* (London, 1984), and B. E. Crawford's contribution (chapter 2—'The Formation of the Scottish Kingdom' with T. Clancy) in *The New Penguin History of Scotland*, ed. R. A. Houston and W. W. Knox (London, 2001). The effects of Viking raids on the church have for long been a subject of concern to medieval historians, and recent contributions by C. Etchingham, *Viking Raids on Irish Church Settlements in the Ninth Century* (Maynooth, 1996) and by D. N. Dumville, *The Churches of North Britain in the First Viking Age* (Whithorn, 1997) have brought fresh interpretations to bear.

General studies of the Viking archaeology of Scotland are more numerous and B. E. Crawford's *Scandinavian Scotland* (Leicester, 1987; to be reprinted), has been recently updated on the archaeological front by J. Graham-Campbell and C. Batey's *Vikings in Scotland: An Archaeological Survey* (Edinburgh, 1997). Historic Scotland has produced two popular publications, *Viking Scotland* by A. Ritchie (London, 1993) and *The Sea Road: A Viking Voyage through Scotland* by O. Owen (Edinburgh, 1999), which present the archaeological evidence very attractively. *The Viking-Age Gold and Silver of Scotland (AD 850–1100)* by J. Graham-Campbell (Edinburgh, 1995) is a specialized study, while the excavation of the Scar boat burial is fully reported and written up within the wider context of Viking archaeology in *Scar: A Viking Boat Burial on Sanday, Orkney* by O. Owen and M. Dalland (Edinburgh, 2001). A preliminary assessment of the excavations at Tarbat, Easter Ross, can be read in 'Conversion and Politics on the Eastern Seaboard of Britain: Some Archaeological Indicators' by M. Carver, in B. E. Crawford (ed.), *Conversion and Christianity in the North Sea World* (St Andrews, 1998). Many different place-name studies are collected together in *Scandinavian Settlement in Northern Britain*, ed. B. E. Crawford (Leicester, 1995).

Turning finally to Wales, a new emphasis since H. R. Loyn's *The Vikings in Wales* (London, 1976) looks to the interaction of Viking elements all round the Irish Sea, particularly focusing on north Wales, as in W. Davies, *Patterns of Power in Early Wales* (Oxford, 1990), and with the new excavations at Llanbedrgoch summarized in M. Redknap, *Vikings in Wales: An Archaeological Quest* (Cardiff, 2000). For the Isle of Man the forthcoming *New History of the Isle of Man*, vol. ii, edited by S. Duffy, will bring together several new contributions on the Viking period; the papers from the Ninth Viking Congress on *The Viking Age in the Isle of Man*, ed. C. Fell et al. (London, 1983) are meanwhile the most comprehensive available.

The most recent standard work on the Danish conquest of England in the second Viking Age is M. K. Lawson's *Cnut: The Danes in England in the Early Eleventh Century* (London, 1993) and a volume of essays on *The Reign of Cnut, King of England, Denmark and Norway* edited by A. R. Rumble (Leicester, 1994). Historical atlases can be invaluable for understanding Viking activity and the best for the Vikings is J. Haywood, *The Penguin Historical Atlas of the Vikings* (Penguin Books, 1995, and reprinted). Viking sculpture is a special field of study and R. N. Bailey's *Viking-Age Sculpture in Northern England* (London, 1980) is still the standard work on the subject, along with J. Lang, 'The Hogback: A Viking Colonial Monument', *Anglo-Saxon Studies in Archaeology and History*, 3 (Oxford, 1984).

Chapter 3

Definitions of towns and commerce can be found in S. Reynolds, *An Introduction to the History of English Medieval Towns* (Oxford, 1977), M. Biddle,

'Towns', in D. M. Wilson (ed.), *The Archaeology of Anglo-Saxon England* (Cambridge, 1976), 99–150, and R. H. Britnell, *The Commercialisation of English Society, 1000–1500* (Cambridge, 1993). *The Cambridge Urban History, i: 600–1540* (ed. D. M. Palliser, Cambridge, 2000) is a major recent contribution to British urban studies, encompassing history, archaeology, demography, and regional case studies. Especially relevant to this chapter are the contributions by G. Astill, 'General Survey 600–1300', J. Blair, 'Small Towns, 600–1270', R. Britnell, 'The Economy of British Towns, 600–1300', J. Campbell, 'Power and Authority, 600–1300', D. A. Hinton, 'The Large Towns, 600–1300', R. Holt, 'Society and Population, 600–1300', and D. Keene, 'London from the Post-Roman Period to 1300'. A very recent work covering the more general social and economic background is C. Dyer, *Making a Living in the Middle Ages: The People of Britain 850–1250* (New Haven, 2002). Themes in early urban history in Ireland are covered in H. B. Clarke and A. Simms (eds.), *The Comparative History of Urban Origins in Non-Roman Europe*, British Archaeological Reports International Series, 255 (Oxford, 1985). For Whithorn, with perhaps Scotland's best claim to urban status before 1100, see P. Hill in *Whithorn and St Ninian: The Excavation of a Monastic Town, 1984–91* (Stroud, 1997).

Coinage and pre-monetary exchange are seldom assessed together as integrated themes; M. A. S. Blackburn (ed.), *Anglo-Saxon Monetary History* (Leicester, 1986) has papers on coins, coin use, and economy in England, but also includes Irish and continental material—H. Loyn's paper was a useful attempt at an overview of the subject (which has inevitably moved on somewhat since 1986). D. M. Metcalf, *An Atlas of Anglo-Saxon and Norman Coin Finds 973–1086* (Oxford, 1998) is a more recent (and also highly informative) contribution. W. Davies, *Wales in the Early Middle Ages* (Leicester, 1996) and T. M. Charles-Edwards, *Early Irish and Welsh Kinship* (Oxford, 1993) include fascinating insights into cultures of pre-monetary economy and exchange in Wales and Ireland.

For studies of individual towns in Britain and Ireland, including excavation reports, see R. Hodges and B. Hobley (eds.), *The Re-birth of Towns in the West 700–1050*, Council for British Archaeology Research Report 68 (London, 1988), which gives a range of urban case studies. The *wics* are surveyed in D. Hill and R. Cowie (eds.), *Wics: The Early Medieval Trading Centres of Northern Europe* (Sheffield, 2001). Years of excavation and research (and numerous specialist reports) on York are summed up in R. A. Hall, *Viking Age York* (London, 1994). R. A. Hall has also provided a recent study of the five Danelaw boroughs: 'Anglo-Scandinavian Urban Development in the East Midlands', in J. A. Graham-Campbell et al. (eds.), *Vikings and the Danelaw: Select Papers from the Proceedings of the Thirteenth Viking Congress, 1997* (Oxford, 2001), 143–56; in the same volume is a detailed study of Lincoln in the Viking Age by A. Vince (157–79). J. Haslam (ed.), *Anglo-Saxon Towns in Southern England* (Chichester, 1984) is a county-by-county overview of the topography of Anglo-Saxon towns; aspects of urban diet and lifestyle are covered in J. Rackham (ed.), *Environment and Economy in Anglo-Saxon England*, Council for British Archaeology Research Report 89 (York, 1994).

The Irish Sea was a dynamic zone for shipping, settlement, and commerce; archaeological evidence from Wales and north-west England is covered in M. Redknap, *Vikings in Wales: An Archaeological Quest* (Cardiff, 2000) and D. Griffiths, 'The Coastal Trading Ports of the Irish Sea', in J. A. Graham-Campbell (ed.), *Viking Treasure from the North West: The Cuerdale Hoard in its Context* (Liverpool, 1992), 63–72, and S. W. Ward, *Excavations at Chester: Saxon Occupation within the Roman Fortress, Sites Excavated 1971–81* (Chester, 1994). For Ireland itself, A. C. Larsen (ed.), *The Vikings in Ireland* (Roskilde, 2001) gives a recent summary. A. T. Lucas's influential paper 'Irish-Norse Relations: Time for a Reappraisal?', *Journal of the Cork Archaeological and Historical Society*, 71 (1966), 62–75 gave a fresh perspective, written before the substantial urban excavations of the late 1960s onwards—P. F. Wallace, *The Viking Age Buildings of Dublin* (Dublin, 1992) shows their exceptional international importance. Waterford is covered by M. Hurley, O. M. B. Scully, and S. W. J. McCutcheon, *Late Viking Age and Medieval Waterford: Excavations 1986–1992* (Waterford, 1997). P. F. Wallace's articles 'The Archaeological Identity of the Hiberno-Norse Town', *Journal of the Royal Society of Antiquaries of Ireland*, 122 (1992), 35–66 and 'The English in Viking Dublin', in M. A. S. Blackburn (ed.), *Anglo-Saxon Monetary History* (Leicester, 1986), 201–21; also J. Bradley, 'The Interpretation of Scandinavian Settlement in Ireland', in J. Bradley (ed.), *Settlement and Society in Medieval Ireland: Studies Presented to F. X. Martin O.S.A.* (Kilkenny, 1988), 49–78, and S. Duffy (ed.), *Medieval Dublin 1* (Dublin, 2000), all give a range of essential insights.

Chapter 4

For further reading on settlement patterns and lordship, see R. Faith, *The English Peasantry and the Growth of Lordship* (London, 1997); J. Blair, *Anglo-Saxon Oxfordshire* (Oxford, 1994); D. Hooke (ed.), *Anglo-Saxon Settlements* (Oxford, 1988); M. Stout, *The Irish Ringfort* (Dublin, 1997); M. A. Monk and J. Sheehan (eds.), *Early Medieval Munster: Archaeology, History and Society* (Cork, 1998); T. Barry, *A History of Settlement in Ireland* (London, 2000); F. Mitchell and M. Ryan, *Reading the Irish Landscape*, rev. edn. (Dublin, 1990); B. J. Graham, 'Early Medieval Ireland: Settlement as an Indicator of Economic and Social Transformation, c.500–1100 AD', in B. J. Graham and L. J. Proudfoot, *An Historical Geography of Ireland* (London, 1993), 19–57; W. Davies, *An Early Welsh Microcosm: Studies in the Llandaff Charters* (London, 1978) and *Wales in the Early Middle Ages* (Leicester, 1982); C. Hurley, 'Landscapes of

Gwent and the Marches as Seen through the Charters of the Seventh to Eleventh Centuries', in N. Edwards, *Landscape and Settlement in Medieval Wales* (Oxford, 1997), 31–40.

For further reading on high-status sites, see A. Williams, 'A Bell-House and a Burh-Geat: Lordly Residences in England before the Norman Conquest', in C. Harper-Bill and R. Harvey (eds.), *Medieval Knighthood*, iv, (Woodbridge, 1992), 221–40; J. R. Fairbrother, *Faccombe Netherton: Excavations of a Saxon and Medieval Manorial Complex*, i, British Museum Occasional Paper 74 (London, 1990); C. J. Lynn, 'Houses in Rural Ireland AD 500–1000', *Ulster Journal of Archaeology*, 57 (1994), 81–94; J. P. Mallory and T. E. McNeill, *The Archaeology of Ulster: From Colonization to Plantation* (Belfast, 1991); T. O'Keefe, *Medieval Ireland: An Archaeology* (Gloucester, 2000); A. O'Sullivan, *The Archaeology of Lake Settlement in Ireland* (Dublin, 1998); B. E. Crawford, *Scandinavian Scotland* (Leicester, 1987); B. E. Crawford and B. B. Smith, *The Biggings, Papa Stour, Shetland: The History and Archaeology of a Royal Norwegian Farm*, Society of Antiquaries of Scotland Monograph Series 15 (Edinburgh, 1999); E. Campbell, 'Llangorse: A Tenth-Century Royal Crannog in Wales', *Antiquity*, 63 (1989), 675–81; D. Longley, 'The Royal Courts of the Welsh Princes in Gwynedd, AD 400–1283', in N. Edwards (ed.), *Landscape and Settlement in Medieval Wales* (Oxford, 1997), 41–54.

For further reading on aristocratic consumption, see R. Fleming, 'The New Wealth, the New Rich, and the New Political Style in Late Anglo-Saxon England', *Anglo-Norman Studies*, 22 (2001), 1–22; C. R. Dodwell, *Anglo-Saxon Art: A New Perspective* (Ithaca, NY, 1982); M. F. Smith, P. Halpin, and R. Fleming, 'Court and Piety in Late Anglo-Saxon England', *Catholic Historical Review*, 87 (2001), 569–602; H. Pryce, 'Ecclesiastical Wealth in Early Medieval Wales', in N. Edwards and A. Lane (eds.), *The Early Church in Wales and the West: Recent Work in Early Christian Archaeology, History and Placenames*, Oxbow Monographs 16 (Oxford, 1992), 22–32, and P. E. Michelli, 'The Inscriptions on Pre-Norman Irish Reliquaries', *Proceedings of the Royal Irish Academy*, 96 (1996), 1–48; P. Harbison, 'Regal (and Other) Patronage in Irish Inscriptions of the Pre-Norman Period', *Ulster Journal of Archaeology*, 58 (1999), 43–54.

For further information on agricultural practices and food, see J. Rackham (ed.), *Environment and Economy in Anglo-Saxon England* (York, 1994); F. Kelly, *Early Irish Farming* (Dublin, 1997); F. McCormick, 'Farming and Food in Medieval Lecale', in L. Proudfoot (ed.), *Down History and Society* (Dublin, 1997), 33–46; N. Brady, 'Labor and Agriculture in Early Medieval Ireland: Evidence from the Sources', in A. J. Frantzen and D. Moffat (eds.), *The Work of Work: Servitude, Slavery and Labor in Medieval England* (Glasgow, 1994), 125–45; C. Rynne, 'Some Observations on the Production of Flour and Meal in the Early Historic Period', *Journal of the Cork Historical and Archaeological Society*, 95 (1990), 20–9; J. Graham-Campbell and C. E. Batey, *Vikings in Scotland: An Archaeological Survey* (Edinburgh, 1998); K. J. Edwards and I. B. M. Ralston (eds.), *Scotland: Environment and Archaeology 8000 BC to AD 1000* (Chichester, 1997); G. F. Bigelow, 'Issues and Prospects in Shetland Norse Archaeology', in C. D. Morris and D. J. Rackham (eds.), *Norse and Later Settlement and Subsistence in the North Atlantic* (Glasgow, 1992), 9–32; J. H. Barrett, R. P. Beukens, and R. A. Nickolson, 'Diet and Ethnicity during the Viking Colonization of Northern Scotland: Evidence from Fish Bones and Stable Carbon Isotopes', *Antiquity*, 75 (2001), 145–54.

Chapter 5

J. Blair and R. Sharpe (eds.), *Pastoral Care before the Parish* (Leicester, 1992) is unusual among works on the church in this period in encompassing both Britain and Ireland and in its comparative approach. K. Hughes, *The Church in Early Irish Society* (London, 1966) remains fundamental for Ireland, although some of its key interpretations have been challenged, most comprehensively in C. Etchingham, *Church Organisation in Ireland AD 650 to 1000* (Maynooth, 1999). There are useful assessments of Scottish ecclesiastical history in this period in A. A. M. Duncan, *Scotland: The Making of the Kingdom* (Edinburgh, 1975) and B. E. Crawford, *Scandinavian Scotland* (Leicester, 1987). On the *Céli Dé*, see P. O'Dwyer, *Céli Dé: Spiritual Reform in Ireland 750–900* (Dublin, 1981), and T. O. Clancy, 'Iona, Scotland, and the Céli Dé', in B. E. Crawford (ed.), *Scotland in Dark Age Britain* (St Andrews, 1996), 111–30. W. Davies, *Wales in the Early Middle Ages* (Leicester, 1982) includes a survey of ecclesiastical developments, which may be supplemented by N. Edwards and A. Lane (eds.), *The Early Church in Wales and the West* (Oxford, 1992). F. Barlow, *The English Church, 1000–1066*, 2nd edn. (London, 1979) and H. R. Loyn, *The English Church, 940–1154* (Harlow, 2000) offer general studies of the church in England, while important changes in ecclesiastical organization are illuminated in J. Blair (ed.), *Minsters and Parish Churches: The Local Church in Transition 950–1200* (Oxford, 1988). Three collections of papers exemplify recent thinking about the tenth-century monastic reformation in England: B. Yorke (ed.), *Bishop Æthelwold: His Career and Influence* (Woodbridge, 1988); N. Ramsey, M. Sparks, and T. Tatton-Brown (eds.), *St Dunstan: His Life, Times and Cult* (Woodbridge, 1992); and N. Brooks and C. Cubitt (eds.), *St Oswald of Worcester: Life and Influence* (London, 1996). For the role of religious women in Anglo-Saxon England, see S. Foot, *Veiled Women*, 2 vols. (Aldershot, 2000), and P. Stafford, 'Queens, Nunneries and Reforming Churchmen: Gender, Religious Status and Reform in Tenth- and Eleventh-Century England', *Past and Present*, 163 (1999), 3–35.

The issues in the continuing debate about the impact of the Vikings on the church and their conversion to Christianity are highlighted in the contrasting approaches of D. M. Hadley, 'Conquest, Colonisation and the Church:

Ecclesiastical Organization in the Danelaw', *Historical Research*, 69 (1996), 109–26 and D. N. Dumville, *The Churches of North Britain in the First Viking Age: Fifth Whithorn Lecture* (Whithorn, 1997). Compare also L. Abrams, 'Conversion and Assimilation', in D. M. Hadley and J. D. Richards (eds.), *Cultures in Contact: Scandinavian Settlement in England in the Ninth and Tenth Centuries* (Turnhout, 2000), 135–53 with J. Barrow, 'Survival and Mutation: Ecclesiastical Institutions in the Danelaw in the Ninth and Tenth Centuries', ibid. 155–76. For Ireland, see C. Etchingham, *Viking Raids on Irish Church Settlements in the Ninth Century* (Maynooth, 1996), L. J. Abrams, 'The Conversion of the Scandinavians of Dublin', *Anglo-Norman Studies*, 20 (1997), 1–29, and D. Ó Corráin, 'Viking Ireland—Afterthoughts', in H. B. Clarke, M. Ní Mhaonaigh, and R. Ó Floinn (eds.), *Ireland and Scandinavia in the Early Viking Age* (Dublin, 1998), 421–52. R. N. Bailey, *Viking Age Sculpture* (London, 1980) remains essential for an understanding of the Christianization and burial practices of Scandinavian settlers in northern England, topics reassessed in D. Stocker, 'Monuments and Merchants: Irregularities in the Distribution of Stone Sculpture in Lincolnshire and Yorkshire in the Tenth Century', in Hadley and Richards (eds.), *Cultures in Contact*, 179–212. Also useful on burial is S. L. Fry, *Burial in Medieval Ireland, 900–1500* (Dublin, 1999). Further aspects of the church's involvement in the lives of the laity are considered in A. J. Frantzen, *The Literature of Penance in Anglo-Saxon England* (New Brunswick, NJ, 1983), D. A. E. Pelteret, *Slavery in Early Mediaeval England* (Woodbridge, 1995), G. Rosser, 'The Anglo-Saxon Gilds', in Blair (ed.), *Minsters and Parish Churches*, 31–4, and W. Davies, ' "Protected Space" in Britain and Ireland in the Middle Ages', in Crawford (ed.), *Scotland in Dark Age Britain*, 1–19. Several contributions to M. Godden and M. Lapidge (eds.), *The Cambridge Companion to Old English Literature* (Cambridge, 1991) deal with religious literature and mentalities, including saints' cults, a subject covered more fully in D. Rollason, *Saints and Relics in Anglo-Saxon England* (Oxford, 1989), A. Macquarrie, *The Saints of Scotland: Essays in Scottish Church History AD 450–1093* (Edinburgh, 1997), and A. Thacker and R. Sharpe (eds.), *Local Saints and Local Churches in the Early Medieval West* (Oxford, 2002).

Chapter 6

There is no single, comprehensive survey of writing and literature in Britain and Ireland for our period. The essential foundation of manuscript studies was laid down by the pioneering Scottish classicist W. M. Lindsay, whose two studies, *Early Irish Minuscule Script* (Oxford, 1910) and *Early Welsh Script* (Oxford, 1912), provided photographic facsimiles (with full transcriptions) of many of the manuscripts mentioned in this chapter. But with just one or two exceptions, his lead was not followed (except by the Lithuanian-American palaeographer E. A. Lowe, and that only for the period up to AD 800). Fac-similes have appeared of individual manuscripts, such as R. W. Hunt's *Saint Dunstan's Classbook from Glastonbury: Codex Biblioth. Bodleianae Oxon. Auct. F.4/32* (Amsterdam, 1961)—possibly the single most important codex of our period for the study of learning in Britain—and more recently H. McKee's two-volume study *Juvencus, Codex Cantabrigiensis Ff.4.42: A Ninth-Century Manuscript Glossed in Welsh, Irish, and Latin*, facsimile edn. (Aberystwyth, 2000), and *The Cambridge Juvencus Manuscript Glossed in Latin, Old Welsh, and Old Irish: Text and Commentary* (Aberystwyth, 2000), together with her summary discussion in 'Scribes and Glosses from Dark Age Wales: The Cambridge Juvencus Manuscript', *Cambrian Medieval Celtic Studies*, 39 (2000), 1–22.

The earliest surviving manuscript prose in Welsh has been re-examined by D. Jenkins and M. E. Owen, 'The Welsh Marginalia in the Lichfield Gospels I, II', *Cambridge Medieval Celtic Studies*, 5 (1983), 37–66 and *CMCS*, 7 (1984), 91–120; D. Jenkins has offered thoughtful musings on the importance of sacred books as repositories for vernacular legal documents in 'From Wales to Weltenburg? Some Considerations on the Origin of the Use of Sacred Books for the Preservation of Secular Records', in N. Brieskorn, P. Mikat, D. Müller, and D. Willoweit (eds.), *Von mittelalterlichen Recht zur neuzeitlichen Rechtswissenschaft. Bedingungen, Wege und Probleme der europäischen Rechts-geschichte* (Paderborn, 1994), 75–88. A similar treatment of the Old English manumissions in the Bodmin Gospels was published by M. Förster in 'Die Freilassungsurkunden des Bodmin-Evangeliars', in *A Grammatical Miscel-lany Offered to Otto Jespersen on his Seventieth Birthday* (Copenhagen, 1930), 77–99. All of these studies touch on specific aspects of the problem of literacy in early medieval societies in these islands, a subject comprehensively treated in the essays edited by H. Pryce, *Literacy in Medieval Celtic Societies* (Cambridge, 1998). Pryce himself has examined the Welsh legal material in a valu-able paper on 'The Context and Purpose of the Earliest Welsh Lawbooks', *Cambrian Medieval Celtic Studies*, 39 (2000), 39–63, which neatly comple-ments T. M. Charles-Edwards, *The Welsh Laws* (Cardiff, 1989), an exception-ally concise but exceptionally useful survey of all the early Welsh legal materials. The Welsh legal texts have been inextricably associated with the personality and cult of the Welsh king Hywel Dda, whose reputation was the subject of a conference and proceedings, *Aberystwyth Studies 10: The Hywel Dda Millenary Volume* (Aberystwyth, 1928); D. Jenkins (trans.), *The Law of Hywel Dda: Law Texts from Medieval Wales* (Llandysul, 1986) provides an invaluable English translation of the Laws, and brings discussion of Hywel's role in their codification up to the present.

By contrast with the situation in Wales (and England) the subject of learn-ing and literature in Ireland in our period has been hopelessly neglected by modern Irish scholars. Nothing of note has appeared since the great pioneering Swiss-German scholar R. Thurneynen's 'Zu irischen Handschriften und Literaturdenkmälern', *Abhandlungen der Königlichen Gesellschaft der Wissenschaften zu Göttingen*, phil.-hist. Kl. 14/2 (1912), and his famous study *Die irische Helden- und Königsage bis zum siebzehnten Jahrhundert* (Halle, 1921), which discussed many of the literary and related vernacular texts of our period, and their manuscript transmissions. The only comparable study in the modern period is T. Ó Concheanainn's 'A Connacht Medieval Literary Heritage: Texts Derived from Cín Dromma Snechtai through Leabhar na hUidhre', *CMCS* 16 (1988), 1–40. A Dutch scholar, H. Oskamp (now sadly deceased), planned a comprehensive survey (with facsimiles) of all surviving Irish manuscripts from the period 1000–1300, but the project never reached fruition; however, his study of 'The Irish Quatrains and Salutation in the Drummond Missal', *Ériu*, 28 (1977), 82–91 gives some idea of what might have been done. A photographic facsimile of one of the most important codices (dating from the 1120s, but containing much older material) was published by K. Meyer, *Rawlinson B 502: A Collection of Pieces in Prose and Verse in the Irish Language, Compiled during the Eleventh and Twelfth Centuries* (Oxford, 1909), while printed facsimiles of the two other most important compilations were published by R. I. Best, O. Bergin, M. A. O'Brien, and A. O'Sullivan, *The Book of Leinster, Formerly Lebor na Nuachongbála*, 6 vols. (Dublin, 1954–83), and R. I. Best and O. Bergin, *Lebor na hUidre: Book of the Dun Cow* (Dublin, 1929). However, there is no satisfactory comprehensive survey of medieval Irish literature to replace D. Hyde's *A Literary History of Ireland from the Earliest Times to the Present Day* (London, 1899), which, though still useful, is badly dated.

For Scotland, very valuable work has been done since K. Jackson's important study 'Common Gaelic: The Evolution of the Goedelic Languages', *Proc. Brit. Acad.* 37 (1951), 71–97, and *The Gaelic Notes in the Book of Deer* (Cambridge, 1972), especially by D. Broun, 'Gaelic Literacy in Eastern Scotland between 1124 and 1249', in Pryce, *Literacy*, 183–201. For the earlier period, the thorny question of Pictish literacy and the supposed loss of Pictish manuscripts and documents has been well covered by D. Dumville, 'Language, Literature, and Law in Medieval Ireland: Some Questions of Transmission', *CMCS* 9 (1985), 91–8, and by J. Higgitt, 'The Pictish Latin Inscription at Tarbat in Ross-shire', *Proc. Soc. Antiq. Scotland*, 112 (1982), 300–21, E. Okasha, 'The Non-ogam Inscriptions of Pictland', *CMCS* 9 (1985), 43–69, and most recently K. Forsyth, 'Literacy in Pictland', in Pryce, *Literacy*, 39–61. Latin literature in Scotland (what there is of it) is discussed by J. MacQueen and W. MacQueen, 'Latin Prose Literature', in R. D. S. Jack (ed.), *The History of Scottish Literature, i: Origins to 1660* (Aberdeen, 1988), 227–44.

The matter of orality and literacy in Anglo-Saxon England is well treated by U. Schaefer, '*Ceteris Imparibus*: Orality/Literacy and the Establishment of Anglo-Saxon Literate Culture', in P. E. Szarmach and J. T. Rosenthal (eds.), *The Preservation and Transmission of Anglo-Saxon Culture* (Kalamazoo, Mich., 1997), 287–311. The same kinds of questions arise, in an early Welsh context, in the papers by P. Sims-Williams, 'The Uses of Writing in Early Medieval Wales', in Pryce, *Literacy*, 15–38, and 'The Provenance of the Llywarch Hen Poems: A Case for Llan-gors, Brycheiniog', *CMCS* 26 (1993), 27–63 (though Sims-Williams tends towards a pessimistic view of the evidence). For England, the question of literacy in particular has been treated by G. Hardin Brown, 'The Dynamics of Literacy in Anglo-Saxon England', *Bulletin of the John Rylands University Library of Manchester*, 77/1 (1995), 119–42, and there is an excellent survey of the manuscript materials in H. Gneuss, 'Anglo-Saxon Libraries from the Conversion to the Benedictine Reform', in *Angli e Sassoni al di qua e al di là del mare: Settimane di Studio del Centro Italiano di Studi sull'alto Medioevo*, 31/2 (1986), 643–88, which is neatly complemented by M. Lapidge, 'Surviving Booklists from Anglo-Saxon England', in M. Lapidge and H. Gneuss (eds.), *Learning and Literature in Anglo-Saxon England* (Cambridge, 1985), 33–89. The subject of bilingualism in English schooling is treated by the same author, 'The Study of Latin Texts in Late Anglo-Saxon England: [1] The Evidence of Latin Glosses', in N. P. Brooks (ed.), *Latin and the Vernacular Languages in Early Medieval Britain* (Leicester, 1982), 99–140. For the study of Anglo-Latin literature in our period, M. Lapidge's various studies are indispensable: *Anglo-Latin Literature, 600–899* (London, 1996) and *Anglo-Latin Literature 900–1066* (London, 1993). Particularly valuable as a demonstration of how texts can be used to illuminate otherwise obscure historical periods is his study 'Some Latin Poems as Evidence for the Reign of Athelstan', *Anglo-Saxon England*, 9 (1981), 61–98; repr. in his *Anglo-Latin Literature 900–1066*, 49–86. The distinctive style of later Latin poetry in England is well brought out by him in his study 'The Hermeneutic Style in Tenth-Century Anglo-Latin Literature', *Anglo-Saxon England*, 4 (1975), 67–111; repr. *Anglo-Latin Literature 900–1066*, 105–49. Also valuable for the light they cast on less well-known aspects of English literacy in our period are D. N. Dumville's studies of liturgical texts: *Liturgy and the Ecclesiastical History of Anglo-Saxon England* (Woodbridge, 1992). He has also contributed important additional research (following the earlier work of T. A. M. Bishop) on the question of the development of new script styles in England in our period, notably in his collected studies *English Caroline Script and Monastic History: Studies in Benedictinism, A.D. 950–1030* (Woodbridge, 1993).

For the development of literary genres in England important studies are M. McC. Gatch, *Preaching and Theology in Anglo-Saxon England: Aelfric and Wulfstan* (Toronto, 1977), G. N. Garmonsway (ed.), *Ælfric's Colloquy*

(London, 1939), and K. Sisam, *Studies in the History of Old English Literature* (Oxford, 1953) (the latter particularly in relation to the important later manuscript collections). The most controversial of all of these collections is re-examined by D. Dumville, 'Beowulf Come Lately: Some Notes on the Palaeography of the Nowell Codex', *Archiv für das Studium der neueren Sprachen und Literaturen*, 225 (1988), 49–63, repr. in D. Dumville, *Britons and Anglo-Saxons in the Early Middle Ages* (Aldershot, 1993), ch. 7.

Literacy and the impact of royalty and government on writing are well discussed by S. Kelly, 'Anglo-Saxon Lay Society and the Written Word', in R. McKitterick (ed.), *The Uses of Literacy in the Early Middle Ages* (Cambridge, 1990), 36–62 and S. Keynes, 'Royal Government and the Written Word in Late Anglo-Saxon England', in McKitterick, *Uses of Literacy*, 226–57. M. B. Parkes's 'The Literacy of the Laity', in *Scribes, Scripts and Readers: Studies in the Communication, Presentation and Dissemination of Medieval Texts* (London, 1991), 275–97 offers an expert palaeographer's view of the question. A magisterial survey for the later part of our period is provided by M. T. Clanchy, *From Memory to Written Record: England 1066–1307* (Cambridge, 1979; 2nd edn. 1993).

The thorny subject of Alfred the Great and his supposed role (almost invariably unquestioned) in the revival of English learning has generated a substantial literature in itself—it has even survived the otherwise delightfully iconoclastic and highly controversial assaults of A. P. Smyth, *King Alfred the Great* (Oxford, 1995). The best general treatment is S. Keynes and M. Lapidge (trans.), *Alfred the Great: Asser's Life of King Alfred and Other Contemporary Sources* (Harmondsworth, 1983), but still useful is E. John, 'The King and the Monks in the Tenth-Century Reformation', in id., *Orbis Britanniae* (Leicester, 1966), 154–80. On the important role of Breton schools in that reform, see 'The English Element in Tenth-Century Breton Book-Production', in Dumville, *Britons and Anglo-Saxons in the Early Middle Ages*, ch. 14. D. Bullough's 'The Educational Tradition in England from Alfred to Ælfric: Teaching *Utriusque Linguae*', repr. in his *Carolingian Renewal: Sources and Heritage* (Manchester, 1991), 297–334 promises only to deceive.

Expert palaeographical studies of manuscript books in England in our period are provided by N. R. Ker, *Books, Collectors and Libraries: Studies in the Medieval Heritage*, ed. A. G. Watson (London, 1985), and Parkes, *Scribes, Scripts and Readers*.

The Irish material from the period *c.*1000 still calls out for a treatment such as A. Gransden's, *Historical Writings in England, i: c.500–1307* (London, 1974) and her *Legends, Traditions and History in Medieval England* (London, 1992), to be supplemented by E. M. C. Van Houts, *History and Family Traditions in England and the Continent, 1000–1200* (Aldershot, 1999). There are some suggestive points of comparison in R. R. Davies, *The First English*

Empire: Power and Identities in the British Isles 1093–1343 (Oxford, 2000) but no Irish scholar has attempted anything on the scale of Thurneysen's great surveys (see above). On the interaction of Irish and British scholars see also M. Lapidge, 'The Cult of St Indract at Glastonbury', in D. Whitelock, R. McKitterick, and D. N. Dumville (eds.), *Ireland in Early Medieval Europe: Studies in Memory of Kathleen Hughes* (Cambridge, 1982), 179–212, and for the evidence of Irish contact with continental schools of philosophy in our period, P. E. Dutton, 'The Uncovering of the *Glosae super Platonem* of Bernard of Chartres', *Mediaeval Studies*, 46 (1984), 192–221. Interesting evidence for Welsh learning of an unusual kind is offered by A. Peden, 'Science and Philosophy in Wales at the Time of the Norman Conquest: A Macrobius Manuscript from Llanbadarn', *CMCS* 2 (1981), 21–45.

Chapter 7

The wider context of this chapter's theme, the 'process of Europeanization', is well set out in R. Bartlett, *The Making of Europe: Conquest, Colonization and Cultural Change* (Harmondsworth, 1993).

The chronology of the process and the nature of the evidence combine to ensure that the ecclesiastical aspects of the subject, and in particular in England, are best represented in the secondary literature. Natural starting points here are two volumes: F. Barlow, *The English Church 1000–1066* (2nd edn. London, 1979) and F. Barlow, *The English Church 1066–1154* (London, 1979). On the two great archbishops of Canterbury see M. Gibson, *Lanfranc of Bec* (Oxford, 1978) and R. W. Southern, *Saint Anselm: A Portrait in a Landscape* (Cambridge, 1990). See also R. Eales and R. Sharpe (eds.), *Canterbury and the Norman Conquest. Churches, Saints and Scholars, 1066–1109* (London, 1995); T. Webber, *Scribes and Scholars at Salisbury Cathedral c.1075–c.1125* (Oxford, 1992); W. M. Aird, *St Cuthbert and the Normans: The Church of Durham, 1071–1153* (Woodbridge, 1998).

For Wales and Scotland these matters have to be teased out of some fine and very wide-ranging books: R. R. Davies, *The Age of Conquest: Wales 1063–1415* (Oxford, 1991); A. A. M. Duncan, *Scotland: The Making of the Kingdom* (London, 1975); G. W. S. Barrow, *Kingship and Unity: Scotland 1000–1306* (London, 1981).

On Ireland see chapter 1, 'The See of Canterbury and the Irish Church', in M.-T. Flanagan, *Irish Society, Anglo-Norman Settlers, Angevin Kingship* (Oxford, 1989), 7–55; A. Gwynn, *The Irish Church in the Eleventh and Twelfth Centuries* (Dublin, 1992); D. Bethell, 'English Monks and Irish Reform in the Eleventh and Twelfth Centuries', *Historical Studies*, 8 (1971), 111–35.

P. Stafford, *Queen Emma and Queen Edith: Queenship and Women's Power in Eleventh-Century England* (Oxford, 1997) illuminates more about pre-1066 political culture than its title suggests.

The kings of England who came from Normandy have been well served in F. Barlow, *Edward the Confessor* (2nd edn. New Haven, 1997), D. Bates, *William the Conqueror* (London, 1989), and F. Barlow, *William Rufus* (New Haven, 1983).

M. Chibnall's *The Debate on the Norman Conquest* (Manchester, 1999) provides a very helpful introduction to the voluminous literature on this subject. See also J. A. Green, *The Aristocracy of Norman England* (Cambridge, 1997); R. Fleming, *Kings and Lords in Conquest England* (Cambridge, 1991); and, for those English who survived, A. Williams, *The English and the Norman Conquest* (London, 1995). On the mirage of feudalism see S. Reynolds, *Fiefs and Vassals* (Oxford, 1994) and D. Bates, 'England and the "Feudal Revolution"', in *Il feudalismo nell'alto medioevo: Settimane di Studio del Centro Italiano di Studi sull'alto Medioevo*, 47 (2000), 611–49.

On the survival and decline of slavery see D. A. E. Pelteret, *Slavery in Early Medieval England* (Woodbridge, 1995). On chivalry in war and politics see M. Strickland, *War and Chivalry: The Conduct and Perception of War in England and Normandy, 1066–1217* (Cambridge, 1996) together with J. Gillingham, 'Thegns and Knights in Eleventh-Century England: Who was then the Gentleman?' and '1066 and the Introduction of Chivalry into England', both in J. Gillingham, *The English in the Twelfth Century* (Woodbridge, 2000). On talking and writing see M. Clanchy, *From Memory to Written Record: England 1066–1307* (2nd edn. 1993). The great buildings of the period have been magnificently analysed and illustrated in E. Fernie, *The Architecture of Norman England* (Oxford, 2000).

Conclusion

The two texts highlighted here are easily available in English translations and are well worth reading: *Armes Prydein*, ed. I. Williams, trans. R. Bromwich (Dublin, 1972); *The Annals of Ulster (to A.D. 1131)*, ed. S. Mac Airt and G. Mac Niocaill (Dublin, 1983). On ethnicities in Europe of the central middle ages, S. Reynolds, *Kingdoms and Communities in Western Europe 900–1300* (Oxford, 1984) is fundamental; for Celtic languages, K. Jackson, *Language and History in Early Britain* (Edinburgh, 1953) is a classic. The concept of the first English empire is most eloquently expressed by R. R. Davies, *The First English Empire* (Oxford, 2000). Women's powers are discussed, in addition to the English references above (pp. 249, 255), by L. Bitel, *Land of Women* (Ithaca, NY, 1996), W. Davies, 'Celtic Women in the Early Middle Ages', in A. Cameron and A. Kuhrt (eds.), *Images of Women in Antiquity* (London, 1983; rev. 1993), and D. Jenkins and M. Owen (eds.), *The Welsh Law of Women* (Cardiff, 1980). By far the best discussion of Celtic myth-making is by P. Sims-Williams, in 'The Visionary Celt', *Cambridge Medieval Celtic Studies*, 11 (1986), 71–96, and 'Celtomania and Celtoscepticism', *Camb. Med. Celtic Stud.*, 36 (1998), 1–35.

Chronology

866–7	The 'great army' moves north and takes York
869	Edmund, king of the East Angles, killed at the battle of Hoxne by Vikings
870–1	Capture of Dumbarton Rock by Olaf and Ivar of Dublin
871	King Æthelred of Wessex and Alfred his brother fight battles with the 'great army'
	Alfred succeeds to the kingdom of Wessex
873	Death of Nobis, 'archbishop' of St Davids
	Death of Ivar, 'king of the Northmen of Britain and Ireland'
874	The 'great army' moves to Mercia and takes over Repton
875–c.883	The community of St Cuthbert abandons Lindisfarne and eventually settles at Chester-le-Street
876	Halfdan takes lands in Northumbria; Viking York established
878	Section of the 'great army' takes lands in north-east Mercia
	Death of Rhodri Mawr of Gwynedd
879	Alfred regroups his forces at Ecgberht's stone and defeats the Vikings at the battle of Edington
880	Viking occupation of East Anglia and sharing out of land
886	London recaptured by Alfred
891	*Anglo-Saxon Chronicle* reports arrival of three Irish *peregrini* in England
899	Death of King Alfred of Wessex
902	Destruction of Viking settlement at Dublin (Kilmainham) and expulsion of the Vikings from Ireland
c.904	Hywel Dda ('the Good'), grandson of Rhodri, becomes king of Dyfed
908	Death of Cormac mac Cuilennáin, king-bishop of Munster and scholar
917	Return of the Vikings to Ireland; refoundation of Dublin (at Woodquay)
	Conquest of East Anglia by Edward the Elder, King Alfred's son
918	Battle on the River Tyne between Constantine II, king of Alba, and Ragnall, grandson of Ivar (king of the Northmen)
920	Submission of the five *burhs* to King Edward of Wessex
927	Death of Máel Brigte mac Tornáin, abbot of Armagh

934	King Athelstan of Wessex/England makes pilgrimage to St Cuthbert's shrine at Chester-le-Street and leads campaign into kingdom of Alba
937	Battle of Brunanburh
942	Hywel becomes king of Gwynedd
943	Olaf (Amlaíb) Cuarán, king of Dublin and York, baptized in England with King Edmund of England as his sponsor
948	King Eadred of England burns Ripon minster
950	Death of Hywel Dda ('the Good')
952	Death of King Constantine II of the Scots at St Andrews, where he had retired to become abbot of the *Céli Dé*
954	Eirik Blood-axe, king of York, expelled and killed at Stainmore
964	Bishop Æthelwold expels clerks from the Old and New Minsters, Winchester, and from Milton Abbas and Chertsey
972	The church of Armagh levies tribute, the 'law of Patrick', on Munster
973	Reform of the Anglo-Saxon coinage
*c.*973	*Regularis Concordia* ('Monastic agreement'), a collection of customs prescribing a uniform observance for the reformed Benedictine monastic houses in England, approved by a council at Winchester
978	Brian Bóruma becomes king of Munster
	Æthelred II ('the Unready') becomes king of the English
984	Death of Æthelwold, bishop of Winchester, a leader of the Benedictine reform movement in England
986	Maredudd ab Owain becomes king of Gwynedd
988	Death of Dunstan, archbishop of Canterbury, a leader of the Benedictine reform movement in England
991	Danes raid East Anglia and defeat levies under Beortnoth at Maldon
992	Death of Oswald, bishop of Worcester, a leader of the Benedictine reform movement in England
994	Swein Forkbeard and Olaf Tryggvason of Norway besiege London
995	The community of St Cuthbert relocates from Chester-le-Street to Durham

Earl Sigurd of Orkney forced to accept baptism by Olaf Tryggvason of Norway

999	Death of Maredudd ab Owain
1002	King Æthelred of England orders massacre of Danes
1004	Invasion of England led by Swein
1005	Brian Bóruma recognizes Armagh's claim to superiority over all Irish churches and declares himself *imperator Scotorum* ('emperor of the Irish')
	Malcolm II becomes king of the Scots
1007	Book of Kells stolen and its cover ripped off
*c.*1010	Death of Ælfric, abbot of Eynsham, monastic scholar and ecclesiastical reformer
1012	Ælfheah, archbishop of Canterbury, murdered by Danes
1013	Northern and eastern England submit to Swein from Denmark
	Death of Swein at Gainsborough
1014	Battle of Clontarf, in which Brian Bóruma is killed
1016	The Dane Cnut, son of Swein, wins back power in England
	Death of Æthelred II, king of the English
1023	Death of Wulfstan, archbishop of York, ecclesiastical reformer
1027	King Cnut makes pilgrimage to Rome and attends the imperial coronation of Conrad II
	Cnut's expedition to Scotland, where three kings submit
1034	Death of Malcolm II; Duncan, son of Malcolm II, becomes king of the Scots
1035	Death of King Cnut
1036	Mutilation of the Atheling Alfred
1039	Gruffudd ap Llywelyn becomes king of Gwynedd
1040	Death of Duncan, king of the Scots; Macbeth becomes king of the Scots
1042	Accession of Edward the Confessor to the English throne
	Diarmait mac Máel na mBó becomes king of Leinster
1049	Pope Leo IX's Council at Rheims
*c.*1050	Bishopric for Orkney established, with see at Birsay
1051–2	Exile and return to England of Earl Godwine and sons
1052	Diarmait mac Máel na Mbó conquers Viking Dublin and makes himself king

1056	Marianus Scottus I, the chronicler, expelled from Ireland
1057	Death of Macbeth, king of the Scots
1058	Malcolm III becomes king of the Scots
1062	Papal legates in England
1063	Death of Gruffudd ap Llywelyn
1065	Consecration of Westminster Abbey church
1066	Battles of Fulford Gate, Stamford Bridge, and Hastings
1067	Muiredach mac Robartaig (Marianus Scottus II) leaves Ireland for Rome
1068	The English Edgar Atheling and family flee to Scotland
1069	Swein Estridsson's invasion of Northumbria
1070	Legatine councils at Windsor and Winchester; papal legates depose English prelates; Lanfranc appointed archbishop of Canterbury
1070s and 1080s	Lanfranc's church councils
1072	King William I of England invades Scotland
	Relocation of see of Dorchester to Lincoln
	Death of Diarmait mac Máel na mBó
	Toirdelbach Ua Briain (Turlough O'Brien) becomes king of Leinster and Munster
1074	Gilla Pátraic, who had been trained at Worcester cathedral priory, appointed bishop of Dublin
1076	Execution of Earl Waltheof
	Muiredach mac Robartaig founds first Schottenkloster in Regensburg
1081	Gruffudd ap Cynan becomes king of Gwynedd
1082	Death of Marianus Scottus I (the chronicler) in Mainz
1085	Cnut, king of Denmark, plans invasion of England
1086	Completion of Domesday Book
	Death of Toirdelbach Ua Briain, king of Leinster and Munster
1087	Death of King William I
1092	King William II of England captures and colonizes Carlisle
1093	Anselm appointed archbishop of Canterbury

	Deaths of Malcolm III and Margaret of Scotland
	Muirchertach Ua Briain acknowledged as king of Leinster and Munster
	Rhys ap Tewdwr killed; Welsh step up resistance to Normans
1095	Death of Wulfstan of Worcester (the last English bishop in office after the Norman Conquest of 1066)
1096	Pope Urban II calls for armed pilgrimage to Jerusalem: the First Crusade
1097	Archbishop Anselm goes into exile
	Edgar, son of Malcolm III and Margaret, made king of Scots
1098	Magnus Barelegs of Norway campaigns in the Northern and Western Isles, Ireland, and Anglesey
1100	King Henry I of England marries Edith/Matilda of Scotland, daughter of Malcolm III and Margaret
	Archbishop Anselm returns from exile
c.1100	Lifris of Llancarfan composes his *Life of St Cadog*
1101	Muirchertach Ua Briain and the papal legate hold an Irish reform synod at Cashel
1102	Council of Westminster; slave trade banned
1103	Death of Magnus Barelegs in Ulster
1111	Synod of Rath Bressail

Glossary

abortive moon: technical term used in computistical texts to describe the earlier of two full moons in a calendar month.

acrostic: poem in which the first letters of every line, when combined, spell out a word or name.

áes dána: learned men of medieval Ireland.

alea evangelii ('gospel dice'): board-game devised for instructing novices in the use of the Eusebian canon-tables (indexes) prefaced to gospel books.

Altitonantis: a Worcester **charter** (q.v.), so called from its opening word.

Anglo-Saxon Chronicle: a simplified description of a series of vernacular Old English chronicles, interlinked but also in important respects independent. As they now survive, they were written between the ninth and mid-twelfth centuries.

apocrypha: deutero-canonical books of the Old and New Testaments.

Benedictine monasteries: monastic communities that sought to follow the Benedictine Rule, composed by St Benedict of Nursia (d. *c.*547) for his monks at Monte Cassino, Italy. The establishment (or, as they saw it, the revival) of Benedictine monasticism was a central aim of the tenth-century monastic reformers in England; see also *Regularis Concordia.*

burgage plot: an individual town landholding, often long with narrow street frontage of regular width.

burh (borough): (1) [Anglo-Saxon] fortified place; (2) settlement with market, mint, and burgage plots, with recognized legal status as a **port** (q.v.) and shire centre.

cáin, pl. *cána* (Irish): (1) law; (2) tax or tribute. Major Irish churches such as Armagh imposed the *cána* of their patron saints on areas under their authority as a means of raising income.

caroline minuscule: the formal bookhand perfected in the age of Charlemagne, from whom it derives its name.

Céli Dé (Irish), literally 'clients of God': a term, anglicized as culdees, for adherents of an ascetic monastic reform movement in the Irish church, originating in the second half of the eighth century, which spread to Scotland by the ninth century and possibly also to Wales.

charter: a written record of the transfer of property rights.

chrism: holy oil, distributed by bishops, used for anointing candidates for baptism and the dying.

cithara: stringed musical instrument of the harp type.

codex: a manuscript book arranged like a modern printed book, in leaves, rather than as a roll.

colloquies (*colloquia*): conversational phrase-books.

computistical manuals: handbooks of mathematical formulas etc. for the calculation of Easter.

culdees see *Céli Dé*.

current minuscule: the common form of handwriting used in liturgical handbooks and schoolbooks in the seventh and eighth centuries.

cursive minuscule: informal, everyday script of antiquity and the middle ages.

demesne: that part of an estate that the lord, with the labour of his dependent peasants and slaves, exploited directly.

dendrochronology: technique used in archaeology to date preserved wood; the pattern of annual tree growth rings can be measured and matched to known regional sequences.

diploma: a term for the most formal type of **charter** (q.v.), often issued by an emperor, pope, or king.

display scripts: uncial and half-uncial, the formal Roman book-hands of late antiquity.

Domesday Book: the record of a remarkably comprehensive and detailed survey of landholdings in England undertaken during 1086 on the orders of King William I. Its name derives from the habit of regarding it as being as authoritative as the Last Judgment.

Easter tables: tables used to find the date of Easter.

englynion: Welsh poetic material based on three-line stanzas, often used for dramatic dialogues and monologues.

Gael (Old Irish *Goídel*): a person in either Ireland or Scotland who speaks **Gaelic** (q.v.); used in the context of Viking Scotland initially of the inhabitants of Dalriada, whose rulers took over power in Pictland *c*.850, and whose language was thereafter dominant throughout the early medieval Scottish kingdom.

Gaelic: the Celtic language used in Ireland and in the Irish/Scottish areas of what is now western Scotland and the Islands.

glossary: a list of rare or unusual words, with their explanations.

glosses: annotations, both between the lines and in the margins of books.

guilds: associations in late Anglo-Saxon England, comprising predominantly laymen, which combined both conviviality and piety; as well as feasting, members made provision for each other's religious needs, especially through employing clergy to perform funeral rites and memorial masses.

hagiography: writings concerning saints.

hermeneutic: a style of Latin writing bristling with archaisms, Graecisms, and sense neologisms.

hide: deriving from the Anglo-Saxon word for a household, it came to mean a unit of land by which tax and other obligations were assessed; grouped into hundreds. Equivalent units in the Danelaw were known as *carucates* and *wapentakes*.

Hisperica Famina: elementary Latin-language instruction, supposedly of seventh-century Irish origin, in which the instructional techniques of the early Insular schools were lampooned in grotesque and exaggerated language.

hithe: quayside or landing place.

Humber: a major river estuary and associated marshlands in England separating what are now Yorkshire and Lincolnshire; a geographical and political boundary of major significance in the early middle ages.

'Irish symptoms': distinctive features in manuscripts that suggest Irish origin or influence.

lay investiture: the ceremony, signifying secular power over the church, by which bishops and abbots received a ring or staff (the symbol of their office) from the king's hands.

Libri paenitentiales: handbooks of penance for use by confessors.

lingua franca: the 'common language' (i.e. Latin) understood by all literate people.

literati: learned men (more correctly, men who could read and write).

Llywarch Hen: reputed author of a cycle of early Welsh poetry (supposedly of seventh-century origin but unlikely to be earlier than the ninth).

longphort: ship fortress; early Viking defended settlement in Ireland.

Mabinogi: a famous cycle of early Welsh prose tales.

magister scholarum: master of a school.

manach, pl. *manaig* (Irish): a term, derived from Latin *monachus*, 'monk', used in early medieval Ireland for the dependants of major churches or monastic tenants.

manumission: document recording the release of slaves from bondage.

martyrology: list of names of individuals remembered in the church as martyrs.

minster (spelt *mynster* in Old English): originally a loanword from Latin *monasterium* and thus denoting a church staffed by a community of clergy, which might or might not contain monks; by the tenth and eleventh centuries the term was often used to refer to a church of superior status, or mother-church, whose clergy (in some cases comprising a community of canons) served a proto-parish or *parochia* (q.v.).

mint: official centre of coin production, consisting of a group of licensed moneyers restricted to **ports** (q.v.) in Anglo-Saxon England. Each mint had a mint signature borne by its coins.

mormaer: a regional ruler or sub-ruler in Scotland, glossed by Old Norse *jarl* by the twelfth century, perhaps evolved from former sub-kingships in Pictland.

mother-church see **minster**.

neologism: a new coinage of a word, or use of a familiar word with new meaning.

Northumbria: a kingdom in Britain stretching north from the **Humber** (q.v.) into what is now southern Scotland, comprising older kingdoms of Deira (roughly modern Yorkshire) and Bernicia. These older units continue to be reflected in tenth-century Viking kingdoms at York and in later patterns of rule by southern kings in the North.

notitiae: written records of charters or other transactions.

oath helping (also known as compurgation): the practice whereby oaths were taken by the supporters of someone involved in judicial process in order to affirm his or her innocence or the truth or justice of his or her case.

ogam: an early medieval Irish alphabet consisting of groups of one to five rectilinear strokes, and one to five notches, relative to a stemline; most frequently surviving on stone monuments.

ordines: liturgical handbooks.

organic preservation: archaeological survival of organic matter in anaerobic conditions, most commonly brought about by permanent waterlogging.

parish see *parochia*.

parochia, pl. *parochiae* (Latin): originally meaning 'sphere of authority', from Greek, in the early middle ages it came to denote the area, usually much more extensive than the parishes of the twelfth century and later, whose inhabitants owed dues to a mother-church or **minster** (q.v.); sometimes also referred to as a proto-parish.

partibility: an inheritance custom recognizing more than a sole heir—e.g. all the sons of a deceased landholder—and dividing the inheritance among them.

patristic texts: writings of the church Fathers (Jerome, Augustine, etc.).

peregrinatio (Latin): literally 'journey'; applied in early medieval contexts to wandering or exile, particularly for spiritual purposes.

planctus (Latin): dirge.

pole: traditional English unit of measurement, equivalent in modern terms to 5.5 yards.

port: in England a legal market and centre of taxation under the authority of a port-reeve, in most cases contiguous with *burh* (q.v.).

quadrivium: the four mathematical subjects of the academic curriculum in antiquity (arithmetic, astronomy, geometry, and music).

Regularis Concordia (Latin): a text approved *c.*973 by a council at Winchester which prescribed a uniform observance, based on the Rule of St Benedict, for the monks and nuns of the reformed monastic houses in England; see also **Benedictine monasteries**.

rubrics: titles or headings of texts (so called from the red ink with which they were written, from Latin *ruber* 'red').

sceatta: broad category for cast silver coin of the seventh to eighth centuries; several varieties were produced in local centres in England and north-west Europe. Numerous and relatively crude, they do not seem to have had a particularly high value.

Scottus, pl. *Scotti*, occasionally *Scoti*: the standard Latin term used to denote 'Irishman' in the early middle ages (until the late eleventh century, after which the term comes to denote also 'Scotsman').

shire: (1) anciently, in England and south and east Scotland, a royal multiple estate; (2) a larger territorial unit, also known as the county, and, as the sphere of duty of the sheriff, an important unit of local government in this period in England.

simony: in canon law the offence of obtaining ecclesiastical office by inappropriate means, most commonly in return for money or political service.

Southumbria: a term used by some northern chroniclers in England to designate Mercians and other peoples south of the **Humber** (q.v.). It emphasizes the significance of the Humber within what became the kingdom of England and is used in this volume to underline that.

telestich: poem in which the first and last letters of every line, when combined, spell out a word or name.

tenement: the holding of a free or unfree tenant, in town or country.

tithe: the tenth of produce payable to the church. In England, payment of tithe was first made compulsory by King Athelstan (924/5–39).

TRE: in the time of King Edward (*tempore regis Edwardi*), i.e. 1066 or before, a common formula in **Domesday Book** (q.v.).

tribute: a payment to a lord that rested on a personal and not a territorial basis.

trivium: classical division of the rhetorical subjects in the academic curriculum of antiquity into grammar, rhetoric, and dialectic.

tuath, pl. *tuatha* (Irish): kingdom or small lordship.

vernacular: indigenous local language (other than Greek or Latin).

wic: place-name possibly derived from Latin *vicus*, associated with seventh- to ninth-century trading settlements in Anglo-Saxon England (alternative contemporary terms include *mercimonium* and *emporium*).

Index